M000309788

Atonement Today

Gospel & Culture (which incorporates The Gospel and Our Culture and the C. S. Lewis Centre) represents a coming together of Christians from many different churches and traditions, united by commitment to Jesus Christ and by a determination to engage with today's culture and to communicate the gospel to it.

We offer resources to help Christians to relate their faith to the real world. These include:

- Lecture tours, workshops and weekend conferences.
- Books, tapes, pamphlets and a journal, *Leading Light*.
- A meeting-point of Christians from a rich diversity of traditions, providing discussion, networking and support.

For more information, write to: Lavinia Harvey, **Gospel & Culture**, Dept of Theology and Religious Studies, King's College London, Strand, London WC2R 2LS.

Atonement Today

A SYMPOSIUM AT
ST JOHN'S COLLEGE, NOTTINGHAM
EDITED BY
JOHN GOLDINGAY

First published in Great Britain 1995
Society for Promoting Christian Knowledge
Holy Trinity Church
Marylebone Road
London NW1 4DU

© The contributors 1995

All rights reserved. No part of this book may be reproduced or
transmitted in any form or by any means, electronic or
mechanical, including photocopying, recording, or by any
information storage and retrieval system, without permission in
writing from the publisher.

British Library Cataloguing-in-Publication Data
A catalogue record for this book is available from the British Library

ISBN 0-281-04894-0

Typeset by
Rowland Phototypesetting Ltd
Bury St Edmunds, Suffolk
Printed in Great Britain by
Redwood Books, Trowbridge, Wiltshire

CONTENTS

Contents

Contributors

Dr Michael Alsford is Lecturer in Theology at the University of Greenwich

Dr Sally Alsford is Lecturer in Theology at the University of Greenwich

Canon Dr David Atkinson is Chancellor of Southwark Cathedral

Dr Christina A. Baxter is Dean and Doctrine Lecturer at St John's College

Dr George H. Bebawi is Chaplain and Lecturer in Doctrine at St John's College

The Revd Dr Christopher Cocksworth is Chaplain at Royal Holloway, University of London, and former student of St John's College

The Revd Dr John Goldingay is Principal and Old Testament Lecturer at St John's College

The Revd Dr Colin Greene is Lecturer in Doctrine and Systematic Theology and Director of Evangelism at Trinity College, Bristol, and former student of St John's College

The Revd John Kelly is Assistant Curate at Normanton-by-Derby and research student at St John's College

The Revd Gordon Oliver is Director of Training in the Diocese of Rochester and former Lecturer in Practical Theology at St John's College

Dr Jenny Sankey is an Anglican ordinand and former Doctrine Lecturer at St John's College

Canon Tom Smail is former Vice-Principal and Lecturer in Doctrine at St John's College

Dr Stephen H. Travis is Vice-Principal and New Testament Lecturer at St John's College

Acknowledgements

Stephen Travis's essay first appeared in *Jesus of Nazareth: Lord and Christ* (I. H. Marshall Festschrift, ed. J. B. Green and M. Turner; Grand Rapids: Eerdmans/Carlisle: Paternoster, 1994). It reappears here with the permission of the publishers.

Lines from 'Do not go gentle into that good night' on page 155 from Dylan Thomas, *The Poems*, published by J. M. Dent. Reprinted by permission of David Higham Associates.

Excerpts from *Atonement and Psychotherapy* by Don S. Browning on pages 249–50. Used by permission of Westminster John Knox Press.

Excerpts from *The Cross of Christ* by John R. W. Stott on pages 65–8 © 1986 by John R. W. Stott. Used by permission of IVP, Leicester and IVP, USA: P.O. Box 1400, Downers Grove, IL 60515.

Biblical quotations are from the New Revised Standard Version © 1989 except where otherwise indicated:
The Revised Standard Version is © 1971 and 1952.
The text of the Authorized Version of the Bible is the property of the Crown in perpetuity.
The New Jerusalem Bible published and copyright 1985 by Darton, Longman & Todd Ltd and Doubleday and Co. Inc.

Introduction

JOHN GOLDINGAY

IN THE JUNE 1990 edition of the *St John's College Newsletter* I wrote a piece on what it meant to be evangelical, referred to the centrality of the cross for evangelical thinking, and commented that 'we need to be wary lest the problem of justifying God in the face of human suffering become more important than the problem of justifying human beings in the face of human sin'.

Tom Smail wrote to comment

> Exactly so! But we shall not do it simply by expounding the scriptural teaching, the way evangelicals often do without ever taking up the theological problems as to how Christ's action can vicariously be effective for us, and what kind of contemporary model can make the whole notion of atonement accessible to people. The biblical ones by themselves will not do it. We need to base ourselves on them to have a norm for what we are saying, but how to say again to our world what they said to theirs is a task that is hardly ever tackled, so that evangelical talk of atonement is either parodied or ignored. The question is what are we going to do about it? . . . Forgive the ramble: can't somebody get some folk together to try to work some of these things through? Can't you?

The letter in Tom's distinctive handwriting sat staring at me from my desk for some weeks; a conversation with Christina Baxter in due course issued in a plan for a week of special lectures and seminars by people with whom the college had links of one kind or another, and for another week in the vacation when the contributors met to discuss the papers further. The result is this book.

It divides into two parts. Part One comprises essays which start more from the Bible, from the church's doctrinal tradition, and from the evangelical tradition in particular, though they do so in a way which is concerned to discover how these resources speak to our age. Stephen Travis and I look at aspects of the way the Bible itself speaks of sacrifice and its significance for understanding atonement, of the fact that Christ died 'for' us, and of the nature of sin and its consequences. Christina Baxter and Tom Smail analyse the notion of penal substitution, considering how the ideas of penalty and substitution can be stated in ways which take account of criticisms and reassert important insights. Chris Cocksworth conducts us through the Letter to the Hebrews in order to identify links between atonement, worship, and life, and Jenny Sankey offers a trinitarian approach to the atonement in the context of the eucharist in particular.

Part Two begins in the contemporary age as a basis for taking soundings back in Scripture and the tradition. Sally Alsford and Christina Baxter take feminist insights and convictions as a starting point for reconsidering the nature of sin and the question whether a male saviour can save women. John Kelly and George Bebawi approach the atonement from issues raised by inter-faith questions and ask what the cross means in the context of dialogue with Judaism and Islam. Michael Alsford and Colin Greene begin from the characteristics of the post-modern age and ask how its ways of thinking hinder and help the preaching of the cross. Finally Gordon Oliver and David Atkinson ask how the models and questions of pastoral theology illumine and are illumined by the doctrine of the atonement.

The book itself cannot convey the difference it made that the symposium took place in our college chapel and in the context of worship, which helped to restore something of the relationship between theology and doxology which the 'modern age' took away from the Christian West. At the same time, one of our students reminded me that symposia started off as drinking parties enlivened by intellectual conversation. It was at least true that a week of the whole college focusing on this central theme of Christian faith enlivened conversation, fellowship, and faith (as well no doubt as raising as many questions as it answered). By a feedback process the comments, questions, and discussions have informed the papers as they now appear. The volume was designed to be and is the fruit of a collaborative venture on the part of 150 people and not merely twelve; the named are glad to acknowledge the contributions of the unnamed, though I should specifically refer to Vernon White, author of *Atonement and Incarnation*, who joined us for the week at St John's and contributed a closing reflection. I am also glad to acknowledge the contribution of my assistant Pat Morris in making the arrangements for the symposium and in ensuring that so much of that informal comment, questioning, and discussion was preserved.

It is also a nice happenstance that the volume is being published in the year when St John's celebrates twenty-five years in Nottingham, whither it moved from London in 1970, and it forms part of that celebration. It is not a statement of the college's position on the significance of the cross; we do not even all agree with each other at every point, nor do we pretend to have handled all the questions that need considering. But we are glad to have had the chance to put together these essays on this subject, because St John's is committed to the conviction that the cross is at the heart of the good news for this generation, as for every generation.

Part One

Focusing on the Tradition

Old Testament Sacrifice and the Death of Christ

JOHN GOLDINGAY

WHAT DO WE mean by 'atonement'? The word itself suggests reconciliation in general ('at-one-ment'), and the New Testament has a variety of images or models for expressing how reconciliation comes about, how atonement works. In English translations of the Bible, at least, 'atonement' can also have a narrower meaning, referring distinctively to reconciliation between humanity and God which is brought about through sacrifice. That has been a central model for understanding Christ's death since New Testament times. In this first chapter I am concerned with atonement in this narrow sense, with what we learn from thinking about Christ's death in the light of the nature of Old Testament sacrifice. I shall consider four approaches to interpreting sacrifice.

I Sacrifice as a Way of Giving a Gift

A man returns home clutching a bunch of cut flowers. He presents these to his wife, who perhaps bursts into tears (or perhaps slaps him in the face). What is going on? In their culture the gift of flowers is recognized as a positive gesture in the context of a relationship. But the gesture may have various significances. It may express or accompany gratefulness for some act, appreciation for the person, hope for some favour, sorrow for some wrongdoing, or regret for some non-culpable failure (he arrived home late because the train broke down). The implicit feelings (e.g. of appreciation or regret) may of course be genuine or false.

Giving a gift is one central aspect of the meaning of sacrifice (see Gray 1925, 1–20). As gifts to God, Old Testament sacrifices can have a parallel range of significances to those of the giving of flowers. A thank-offering expresses gratitude for some act on God's part. A whole offering suggests the commitment of the person to God; the offerer surrenders every part of the animal. Sin offerings and guilt offerings provide ways of finding cleansing when one is stained, and of making up for the consequences of failure. Parallel to the gift of flowers in human relationships, then, sacrifices give the appropriate concrete, material, symbolic expression and evidence of a response to God of commitment, appreciation, gratitude, hope, shame, and regret. Without the attitude, the sacrifice would be meaningless; without the sacrifice, the attitude would be a mere head-trip.

The analogy with a practice such as the giving of flowers may help North Atlantic urban Christians to appreciate some aspects of the logic of sacrifice. First, the practice presupposes a framework of interpretation within a culture; as with other aspects of Western culture, someone from outside might find it puzzling. The significance of the practice is assumed rather than stated.

Second, Protestant interpreters have understood passages in the prophets and the Psalms which raise questions about sacrifice to be suggesting that there is no need for sacrifice in principle. One might similarly argue that there is no need for a man to give his wife flowers, especially as this can easily be a substitute for real commitment, or a disguise rather than an expression of feelings, or a sexist gesture. One fault in that argument lies in its failure to take account of the fact that men and women are material human beings and that symbolic gestures are built-in to being human. It is appropriate for people to have concrete and outward, practical and symbolic, ways of expressing attitudes of will, mind, and feeling. In a parallel way people relate to God by actions as well as by words, thoughts, and feelings. The analogy with the giving of a gift such as flowers hints at the person-to-person nature of the relationship between God and people. To put it another way, a gift is an act which does something. The giving of flowers can have a magical effect on a relationship; sacrifice, too, can act like magic. Something happens when either offering is made.

Third, it is not merely their inherent commercial value which gives the gift of flowers its significance and its effectiveness, but the gift's symbolic significance in a culture. If the giver had caused his wife some loss (e.g. had crashed her car) he would need to put that right; the gift of flowers adds to this practical act rather than replacing it. On the other hand, if the loss he had caused could not be made up (as when I accidentally threw away a package of photographs of our wedding and honeymoon) some symbolic gift may help to compensate for it (though I do not remember making one). In the Day of Atonement ritual, two goats correspond to the entire body of wrongdoing committed by the community in a year.

Fourth, both forms of gift also presuppose that right attitude of spirit and will is indispensable if the gift is to be significant and effective. The gift only 'works' if it is the symbolic expression of a personal attitude which characterizes the giver's life as a whole. A woman whose husband brings her flowers which she has reason to believe hide rather than express his true attitude may well respond 'Stuff your bloody flowers'. In a parallel way Yahweh says 'Stuff your bloody sacrifices' in equivalent circumstances.

Fifth, it is possible for the giving of flowers to be the beginning of a relationship, as in a memorable British television advertisement, but more commonly it belongs in the context of an existent one. Sacrifice, too, is not a means of establishing the relationship between people and God but a means of expressing, developing, and healing it (cf. Kidner 1952, 23).

Sixth, when the man offers his flowers to his wife, as much significance attaches to their reception as to their being offered. In parallel, a ' "theology of acceptance" pervades Old Testament attitudes towards sacrifice' (Daly 1978, 23). This begins with Genesis 4. The story of Cain and Abel already illustrates that acceptance cannot be presupposed, that everything depends upon it, and that questions of moral stance and questions of acceptance interweave, though not always in the way we might expect (see further Jer 6.20; Hos 9.4; Amos 5.22).

God offered Jesus Christ as a sacrifice, Jesus offered himself as a sacrifice. What does this statement suggest regarding the significance of his death?

First, the offering of Christ was an outward act. Admittedly the actual statement that Jesus's death was a sacrifice is a metaphorical one. Jesus was not literally a priest, his offering did not take place in a temple, and he did not kill himself. Describing his death as a sacrifice is a way of gaining an understanding of its deep significance. It is an example of typological thinking. But as a sacrifice Jesus's person, his life, and his death – the totality of his self-offering – were concrete, outward, historical, this-worldly events.

Second, the offering of Christ took place within the context of a person-to-person relationship. To see Christ's death as effecting the satisfaction of God's honour or the achievement of God's victory or the redemption of God's possession or the acceptance of God's punishment sets it in the context of intrinsically hierarchical and/or contractual webs of relationships, those of authority, power, business, or law. To see Christ's death as a gift offered to God sets it in the context of a person-to-person relationship of mutual commitment with its potential for love, favour, generosity, self-sacrifice, gratitude, and forgiveness (as opposed to pardon) (see Brümmer 1992 for further analysis).

Third, this relationship in whose context Christ's offering took place is an already existing one. It is not the case that people were unable to relate to God before Jesus's act of self-offering to the Father. It is precisely because they were in relationship to God that there needed to be an offering of themselves to God in appreciation, gratitude, joy, commitment, hope, penitence, and recompense, expressed in the self-offering which characterizes Christ's life as a whole.

It was because God chose us that God gave Jesus for us, rather than vice versa. Sacrifice was the seal of a relationship rather than the means to it. Because my wife is disabled and cannot get out to the shops on her own, when Christmas draws near I say to her 'Would you like to give me that shirt?' And if she likes it too, I buy it, wrap it, attach a tag which says it comes from her to me, put it with the other family presents, and in due course receive it from among them as a gift from her which I know she is glad to give me.

The same point may be made by noting that Christ is both priest and victim at his sacrifice. He is not given by someone else. When this form of self-sacrifice is required by the path he has to walk, he freely gives himself; it is a positive act of self-giving rather than a hopeless giving up. Indeed, we may go further. It was already the case that Old Testament sacrifices involved the offering of something God provided. The point is particularly explicit in the prayer with which Israel brought first-fruits (Deut 26.10–11) and in David's prayer regarding the offerings for building a temple (1 Chron 29.14). God is the origin of Christ's sacrifice in a more direct or specific sense. Such sacrificial notions are implied when the New Testament says that God 'gave his only Son' (John 3.16) or 'put [Christ] forward as a sacrifice of atonement' (Rom 3.25) or 'did not withhold his own Son, but gave him up for all of us' (Rom 8.32, following the language of Abraham's offering of Isaac) (Gunton 1988, 125; Dunn 1991a, 41).

2 Sacrifice as a Way of Finding Cleansing and Restoration

The giving of flowers, then, can have various meanings. These are not confined to the expressing of sorrow for some failure, but they do include that. Likewise some sacrifices expressed to God people's commitment, gratitude, appreciation, or need. Others were more concerned with the problems caused by human wrongdoing. Indeed, the account of Israel's sacrificial system in Leviticus does hint at a general concern to allow for the fact of human failure. It may suggest the idea that even in expressing our commitment, gratitude, appreciation, and prayer, we do so as people sharing in this failure.

In Richard Swinburne's analysis (1989, 74), in human relationships doing wrong to someone has two sorts of moral consequences. It puts us in a situation in relation to them something like that of a debtor: there is a wrong which needs

2 dimensions to sin
relational
understanding of sin
1) debtor to another
2) unclean in ourselves

righting. In addition we acquire a status 'something like being unclean'.

Leviticus 4—5 presupposes an equivalent dynamic in our relationship with God, and provides for two corresponding forms of offering. They have traditionally been called the 'sin offering' and 'guilt offering', but 'purification offering' and 'restitution offering' are better renderings of the words (see e.g. Wenham 1979, 88–9, following e.g. Milgrom 1971 and Levine 1974, 101–5). The first deals with the stain that some acts can bring on a person (or a place), the second with the position of indebtedness it puts them in. They apply whether or not the event involved moral blame on the person's part (that is, they deal with events that were objectively wrong whether or not the person was culpable), and they offer ways of finding cleansing and of making up for the wrong in certain respects. It is the restitution offering with which the servant's death is metaphorically identified in Isaiah 53.10. Here sacrifice is already spoken of typologically within the Old Testament. Misunderstanding of Isaiah 53.5–6 and 10–12 as if it implied a punitive understanding of sacrifice is one root of the idea that there is a link between atonement and punishment (see Calvin, *Institutes* II.16.5–6; Barth 1956, 253). Indeed, Isaiah 53 (misunderstood) and Hebrews form the restrictive prism which has dominated Christian thinking about the atonement.

The notion that wrongdoing leaves us in debt or under obligation to the person we have wronged is a familiar one, and the giving of flowers as a recognized expression of contrition and of the desire to 'make up for' what we have done illumines some aspects of the logic of sacrifices concerned with sin. Swinburne's analysis and the comparison with the Levitical offerings draws attention to another aspect of the problems caused by our failure and wrongdoing: the stain it leaves. Contact with blood and with death was a major cause of stain as well as indebtedness in Israel. It parallels our own sense of stain as well as indebtedness when we are in contact with blood or death or are (even unwittingly) the cause of injury or death (cf. Caird 1980, 17; Ricoeur 1969, 25).

It is not that we first experience failure and then consciously utilize the imagery of pollution to express its significance. If a child escaped its mother's grasp and ran into the road, and I could not avoid running it over, I would instinctively feel stained by its blood. I would find myself distasteful. I would be guilty of killing someone, even though it was not my fault, and would feel the shame of guilt. This would be the case all the more, of course, if I were slightly exceeding the speed limit at the time, as is likely, for then I have to accept more responsibility for the event; but even without that, guilt, stain, and shame are involved (cf. Swinburne 1989, 73–4). If a wife discovers her husband has been unfaithful to her, among other things he may well seem stained to her. Even if in fact he takes the initiative, confesses the wrongdoing, and seeks a new beginning to the relationship, he may well nevertheless seem stained both to her and to himself, and she may find it difficult to approach him. In neither case are we speaking of a mere subjective feeling of stain. And in either case, the mere giving of flowers would have no effect. How does the stain come to be removed?

If I am morally in the wrong and am stained, restoration and cleansing may involve at least five factors (I partly follow the analysis in Swinburne 1989, 81–4). There is repentance, in the two Hebrew senses of regret and turning to a new pattern of behaviour, and also in the Greek sense of a change of attitude. There is the open expression of that repentance in acknowledgement of the wrongdoing as what it was, in confession or apology. There may be some symbolic act of which the gift of flowers is a trivial example. There needs to be some substantial act which replaces my wrongdoing with something positive. Where possible this involves at least the restoring of the situation to what it was before (if I have crashed your car, I see it is repaired). Of course in the situations which trouble us most (such as death or unfaithfulness) that is impossible, and some other more imaginative act may be required. Finally, there is time, for somehow restoration cannot be instant.

A similar set of factors may be identified in relationships between human beings and God. Deliberate wrongdoing in defiance of God's word must issue in being cut off from the community, and sacrifice alone cannot make up for such

9

wrongdoing (Num 15.30–1). If a person repents of their wrongdoing and confesses, they cease to be in defiance of God, but this does not solve the entire problem, and they must also make restitution for their wrongdoing in relation to human beings who were involved and in relation to God. They also have to take the appropriate action with regard to the defilement which their action has brought upon them; in itself their repentance and confession cannot remove that, but it puts them into a position like that of an inadvertent offender who can offer the customary sacrifice in connection with their offence and thereby find purification (Lev 6.1–7) (Milgrom 1975). With offerings for purification, too, time is one of the great healers: 'purification is achieved principally by an appropriate ritual and a lapse of time' (Jensen 1992, 165). And if the offering is not set in the context of the right attitude, to judge from the prophets, Yahweh may indeed say, 'Stuff your bloody sacrifices'.

Directly or indirectly a giver is personally identified with their gift. Usually the husband personally hands over the flowers; commonly the offerer lays hands on the offering. Like flowers, offerings do not generally substitute for people (except in the case of the dedication of the first-born) but neither do their offerers merely own them. The laying on of hands identifies offerers and offerings and indicates that they truly represent them; something of themselves passes over with the gift to the recipient (cf. Dunn 1991a, 44–5). In the case of a purification offering and of the Day of Atonement ritual, the stain is transferred to the offering (cf. Lev 16.21) and is destroyed in it. Here there is indeed a sense in which the offering substitutes for the offerer, though it is not that the offering is vicariously punished. The idea of punishment belongs in the framework of law rather than the framework of worship, and we get into difficulties when we mix ideas from the different frameworks such as these. Sacrifice does not involve penal substitution in the sense that one entity bears another's punishment. By laying hands on the offering, the offerers identify with it and pass on to it not their guilt but their stain. The offering is then not vicariously punished but vicariously cleansed. (In Chapter 3 I consider the question whether the offering propitiates God's wrath.)

A common illustration of the need and achievement of atonement pictures God and humanity on either side of a chasm carved out by human sinfulness; the cross then makes it possible for the chasm to be bridged and for human beings to be one with God. The sacrificial model presupposes that God and human beings stand together in love and mutual self-offering. Insofar as sin becomes a problem in the relationship, in the sacrificial system God provides the way for it to be handled – even while drawing attention to it – as part of providing the means in general for expressing and developing a relationship with people. Our situation is not one in which God and ourselves are set over against each other with sin causing a gulf between us, but one in which God is on the same side as us over against all that spoils and offends. 'When deeds of iniquity overwhelm us, you forgive our transgressions' (Ps 65.3). Of course people could decline to turn back to God, to seek forgiveness, and to offer the appropriate sacrifice, and then the relationship would remain disturbed. There would be enmity between them and God. It is that resistance to God which means that we do not stand together on the same side over against sin.

[handwritten marginal note: God stands with us against sin]

In Christ, as happens in connection with a purification offering or the Day of Atonement ritual, God is willing to transfer to something else the stain which rests on human beings so as then to destroy it and render the people clean. A sinless one is 'made sin', or perhaps 'made a sin offering' (2 Cor 5.21; cf. de Vaux 1961, 420). What was polluted can be restored through contact with the clean, as is announced by Jesus's unhesitating willingness to reach out to touch the polluted. They are no danger to him; he brings cleansing and restoration to them (Daly 1978, 26–7).

Christ offers himself on our behalf; his self-offering becomes effective for us as we associate ourselves with it. It would be natural for the woman whose child I killed to feel negative towards me and for me to share that feeling towards myself. Imagine that God brought the child back to life and gave it to me to restore to its mother. As I did so, my stain would surely go, and this would be recognized by her and by me. Indeed, the relationship between us might now gain a depth it would never otherwise have had (though all this only if God brought me into the process of restoring).

3 Sacrifice as a Way of Enabling Movement between this World and the Realm of the Holy

Sacrifice, then, is a way of making a gift and a way of bringing about restoration. But it commonly involves the gift's destruction, a strange way of making a gift. Why is this so?

As with the giving of flowers (which also die as a result of becoming a gift), one can suggest a down-to-earth reason. There is a substantial overlap between sacrifice and feasting, and an animal has to be killed before it can be eaten. Generally the killing of the animal was a preliminary to the rite at the altar, undertaken by offerer rather than a priest. In the Old Testament, at least, it is not the case that the animal's death is the climax of the rite (contrast Beattie 1980, 34). What is central is what is done with its blood and with fire.

The varied acts involving blood indeed emphasize that sacrifice is about life poured out in death. Perhaps this reflects a distinctive feature of this occasion of giving. The gift is given to someone invisible, someone who belongs in a realm other than the earthly: the one who inhabits eternity, whose name is holy. There is a metaphysical distinction between the offerers and the recipient (even apart from any moral distinction). To describe God as the holy one is to acknowledge this distinction: God is spirit, humanity is flesh. If sacrifice is to be a means of expressing their mutual relation and of facilitating the step of faith into the unseen world of spirit, it has to belong to both realms (cf. Ashby 1988, 1). Fire takes the offering from the material, earthly realm to the immaterial, heavenly one (cf. Hubert and Mauss 1964, 97). It crosses the threshold between the visible and the invisible.

In Eden God takes the initiative in providing a sacramental means whereby the divine life is shared with human beings through their eating the fruit of a certain tree. East of Eden human beings follow God's example and offer God of their produce and their flocks. The mutual giving of fruit, produce, and flocks is designed to express the relationship between God and humanity, to facilitate movement between people and God. In practice it actually contributes to the process whereby the metaphysical distinction is turned into a moral one as it tempts the human beings into misplaced assertiveness and aggression.

Sacrifice facilitates movement between different worlds. It is a ferry boat between heaven and earth (see Ashby 1988, 24–5, quoting S. Lévi, 1966). Sacrifice is a *'rite de passage'* (van Gennep 1960: a ferry boat is a *bateau de passage*). The imagery has been extensively used this century, but in Chapter 7 Christopher Cocksworth notes that it already appears in Luther's comments on Hebrews 10.19–22, where Christ is the ferryman who transports us safely from this realm to that of heaven.

Sacrifice can also be part of a *rite de passage* in another sense, in that it can facilitate movement at moments of transition in the life of individuals or communities (Leach 1976). There is thus a sacrifice associated with birth and with the rite of circumcision. It is striking, however, that there are no such sacrifices associated with other transition events such as puberty, marriage, and death, nor is it the case that the regular Old Testament sacrifices belonged in this context. Again, the Day of Atonement takes place in October in proximity to the New Year and thus facilitates the transition from one year to the next as God's means of ensuring that one year's failures are eliminated as a new year begins. But it is also striking that Leviticus 16 and 23, far from making anything of this point, date the Day of Atonement, like other festivals, not by the autumn calendar but by the spring calendar, in which it comes in the seventh month (see Rogerson 1980, 35 for further critique).

Exodus 12 similarly begins by asserting that Passover comes at the beginning of the year, implying that if the Israelite calendar year has a transition point, this occurs in the spring, with Passover as its transition ritual (so Segal 1963, 186–7; though it must be noted that the move to a spring calendar is usually reckoned a relatively late, seventh-century development brought about by Babylonian influence). Passover marks the transition from the old year to the new, symbolized by the clearing out of the old leaven in favour of the new. It also marks the transition from the rainy season/winter to the dry season/summer. More importantly in the the Old Testament's explicit commentary, it also commemorates the Israelites' passing from bondage to freedom, from Egypt to Canaan, and from death to life. The rite takes place chronologically at the transition point from one day to another, at midnight, and geographically emphasizes the transition point from inside to outside, the door of people's houses where the blood is daubed. Historically and then experientially these transitions are facilitated by means of sacrifice.

Christ relates to us not merely by taking our place in a legal or cultic transaction between humanity and God but by being our 'representative or mediator who in his very person presents or mediates God to us and us to God, thus showing the vital differences between the creator and the creation not to be a lethal separation: in and through him we, though mortal beings, live in the eternal community with the immortal God' (Dalferth 1991, 321). He 'is our substitute because he does for us what we cannot do for ourselves', because we need to have our being formed not by ourselves but by God, but he substitutes for us in order to free us then to be ourselves and to go where he has gone, into God's presence (Gunton 1988, 165–6). His death makes possible our movement into God's presence.

In theory, the dying of Christ thus fulfils and terminates any need for special places, rites, castes, or times. In Christian faith there is no longer shrine, sacrifice, priesthood, or sabbath, because there is now open access to God for all time, people, and places.

In practice, the Christian church found itself reinventing holy place: churches became the house of God, commonly following the threefold architectural structure of the Jerusalem temple, and not merely convenient places for the temple of God to meet. It reinvented holy time: Sunday as the sabbath and not simply resurrection day. It reinvented holy caste – a structured patriarchy of bishop, priests, and deacons corresponding to that of high priest, priests, and Levites – rather than the more egalitarian male and female apostles, prophets, teachers, and leadership groups of the New Testament. It reinvented holy rites: baptism in the street and eucharist in the home become holy baptism and holy communion.

Is it the same instinct which underlies the notion of eucharistic sacrifice? If we accept the notions of Christian sabbath, priesthood, and church buildings, do we also have to accept that there needs to be some continuing outlet for the God-approved instinct which led to the institution of sacrifice? Or is sacra*ment* enough? Passages such as Romans 12, Romans 16, and 1 Peter 1 imply that there is indeed a continuing expression of the sacrificial death of Christ, but it is one which is made in the world rather than in the church building. Sacrifices are offered in service, proclamation and winning people for Christ. If this is so, is there a place in Christian faith for holy place, holy time, or holy caste? I think not.

4 Sacrifice as a Way of Handling the Fact of Violence in the Community

It is suggestive that humanity's first sacrifice leads to humanity's first act of violence, the act which Genesis itself describes as the occasion of a fall and of the first sin (Gen 4.5–7). The essence of sin East of Eden seems to lie in violence; it is for the pursuit of violence that Lamech adapts the first technology, and for the glorification of violence that he adapts the first art (Gen 4.23–4). It is because the world is filled with violence that God determines to destroy it (Gen 6.11–13). The Old Testament's hope is of an era of peace when everyone is free to sit under their own vine and figtree.

Animal and human sacrifice by their very nature involve violence, on an object which did not 'deserve' it. The substitutionary aspect to sacrifice is clearest in the Day of Atonement ritual, where one goat is sacrificed and another 'scapegoat' is driven into the open country. The rite is an act of catharsis (cf. Beattie 1980, 43). The link between sacrifice and violence is also hinted at by the Passover festival, which in Israel's own history with God begins with a reversal of the violence of Egypt.

In *Violence and the Sacred* René Girard has made the link

with violence the key to understanding sacrifice. Even less than other understandings is this overt in the Old Testament (in that respect it is reminiscent of Freudian or Marxist understandings of aspects of Scripture), but it is a suggestive thesis. Violence has the same contagion as pollution. It has the power to spread its contamination. It is infectious. The only power that can counter violence is – more violence, but then

> whether we fail or succeed in our effort to subdue it, the real victor is always violence itself. . . . The more men strive to curb their violent impulses, the more these impulses seem to prosper. The very weapons used to combat violence are turned against their users. Violence is like a raging fire that feeds on the very objects intended to smother its flames (Girard 1977, 31).

Blood speaks of violence and pollution. This is possibly one reason why even menstrual blood causes pollution and requires a purification sacrifice, though this perhaps also hints at some deeper link between sex and violence, hinted at further in a book such as Judges which interrelates the two so systematically (Bal 1988; see further Ricoeur 1969, e.g. 28, 36 on the link between them in the symbolism of pollution). Our own culture has become newly aware of the link between sex and violence within marriage and outside it. 'Sexuality leads to quarrels, jealous rages, mortal combats. It is a permanent source of disorder even within the most harmonious of communities' (Girard 1977, 35). Gunton (1988, 119) notes that rapists are often motivated by a desire to defile and pollute their victims. The nature of the manifold links between blood, sexuality, and violence gives gloomy plausibility to 'the proposition that all masculine relationships are based on reciprocal acts of violence' (Girard 1977, 48) which is disturbingly paralleled by the feminist proposition that violence is a distinctively male problem, the converse of the characteristic female need to emerge from passivity.

Sacrifice channels violence, gives it a legitimated context for ritual expression, and thereby exercises a measure of control over its effects in the community. Sacrifice is thus a means of maintaining order in the community (cf. Davies 1977, from an anthropological perspective). Sacrifice and violence are therefore alternatives. A community given to violence gives acted testimony to the inefficacy of its sacrifices, as is reflected in the famous contempt for people's sacrifices shown by prophets such as Amos, Micah, Isaiah, and Jeremiah in the midst of communities characterized by violence (Girard 1977, 43).

Now Jesus's death was not actually effected in a ritual context but in a political one. He was killed by soldiers, not priests – Old Testament law of course had no place for the sacrifice of a human being (Gunton 1988, 122). And he was killed as a result of a judicial process: his death was indeed punitive or penal, but to satisfy human rather than divine justice. Whereas sacrificial animals were not killed particularly 'violently' (Girard's interpretation looks beneath the surface of what is going on symbolically), Jesus's sacrificial death was a more intrinsically violent event.

Admittedly there are normally ritual features about an execution, particularly when the charge has a religious aspect, as was the case with Jesus (Bourdillon and Fortes 1980, 13–14, 27). Jesus's death was a political event, but at the same time a religious one because of the interweaving of religion and politics. To say that the people who brought it about were Jews can imply that Jews rather than Gentiles bear responsibility for it, and this can encourage and has encouraged anti-Semitism. To guard against that, it is now common to emphasize that Romans rather than Jews were responsible for Jesus's death. Historically this is a half-truth; Jewish and Roman leadership surely collaborated in the event, and the New Testament attributes responsibility to both parties. Further, there were both Jews and Romans who tried to avoid Jesus being killed; that in itself suggests that responsibility does not lie with a particular national group as such. Theologically the significant point is not nationality but status. Jesus's death was a religio-political event. It was the desire of the members of his own religious group, but in particular of their leadership, who were able to enter into alliance with the political leadership of the secular power.

Jesus did not simply die. He was killed. Now sacrifice

intrinsically involved bloodshed and death, but not suffering or cruelty. Jesus's death was a deliberately violent, unpleasant event. His killing was an act of violence against him, but not merely for his own sake. He claimed to represent God, and did. Whether people recognized it or not, their violence against Jesus was violence against God. 'At the cross our human righteousness and piety found themselves ranged in murderous enmity against the God whom they proposed to honor' (Newbigin 1978, 200). Certain religious who exhibit 'passionist' manifestations present themselves as a sacrifice to the destructive impulse in the world rather than 'hitting back' (Masterman 1947–8, 88; Ann Loades [1991, 247–8] instances Simone Weil). God's own reaction to the violence of the world was to reckon that the power of evil needs to be neutralized and brought to nothing by being absorbed; hence the significance of Jesus's not defending himself when attacked. Forgiveness is 'a certain way of absorbing pain', one that refuses to let it engender bitterness, resentment, hatred, and revenge (Hodgson 1951, 63–4). God 'comes into the world as the "Innocent Victim"' and 'defends and frees victims' (Williams 1991, 2). In the end the death of the victim had to be a death of this kind of victim and not merely a ritual one. In the end the Old Testament sacrifices were indeed but types of the real thing.

According to Hosea God desires faithfulness not sacrifice, and according to Matthew Jesus concurs (Hos 6.6; Matt 12.7). Elsewhere Jesus makes comments which, Mark observes, abolish the categories of cleanliness and pollution (Mark 7.19). Why, then, does God offer and accept the sacrifice of Jesus, or accept an interpretation of his death along such lines? Perhaps God is characteristically condescending to where humanity is: we desire sacrifice, so God gives it, as was the case with the gift of the temple and the institution of the monarchy in Israel. 'We strain to glimpse your mercy seat and find you kneeling at our feet' (Brian Wren 1983; from the hymn 'Lord God, your love has called us here').

It is tempting to believe that we live in a century of unprecedented human violence. This includes the political violence of two intercontinental wars, of Vietnam and the Balkans, of

Ireland and the Middle East, and of oppression within the USSR and China and within Latin American and African states. The killing of human beings as a ritual sacrifice was an unusual event in the ancient world; the killing of human beings as a metaphorical sacrifice has become a more common phenomenon in the national warfare of the modern world. The violence of our century also includes interpersonal violence, in particular marital violence, sexual violence, and parental violence, but also violence in connection with theft, and police violence.

The fact that we belong to such a violent humanity must give great significance for us to the fact that the Old Testament understanding of human life gives a prominent place to national and interpersonal violence. Its spirituality is a spirituality of violence, one whose prayer often focuses on violence received and seeks for God to reverse it. In talking about the Psalms, I often find clergy offended at the violence of the Psalms, but I then suspect that this reflects their not having come to terms with the violence in their own spirits. Walter Brueggemann (1982, 68) has commented that the real problem lies not in the presence of violence and anger there in the Psalms but in their presence within and among us, and observes how attuned the Psalter thus is to what goes on among us: there is 'an acute correspondence between what is written there and what is practiced here'. The Torah and the Psalms offered people the opportunity to face their violence and anger and to express it in ritual and in words rather than in ordinary actions. The cross is also God's affirmative response to the Psalms' prayer for violence.

If ours is a century of unprecedented violence, might it be no coincidence that it is also an unprecedentedly post-Christian century?

When the religious framework of a society starts to totter, it is not exclusively or immediately the physical security of the society that is threatened; rather the whole cultural foundation of the society is put in jeopardy. The institutions lose their vitality; the protective façade of the society gives way; social values are rapidly eroded, and the whole cultural structure seems on the verge of collapse. The hidden violence of the sacrificial crisis eventually succeeds in destroying distinctions, and this destruction in turn fuels the renewed violence. In short, it seems that anything that adversely affects the institution of sacrifice will ultimately pose a threat to the very basis of the community, to the principles on which its social harmony and equilibrium depend (Girard 1977, 49).

Might the preaching of the cross as God's once-for-all absorbing of human violence be the key to the peace of the world? But does that preaching first have to be heard by the Christian community (that locus of violence), so that it may then be preached in its life?

In this connection, my colleague Colin Hart points out to me how people in Christian ministry are often on the receiving end of anger and violence, much of it transferred from the appropriate object. The first temptation for them, as for anyone else, is to retaliate. The second temptation is by superhuman effort to absorb and neutralize the violence and thereby end the cycle of violence. It is a temptation, because the mere effort to imitate Jesus, at this point as at others, is ultimately bound to fail. There needs to be an intimate interrelation between this imitation and Jesus's own atoning death which enables us to pass on the violence and anger to Jesus on the basis of his actually having already absorbed it, rather than keeping it within ourselves where it can continue its negative work.

2

Christ as Bearer of Divine Judgement in Paul's Thought about the Atonement

STEPHEN H. TRAVIS

Paul's vocabulary expresses the results of Christ's death rather than its character, and this fits in with New Testament thought in general, which is more concerned with the nature of salvation than the precise way in which it has been achieved.

THOUGH MOST WOULD agree with these words of Howard Marshall (1990, 250), the history of exegesis and of dogmatic theology is laden with attempts to explain in detail the rationale of Paul's understanding of the death of Christ. My aim here is to explore to what extent statements in Paul's letters can bear the weight of those interpretations of Christ's death which speak in terms of 'Christ bearing our punishment'.

In *Christ and the Judgment of God* I argued that in Paul's understanding of divine judgement ideas of 'punishment' or 'retribution' lie on the periphery of his thought. He thinks not so much of God imposing a retributive penalty for human sins, but of people experiencing the God-given consequences of their choices and actions. He understands both salvation and condemnation primarily in relational terms: people's destinies will be a confirmation and intensification of the relationship with God or alienation from him which has been their experience in this life. In that study, for fear of over-complicating the argument, I chose not to discuss passages in Paul which seem to bring retributive ideas into relation with the death of Christ. In attempting now to make good the omission I hope to clarify some aspects of Paul's view of the atonement, as well as to complement my earlier discussion of Paul's statements about divine judgement.

1 History and Definitions

In Anselm's understanding of the atonement it is axiomatic that if injustice remains unpunished the integrity and credibility of God are in question. Sinners cannot put themselves right with God, yet justice requires the 'satisfaction' of God's demands. The death of Jesus, offered freely as a gift to the Father, out-weighs in value and therefore compensates for all the sins of humanity (see Gunton 1988, 87–93). The Reformers shifted the focus from satisfaction to more strictly penal categories by speaking of Christ undergoing vicarious punishment to meet the claims of God's punitive justice, as when Calvin writes: 'This is our acquittal: the guilt which held us liable for punishment was transferred to the head of the Son of God' (*Institutes* II.16.5).

Among twentieth-century writers who speak of Christ bearing the penalty or punishment for sin are Emil Brunner and Karl Barth (though Barth goes on to reject the theory of penal substitution). P. Stuhlmacher sees in Romans 4.25 the idea that 'the death of Jesus is the punishment "for our trespasses"'. And L. Morris insists on a retributive understanding of the penalty which Christ has borne on behalf of humanity. (See Brunner 1934, 473; Barth 1956, 253; Stuhlmacher 1986, 79; Morris 1966, 382–8).

Before proceeding to a study of certain texts in Paul's letters, we need to clarify what we are looking for. The word 'retribution' is often used loosely, to refer to any kind of unpleasant consequences which arise from human actions. But in what follows I shall use the word in its strict sense, to refer to a penalty which is inflicted on the offender *from outside*, not intrinsically 'built into' the acts to which it is attached; and to imply some *correspondence* or *equivalence* between punishment and the deed which has evoked it (see further Travis 1986, 2–5). To what extent, then, do such ideas underlie Paul's references to the saving significance of Christ's death? The following discussion takes these passages in their probable order of writing, though nothing crucial hangs on their being taken in this order.

2 Key Passages in Paul's Letters

Christ redeemed us from the curse of the law by becoming a curse for us – for it is written, 'Cursed is everyone who hangs on a tree' (Gal 3.13).

This text forms part of Paul's argument against those who would insist that Gentiles submit to circumcision and the food laws – those marks of Jewish identity referred to as 'works of the law' (Gal 3.10). The intention is to show that it is 'in Christ Jesus' and 'through faith' that Gentiles may share in the blessings promised to Abraham (Gal 3.14). N.T. Wright has illuminated in the following way the route whereby Paul moves from verse 10 to verse 14. Paul is working with the theme of the covenant: Genesis 15 and Deuteronomy 27, both quoted here, are great covenant passages. In line with Jewish writers of the period (e.g. Damascus Document 1.5–8) he believed that the Jewish people was still experiencing the curse of exile predicted in Deuteronomy 27, and this left in doubt how the blessings to Gentiles, promised to Abraham, could ever be fulfilled. But now the problem has been dealt with. 'The covenant has reached its climax in the death of the Messiah.' When Paul says, 'Christ has redeemed us', he means Jews, who were under the judgement decreed by the law. And the purpose of their redemption was that their exile – their being distanced from God and his blessing – should be ended and the blessing be conveyed to Gentiles.

It is important to recognize here that Paul is concerned not so much with the sins of individuals incurring God's judgement, but with Israel as a whole which has failed to observe the Torah. And he can say that Christ has endured the curse on Israel's behalf because he sees him as representative of Israel.

Christ, as the representative Messiah, has achieved a specific task, that of taking on himself the curse which hung over Israel and which on the one hand prevented her from enjoying full membership in Abraham's family and thereby on the other hand prevented the blessing of Abraham from flowing out to the Gentiles (see Wright 1991, 137–56; quotations from 143 and 151).

Paul's argument is not a statement about atonement in general or about the salvation of individuals. His concern is not so much to explain how the death of Christ makes atonement for individual sinners as to show how it makes possible the coming of God's blessing to Gentiles (Gal 3.14).

So we must not read verse 13 as a general statement about atonement. If it is to shed light on our understanding of the atonement this must be by extrapolation from Paul's argument which is here specific to the situation of Israel-in-exile. We may say, perhaps, that just as Jesus, Israel's representative Messiah, through his death finally exhausted the curse of exile for the Jewish people and thus brought about the renewal of God's covenant with Israel (cf. 1 Cor 11.25) and opened the way for Gentiles to enter into union with Christ (Gal 3.14), so he took upon himself for all of us the consequences of our sinfulness and identified with our alienation from God in order to bring us into union with him.

Moreover, we may wonder whether Paul – despite the very specific reference of Galatians 3.10–14 to the situation of Israel-in-exile – had not already been doing some such theologizing himself. The fact that other New Testament writers allude to Deuteronomy 21.23 (as is evidenced by the description of the cross as a 'tree' in Acts 5.30; 10.39; 13.29; 1 Pet 2.24), though without making use of the covenant theology found in Galatians 3, suggests that there had already been some debate among Christians about the significance of that text in relation to the death of Jesus. There is evidence also in the Qumran Scrolls of the application of Deuteronomy 21.23 to instances of crucifixion. So it is likely that the question whether someone who had been 'hanged on a tree' in crucifixion and had thereby apparently come under God's curse could possibly be the Messiah had already been a point of controversy between non-Christian Jews and followers of Jesus (see Lindars 1961, 232–4; Wilcox 1977, 85–99). In view of the likelihood of such debate among Christians and between Christians and Jews, it seems plausible that Paul was aware of broader interpretations of Deuteronomy 21.23 than that which suited his specific purpose in Galatians 3. But we cannot be sure whether he would have found it appropriate to apply this theme of the covenant curse to Gentiles, or whether he felt that the 'curse of the law' was something peculiar to Jews. Certainly we do not find him reusing this particular imagery in any other letter.

Did Paul regard the curse of the law as a retributive punishment? It is true, of course, that the curses of Deuteronomy 27 are followed in Deuteronomy 28—31 with threats of retribution – predictions of exile and numerous warnings that 'the Lord will smite you . . .', 'the Lord will cause you to be defeated . . .', etc. On the other hand, divine judgement is also expressed there in non-retributive terms of God's 'hiding his face' (Deut 31.17–18; 32.20) so that his people, deprived of his protection, become oppressed by enemies of all kinds (see Travis 1986, 12). We can hardly know whether such details were in Paul's mind. But we can observe that in his citation of Deuteronomy 21.23 Paul alters 'accursed by God' to 'cursed' (*epikataratos*). Is this because he wants to put a certain distance between Christ's experience of forsakenness and the thought that this is specifically inflicted by God?

There is of course a certain equivalence or correspondence (part of my definition of retribution) expressed in Galatians 3.13 between the curse which threatened Israel and the curse which Christ endured on their behalf. But this does not imply a quantitative equivalence between the sins of men and women and the sufferings of Christ. It is part of the rhetoric by which Paul makes his point, an expression not of equivalence but of 'interchange', as M. D. Hooker has expressed it. And she notes that 'the experience of Gal 3:13 is not a simple exchange. It is not that Christ is cursed and we are blessed. Rather he enters into our experience, and we then enter into his, by sharing in his resurrection' (Hooker 1990, 16).

In saying that Christ 'became a curse for us' Paul is showing knowledge of the Hebrew text of Deuteronomy 21.23, which says that a hanged man is 'a curse of God' or 'an affront to God' (*qllt 'lhym*; cf. Jer 24.9; 42.18; Zech 8.13). Such daring use of language is found also in the next passage to be considered.

Having spoken of Christ's death 'for us' (*huper hēmōn*), Paul moves on to speak of blessing 'in Christ Jesus'. This combination of 'representation' or 'substitution' language with 'participation' language is something else to which we shall return.

For our sake he made him to be sin who knew no sin, so that in him we might become the righteousness of God (2 Cor 5.21).

Here again Paul uses extremely paradoxical language to speak of Christ's saving work. He is probably re-working traditional material (see discussion in Stuhlmacher 1965, 74–7; Martin 1986, 138–41, 156). But the formulation is consistent with Paul's own love of paradoxical expressions: in 2 Corinthians we find, for example, power through weakness (12.9), life through death (4.12), wealth through poverty (8.9).

God made (NB the divine initiative, cf. 2 Cor 5.19) to 'be sin for our sake' (*huper hēmōn* again) the one who 'knew no sin'. Several commentators understand this clause as an allusion to the sin offering – either to the unblemished animal sacrifice of Leviticus 4 or to the metaphorical use of sacrificial language ('*šm*) in Isaiah 53.10 (cf. Cyril of Alexandria, *Epistle 41*; Augustine's *Lectures on St John* xli.5–6, on John 8.31–6; Furnish 1984, 351; Martin 1986, 157; Dunn 1991a, 42–3). Others insist that it would be impossible for Paul to use *hamartia* in the two different senses of sin and sin offering in the space of three words and that the shocking mystery of Paul's language should be left to make its own impact (cf. Hughes 1962, 214–15; Barrett 1973, 180; Hooker 1990, 13). But in either case the essential point is that Christ has experienced the sinner's estrangement from God, he has absorbed and thereby taken away sin, so that we might be brought into a right relationship with God.

Once again language about Christ being offered 'for us' is linked with the statement that 'in him' we find righteousness. In identifying with sin for us as our representative Christ breaks its power and thereby frees those who are in him to share his righteousness (cf. the similar ideas in Rom 5.19; 6.10–11).

In his discussion of this passage Marshall comments: 'It is hard to understand this [Christ's becoming sin for us] in any other way than that in dying Christ exhausted the effects of divine wrath against sin' (1990, 264); he is influenced partly by the use of 'reconciliation' language in 2 Maccabees, on which we shall comment in connection with the next passage. But God's wrath is not mentioned in the context, and the focus is in fact on Christ's death absorbing or neutralizing the effects of sin. And that does not involve notions of retribution.

The formal correspondence of language between 'knew no sin' and 'righteousness' and between 'sin' and 'sin' evokes the same comment as was made above on Galatians 3.13. It is a stylistic device, not an expression of equivalence between sin and suffering. It could provoke eloquent expressions of worship, as in the *Letter to Diognetus*: 'O sweet exchange! O unsearchable operation! O benefits surpassing all expectation! that the wickedness of many should be hid in a single Righteous One, and that the righteousness of One should justify many transgressors' (ch. 9). But that is, appropriately, the language of wonder and worship rather than of theological precision.

. . . Christ Jesus, whom God put forward as a sacrifice of atonement by his blood, effective through faith. He did this to show his righteousness, because in his divine forbearance he had passed over the sins formerly committed; it was to prove at the present time that he himself is righteous and that he justifies the one who has faith in Jesus (Rom 3.24–6).

Here is yet another passage in which Paul makes use of traditional formulations in an exposition of the meaning of Christ's death. Discussion of these formulations is summarized by Dunn (1988, 163–4). There is dispute about precisely where the traditional material begins and ends, and how Paul has adapted it. But it seems misguided to suggest, as some do, that in verse 26 Paul is deliberately correcting earlier tradition. One may safely assume that Paul uses the tradition because he is happy to make it his own – or at least that if he were correcting it he would have made this a little more obvious to his Roman readers!

The particular questions which concern us are the meaning of *hilastērion* (verse 25: NRSV 'sacrifice of atonement'), and the implications of the double reference to God's righteousness in verse 26.

The debate as to whether *hilastērion* should be translated as 'expiation', 'propitiation' or 'mercy-seat' has become something of a war of attrition (Dunn 1988, 161–2, 171–2, gives references to most of the relevant literature). Clearly Paul is using sacrificial imagery to express the significance of Christ's death. But is he saying that this death serves to expiate or take away sin, or that it turns away God's wrath? The main arguments of those who opt for 'propitiation' are that the word group has this meaning at least sometimes in the Old Testament (e.g. Num 16.46; Dan 9.16), and that the whole context of Paul's exposition, beginning with the revelation of God's wrath in Rom 1.18–32, *requires* reference to the turning away of that wrath in the explanation of Christ's saving work in 3.21–6. Arguments in favour of 'expiation' are that in many Old Testament instances of the related verb *hilaskomai* the object is not God but human beings or their sins (e.g. 2 Kings 5.18; Ps 24.11); and that Paul here has God as the subject of the action. 'If God is the subject, then the obvious object is sin or the sinner. To argue that God provided Jesus as a means of propitiating God is certainly possible, but less likely' (Dunn 1991a, 49). Dunn has made out a strong case for the view that according to Paul's 'theology' of sacrifice Christ's death cancels out human sin by destroying it. However, the *effect* of sin being destroyed in this way is of course that the wrath of Rom 1.18–32 no longer hangs over those who identify with Christ as their representative. So it is possible to say that expiation leads to propitiation, and to avoid polarizing the two ideas (cf. Barrett 1957, 78).

However, to admit that a reference to God's wrath underlies Paul's use of *hilastērion* is not to introduce the idea of retribution. For if we ask what is the nature of the wrath described in Rom 1.18–32, we find that it is not the retributive inflicting of punishment from outside, but God's allowing of people to experience the intrinsic consequences of their refusal to live in relationship with him. 'God gave them up . . .' (Rom 1.24, 26, 28). God's wrath is his judgement experienced as alienation from God (see Travis 1986, 31–3, 36–8; 1992, 996–7). As *hilastērion* Christ does not suffer punishment from God and thereby avert his wrath; he enters into humanity's experience of sin's consequences to destroy sin and thus restore people to relationship with God.

Several scholars have sought to shed light on Paul's use of *hilastērion* here by appealing to the martyr theology of 2 and 4 Maccabees, where the deaths of the Maccabean martyrs are understood as having atoning, or propitiatory significance. In 2 Maccabees 7.37–8 the youngest of the seven brothers says to his enemies:

> I, like my brothers, give up body and life for the laws of our ancestors, appealing to God to show mercy (*hileōs genesthai*) soon to our nation and by trials and plagues to make you confess that he alone is God, and through me and my brothers to bring to an end the wrath (*orgē*) of the Almighty that has justly (*dikaiōs*) fallen on our whole nation.

In 4 Maccabees 6.28–9 Eleazar prays: 'Be merciful (*hileōs genou*) to your people, and let our punishment suffice for them (*arkestheis tēi hēmeterāi huper autōn dikēi*). Make my blood their purification, and take my life in exchange (*antipsuchon*) for theirs.' And 4 Maccabees 17.21–2 says that the seven martyrs have

> become, as it were, a ransom (*hōsper antipsuchon*) for the sin of our nation. And through the blood of these devout ones and their death as an atoning sacrifice (*dia . . . tou hilastēriou [tou] thanatou autōn*), divine Providence preserved Israel.

I do not wish to dispute the suggestion that Jewish martyr theology of this kind influenced early Christian thinking about the death of Jesus. But it seems to me a mistake of method to look to such texts for an explanation of what Paul's use of *hilastērion* means. The fact that the retributive ideas of 2 and 4

Maccabees are not explicit in Romans 3 strongly suggests that he does not accept the assumptions of those writers. Whereas these and other Jewish writings often suggest that the persecutions experienced by God's people are divine punishment for their sins, Paul nowhere expresses this assumption about the persecution of Christians. Is that because he believes that Christ has taken on himself the sufferings which would otherwise be due to Christians, or simply because he is working with a different set of assumptions? (see Travis 1986, 83–5).

In contrast to 2 and 4 Maccabees, but in line with the sacrificial cult of the Old Testament, Paul stresses God's initiative in providing the sacrifice. Hence it is likely that his primary reference is to the Jewish sacrificial cult itself as an image of Christ's death.

To elucidate the issues in Romans 3.25b–26 I will summarize two contrasting interpretations represented by the commentaries of C. E. B. Cranfield and J. A. Ziesler. According to Cranfield,

> Paul is saying in these two verses that God purposed (from eternity) that Christ should be *hilastērion*, in order that the reality of God's righteousness, that is, of His goodness and mercy, which would be called in question by his passing over sins committed up to the time of that decisive act, might be established.

He is taking *eis endeixin* to mean 'to prove', and *paresis* to mean 'passing over, leaving unpunished'. God's patient holding back of his wrath might have been interpreted to mean that he was indifferent to human sins – which would be a denial of his own nature. But now he demonstrates through the cross his decisive dealing with sin. God has done this so that he might be righteous even in justifying the one who believes in Jesus (verse 26b). He has maintained his own righteousness without compromise because in Christ's work as *hilastērion* he has himself borne the intolerable burden of evil and disclosed both his full hatred and his complete forgiveness of human evil (see the whole discussion in Cranfield 1975, 211–18; the quotation from 212). Cranfield does not say that Christ was bearing the punishment for sin, though he does insist on 'propitiatory sacrifice' as the meaning of *hilastērion*. But others who follow this general line of exegesis do make explicit use of retributive language. N. T. Wright says: 'Justification in the present depends on the achievement of an objective atonement in which sins are not ignored but dealt with in the proper way, by punishment. That punishment had not been meted out before (3:24ff). Now, on the cross, it has.' And Morris concludes that the New Testament writers 'see Christ as suffering in such a way as to remove from God the stigma of being unjust in remitting our penalty' (Wright 1980, 24; Morris 1966, 388; cf. Piper 1983, 115–30; Hill 1967, 158).

Ziesler, on the other hand, sees each instance of 'righteousness' and 'righteous' in verses 25 and 26 as expressing the same meaning as the initial declaration of God's righteousness in Romans 1.17. It is, as we have learnt from the Old Testament scholars, his loyalty to his covenant by which he commits himself to restore and sustain Israel; but now in the gospel this covenant loyalty is seen to embrace a saving purpose for all who have faith – Gentiles as well as Jews (1.16–17). Taking *paresis* to mean 'forgiveness', Ziesler sees God's saving righteousness as being demonstrated by his forgiving the sins formerly committed by people who are now receiving the gospel. To say that God 'is righteous (*dikaion*) and that he justifies (*dikaiounta*) the one who has faith in Jesus' means that he demonstrates his faithfulness and promise of salvation by accepting those who trust in Jesus (Ziesler 1989, 115–16; see further Ziesler 1972, 193–4).

How is one to choose between these two basic approaches, both of which could be elaborated with lists of supporting scholars and with details of argument about the numerous exegetical dilemmas lurking in this dense passage? For our present purposes, we may suggest that the first approach has an inner consistency and a long pedigree of interpretation. But its consistency does seem to depend on understanding *hilastērion* as the turning away of retributive wrath. And we have seen reason to question whether that is what Paul intends. The second approach does not underplay the seriousness of the human condition apart from divine grace, and sees the death of Christ as the supreme demonstration of God's commitment to bring human beings into relationship with himself. But it does not imply a retributive understanding of the sufferings which Christ endured on the cross.

> Much more surely then, now that we have been justified by his blood, will we be saved through him from the wrath of God. For if while we were enemies, we were reconciled to God through the death of his Son, much more surely, having been reconciled, will we be saved by his life (Rom 5.9–10).

Here again Paul moves from sacrificial language ('blood') to the idea of sharing Christ's life. The juxtaposition of a reference to wrath ('of God' is not in the Greek text, as the NRSV margin notes) and to the reconciliation of enemies raises the question whether the enmity lies entirely on the human side, or whether Paul thinks of a hostility of God towards human beings (Käsemann 1980, 139, lists scholars on either side of this debate). Most scholars deny that there is any hostility on God's part, pointing out that Paul never uses the verb 'to reconcile' with God as the object. This is in contrast to passages such as 2 Maccabees 1.5; 7.33; 8.29, which certainly speak of God being reconciled to his people after expressing his wrath towards them.

As in the case of *hilastērion*, it would be dangerous to allow meanings in 2 Maccabees to determine exegesis of Paul. But since the logic of Paul's argument is that the sacrificial death of Christ was necessary to bring about our justification and reconciliation, there is more than a hint here of a hostility on God's part towards human sinfulness. Certainly in Romans 11.28 God is said to be the subject of hostility towards people. But that hostility is not to be conceived of as desire to inflict punishment. Rather is it an absence of relationship between God and human beings, which he has taken the initiative to overcome.

3 Some Further Considerations on Paul's Understanding of the Death of Christ

We have now, I believe, considered all of the passages in Paul's letters where a retributive understanding of the sufferings of Christ on the cross may be considered a serious possibility. And we have seen reason to believe that in each case a retributive interpretation is not the most likely one. This is not to deny that, according to Paul, God takes human sin with absolute seriousness, or that Christ on the cross experienced divine judgement on our behalf. But it is to suggest that to speak of Christ on the cross suffering our 'punishment', or enduring a retributive penalty for our sins, is to go further than Paul himself goes.

It is true, of course, that Paul has many allusions to Christ's death which *might* be interpreted in line with a retributive understanding of what he suffered. For example, if a retributive understanding were established on other grounds, all the statements that Christ died 'for our sins' (*huper tōn hamartiōn hēmōn*, e.g. Rom 4.25; 1 Cor 15.3; Gal 1.4) or 'for us' (*huper hēmōn*) or similar expressions (e.g. Rom 5.6; 8.32; 1 Cor 8.11; 11.24; Eph 5.2; 1 Thess 5.10) could be regarded as expressions of the same theological perspective. But such brief statements do not on their own establish such a doctrine, and they are capable of other interpretations. I want now therefore to make some observations about Paul's understanding of the death of Christ in order to try to set the passages discussed above in a broader framework.

1. Paul has more than one framework for understanding the significance of Christ's death. For instance, he can speak of Christ's sufferings as the beginning of the 'messianic woes' which herald the new age of salvation. D. C. Allison (1985, 65–6) finds allusions to this idea in e.g. Colossians 1.24; 2 Corinthians 1.5. Or he can use the image of sacrifice. Although attempts are made occasionally to minimize the significance of sacrificial imagery for Paul (see Käsemann 1969, 43–4), it is difficult to deny that he sometimes compares the death of Christ to the sin offering (Rom 8.3; see Wright 1991, 220–5), the Passover sacrifice (1 Cor 5.7) and the covenant sacrifice (1 Cor

11.25). As we have seen, sacrificial imagery crops up particularly when Paul is making use of traditional formulae, but it is by no means confined to these. He makes some use of the suffering servant theme – already itself a metaphorical application of sacrificial ideas – as when he uses phrases such as 'he was handed over to death for our trespasses' (Rom 4.25) and God 'gave him up for all of us' (Rom 8.32; cf. *kurios paredōken autōn tais hamartiais hēmōn*, Isa 53.6 LXX; *dia tas hamartias autōn paredothē*, Isa 53.12 LXX). Or he can refer often to our participation in Christ's death and resurrection (e.g. Rom 6.3–4) – a theme to which we shall return. In the context of the range of language and imagery used by Paul, it is important to notice how comparatively few are the passages where we have been able to find even the possibility of a retributive framework of understanding.

2. Insofar as it is possible to discern a rationale of sacrifice in Paul's use of this imagery, the rationale seems not to be one that fits comfortably with a retributive framework. In Chapter 1, John Goldingay has noted that there is no clear rationale of how the Jewish sacrificial system worked within the Old Testament itself. But Dunn (1991a, 43–7) believes he can reconstruct Paul's understanding of what sacrifice signified from his references to Christ's death as sacrifice. He finds that the sin offering, like Jesus's death in Romans 8.3, was meant to deal with sin; that, as Jesus in his death represented humanity in its fallenness ('in the likeness of sinful flesh' Rom 8.3), so the sin offering represented sinners in their sin; and that the death of the sacrificial animal was seen as the death of the sinner *qua* sinner – that is, the destruction of the person's sin (in Rom 8.3 it is *sin* which is 'condemned', i.e. destroyed, done away with). Dunn acknowledges that aspects of his argument are vigorously contested, but his understanding of the matter does seem to fit with the hints given by Paul himself.

If this explanation holds good, there is no place for the popular idea that in the sacrificial ritual God is somehow *punishing* the animal so that the punishment should not fall on the sinner who presents the sacrifice, or for the inference that something parallel to that is happening in the sacrificial death of Christ.

34

The point is rather that as the sinner identified with the sacrificial victim the sin was transferred to the animal and destroyed through its death (cf. Gunton 1988, 120).

3. Already within the Old Testament and Jewish literature sacrifice had begun to be spiritualized in terms of obedience. The prophetic demand for obedience *rather than* sacrifice is well known (Isa 1.10–17; Jer 7.21–3; Hos 6.6; Amos 5.21–5; Mic 6.6–8; Ps 40.6–8; 50.7–14; 51.16–17). But a passage such as Ecclesiasticus 35.1–5 expresses the idea that obedience to the moral demands of God 'fulfils' or 'serves as' or 'substitutes for' sacrifice: 'The one who keeps the law makes many offerings; one who heeds the commandments makes an offering of well-being. The one who returns a kindness offers choice flour, and one who gives alms sacrifices a thank offering. . . .' Within the New Testament the Letter to the Hebrews, for all its detailed allusion to priesthood and sacrifice, explains that the sacrificial system has been superseded by Christ's obedience, citing Psalm 40: 'Sacrifices and offerings you have not desired . . . Then I said, "See, God, I have come to do your will, O God"' (Heb 10.5–10) (cf. Caird 1980, 71–2).

In the Pauline literature the obedience of Christ is perhaps not explicitly described in terms of the fulfilment of sacrifice (though 2 Cor 5.21 and Eph 5.2 come close). But certainly Christ's obedience is a key motif in the presentation of the significance of Christ's death in Romans 5.18–19. (Is there here an allusion to Isa 53.11, which also speaks of 'the many' being made 'righteous' – through the 'sacrificial' self-giving of the servant?) In obedience to the Father, Christ identified with Adam's race, shared in Adam's death, and attained to vindication and resurrection as the head of a new humanity. 'The many' share in his vindication and new life by identification with him as their representative Head.

4. This brings us to the connection between Christ's death and our 'union with him' or 'participation in him'. Although D. E. H. Whiteley overemphasized this theme in Paul in his anxiety to minimize the notion of substitutionary atonement, Paul is particularly fond of it as a way of talking about how Christ's death affects men and women (see Whiteley 1964, 130–

51). E. P. Sanders has been somewhat unfairly criticized for implying that Paul's 'participationist' language has not been properly integrated with his 'juristic' language (see Sanders 1977, 466, 507–8, 519–20).

It is notable how often Paul refers to Christ's death with a brief sacrificial allusion and then goes on to elaborate its purpose in terms of participation in Christ. Several times he uses sentences in the form: 'Christ gave himself for our sins (or similar) *in order that* we might live in him (or some such 'participationist' expression)'. For example: '. . . Christ, who died for us, so that . . . we may live with him' (1 Thess 5.9–10; cf. Rom 8.3–4; 14.9; 2 Cor 5.15, 21). An alternative formulation is found in 2 Corinthians 5.14, 'One has died for all; therefore all have died'. And if Paul can say we are 'justified by his blood' (Rom 5.9), he can equally well speak of our being 'justified in Christ' (Gal 2.17).

Two things should be noted here. First, 'participation in Christ's death and resurrection' is a central theme in Paul's presentation of Christ's death and its effect on humanity. When he talks about our being 'crucified with Christ' (Gal 2.19) or 'buried with him by baptism into death' (Rom 6.4), he means that we enter into his obedience so that we may also share in his resurrection life. 'Participationist' language such as this is far more frequent in Paul than language which might be understood as retributive in the sense discussed earlier.

But, second, the formulation of those sentences in the form, 'Christ gave himself for our sins *so that* . . .' (1 Thess 5.9–10 etc.) implies that in his death Christ achieved something objectively *before* the fruits of it were available to the subjective experience of those who have faith in him. Our 'participation' in Christ crucified and risen *depends* on his first 'dying for us'. It was while we were 'weak', 'ungodly', 'sinners', 'dead' that Christ died for us (Rom 5.6, 8; Col 2.13–14). The varieties of Paul's language about Christ's death cannot simply be collapsed into the theme of participation (cf. Packer 1974, 31–4). Rather, it should be recognized that the varieties of expression find their unity in the idea of Christ as representative Man, who identifies with sinful humanity and with whom we may identify ourselves

– in whose death and resurrection we may participate – through faith. (For a helpful exploration of the need for balance between 'objective' and 'subjective' in theories of the atonement, see Fiddes 1989.)

4 Conclusions

I have argued that Paul's understanding of the death of Christ does not include the idea that he bore the retributive punishment for our sins which otherwise would have to be inflicted on us. To understand the atonement in those terms is to misunderstand what Paul means by 'the wrath of God'. It is to press too far the implications of his legal metaphor. It is to risk driving a wedge between the action of God and that of Jesus (cf. Gunton 1988, 65; for forceful statements on the difficulties involved in retributive language see Lampe 1962 and 1968).

Rather than saying that in his death Christ experienced retributive punishment on behalf of humanity, Paul says that he entered into and bore on our behalf the destructive consequences of sin. Standing where we stand, he bore the consequences of our alienation from God. In so doing he absorbed and exhausted them, so that they should not fall on us. It is both true and important to say that he 'was judged in our place' – that he experienced divine judgement on sin in the sense that he endured the God-ordained consequences of human sinfulness. But this is not the same as to say that he bore our punishment. It is a perspective on the atonement which, I believe, confirms the understanding of divine judgement for which I argued in *Christ and the Judgment of God*: that judgement is not inflicted by God 'from outside, but is the intrinsic outworking, under God's control, of the consequences of human choices and actions, and that Paul's primary category for understanding salvation and condemnation is that of relationship or non-relationship to God.

Such an approach does not regard the human condition as any less serious than approaches which rely on retributive categories. But it is more in line with Paul's understanding of sin as a relational concept. It is very striking that Paul almost always uses his normal word for 'sin' (*hamartia*) in the singular. Of sixty-two instances, only nine are in the plural and at least four of these are in Old Testament quotations or are dependent on early Christian tradition (Rom 4.7; 11.27; 1 Thess 2.16; 1 Cor 15.3). This is because he understands sin not as a collection of individual acts but as a relationship of hostility towards God (cf. Kittel 1964, 309–10). It is that hostility, that whole mass of opposition to God, which Christ absorbed in his death. The danger with a retributive framework of thought is that it tends to regard sins as individual deeds, each requiring a corresponding penalty.

The retributive doctrine is right in its insistence that forgiveness cannot take place without a cost being borne. It is no light or easy thing to forgive and to restore broken relationships. A person who forgives another takes into himself or herself the hurt and the pain which has been caused, rather than throw it back at the offender in retaliation. The meaning of the cross is that in Christ God himself took responsibility for the world's evil and absorbed its consequences into himself. He was not punishing his Son in order to avoid punishing his creatures. Admittedly, we may sometimes speak of athletes or academics 'punishing themselves' in order to achieve some great goal, but we know we are using such language in a highly figurative way. And it would not clarify our understanding of the atonement to use such extreme imagery with reference to God. Given the helpful distinction between 'price' and 'cost' in language about redemption (Marshall 1990, 251), we may rather speak of God 'absorbing the cost' of remaking our relationship with him (cf. Moule 1971).

3

Your Iniquities Have Made a Separation between You and Your God

JOHN GOLDINGAY

THERE IS A sense in which no Christian doctrine can be discussed in isolation from all the others, for Christian belief is a coherent whole rather than an assembly of unconnected modules. The death of Christ cannot be understood independently of his resurrection, nor atonement in isolation from Christology or from the Trinity. Insofar as atonement is concerned with the solving of a problem, the reconciliation of humanity and God when they were separated, in particular we need to discuss the nature of that separation if we are to understand the at-one-ment.

I   The Symbolism of Sin

Scripture has a telling range of terms for sin: to list the most common of these, sin means failure, rebellion, transgression, trespass, turning from the right road, stain, infidelity. Each of these terms is a symbolic expression – it takes some deeply significant human experience and utilizes it to illumine aspects of the nature of our relationship with God. I should not imply that this illumination is all one-way traffic: no doubt inner awareness of such features in our relationship with God helps us to understand our ordinary human experiences and relationships, as the notions of fatherhood and family start with God and move from there to humanity rather than vice versa, according to Ephesians 3.14–15. But we actually go about conceptualizing and articulating our relationship with God in the light of the deep and significant human experiences to which we have more immediate access. The human experiences provide us with our symbols for thinking and communicating. And as is often the case with symbols, any individual expression opens a window on a broader symbolism or on a story of which it freezes a single frame. Each symbol belongs to a comprehensive picture of relations with God.

We are familiar, for instance, with the human experience of accepting the political authority of an imperial power for the sake of the benefits of security and order such a relationship can bring. The treaty relationship places us under obligation of allegiance to this power and limits our freedom in relation to other powers, both great imperial powers to whom we might submit and other powers of equivalent status to our own with whom we might ally on equal terms for mutual benefit. To transfer our allegiance to some other authority or to ally with other states independently of our relationship with that supreme authority or to adopt some other policy unapproved by the imperial power counts as rebellion (e.g. 2 Kings 1.1; 18.7). It is likely to attract the imperial power's attention and provoke it to 'pay us a visit', as the delightfully mafia-like Hebrew expression puts it, to brings us back into line. Such vengeance may possibly be averted if we terminate the rebellion and pledge renewed allegiance; the imperial power may then be willing to grant us pardon. God, then, is like an imperial power (God is Lord), our covenantal relationship with God involves allegiance to the exclusion of other allegiances, sin is like the rebellion which breaks such a covenantal relationship (e.g. Hos 8.1), it puts us in danger of God paying us a visit to put us in our place, but repentance can open up the possibility of pardon. The two Hebrew terms for rebellion are *pesha'* (often translated 'transgression' in English Bibles) and *mered*. The word 'rebellion' appears strangely rarely in the English New Testament, translating the Greek word *parapikrasmos*, but it seems likely that the more common word translated 'sin', *hamartia*, also has this connotation (in the Greek Old Testament *hamartia* often translates *pesha'*).

In this example, as in the ones that follow, in various ways

I schematize for the sake of clarity. The Old Testament speaks of 'rebellion' in the context of parent-child relationships, for instance (see Isa 1.2), as well as those of political relationships. No doubt the word for rebellion gained a theological life of its own; people who used it were not immediately aware of the whole story I have just summarized. We ourselves will often use expressions such as 'Christ's redemption' without being consciously aware that we are thinking in terms of someone anointed by God buying back a slave from bondage. Yet these are not merely dead metaphors, but symbols which still carry freight – as we can see from their usage in other contexts.

The example also points to the limitations as well as the potential in all such symbols. Talk in terms of political authority-allegiance-rebellion-pardon illumines some aspects of our relationship with God but obscures others, as critique of the 'monarchic metaphor' notes (cf. Wren 1983). Any one family of symbols needs to be set in the context of the others so that we can avoid being led astray by some features of it. There are limitations to a comparison of God and the mafia Godfather.

Alongside the symbolism of rebellion is thus that of infidelity (Hebrew *meshubah*, literally 'turning' [to someone else]; Greek *apistia*). So the relationship between God and humanity is like a marriage: 'I belong to my lover and my lover belongs to me' has as its equivalent 'I belong to you as your God and you belong to me as my people'. One basic requirement of this relationship is a committed faithfulness which excludes other partners. Sin is then like the infidelity which makes a man or a woman behave as if they have the same rights over themselves as they had before they married, as if they are still free to give themselves to someone else. The imagery is used especially powerfully in Jeremiah 3. Such action probably indicates that there was already some breakdown in the relationship; when uncovered, the breakdown is deepened and is on the way to becoming separation and divorce. Reversing that process requires a desire to heal the relationship, a willingness to resume that exclusive mutual commitment, and a forgiveness on the part of the wronged party.

Or sin is like some equivalent act of disloyalty which wrongs a friendship (e.g. Jer 5.11; the Hebrew noun is *beged*, the Greek adjective *asunthetos*). So God is a friend who shares the mutual love of friendship with us. While friendship does not require exclusive loyalty in the manner of marriage, it presupposes a form of mutual commitment. Speaking ill of a friend, or taking advantage of the friendship, or acting in a way calculated to bring loss to the friend, imperils the friendship. It risks replacing friendship by anger, conflict, and enmity, which are so often the other side of hurt when a friend treats us in a way which suggests that the relationship means nothing to them. For the friendship to be restored requires mutual reconciliation. Our friendship with God is likewise imperilled by our behaving in a way which suggests that the relationship means nothing to us and which provokes that anger which is the other side of hurt. Its restoring depends on mutual reconciliation.

Or sin is like the ungrateful forgetfulness of a child. Hosea 11 relates the classic pained testimony of a mother or father who has given all the attention required of a parent in bringing up a child and has met with no response. Paul strikingly includes ingratitude as a damning feature of the attitude to God shown by humanity as a whole, which leads to its standing under God's wrath (Rom 1.21).

Or sin is like getting dirty (Isa 6.5; Lam 1.9). In the Old Testament this symbol is linked with the holiness of God. That holiness which suggests God's majesty, heavenliness, and glory is the characteristic which marks God off from human beings. We noted in Chapter 1 that it is originally not a moral category but a metaphysical one; it suggests supernatural transcendence, the distinctiveness which differentiates Creator from creature. It requires a parallel distinctiveness on the part of people who associate themselves with God. Such distinctiveness is imperilled through contact with the realm of blood and death which stains and pollutes. The stain (in Hebrew *tum'ah*) or impurity (in Greek *akatharsia*) spoils the relationship and requires cleansing.

Or sin is like wandering out of the way (the Hebrew term is '*avon*, a common expression usually rendered 'iniquity'; the less common equivalent Greek term is *planē*). So God is a guide who points out the right way to go if we wish to reach a certain destination. The relationship of travellers to their guide is that they take care to follow the way the guide points. But distractions or alternative advice or inattention may lead to their accidentally losing their way or deliberately turning out of the right way (cf. Isa 53.6; Jer 3.21). Instead of being straight, their journey becomes tortuous, twisting, and twisted. They err and go the wrong rather than the right way and as a result get lost or find themselves in exile. The nature of being lost or exiled is to make it difficult or impossible to get back to the right road or to return to one's home; we need the guide to follow us and restore us.

Or sin is like trespassing on someone's property or rights or honour (e.g. Josh 22.16–31; Rom 4.5; 5.6). A human being is likely to possess home and land and rights such as honour, freedom, and privacy; God, too, is one who has rights that require respect. God's own person deserves honour. Sin involves trespassing on God's rights (in Hebrew *ma'al*), refusing to recognize God's majesty (in Greek *asebeia*), and putting oneself into God's debt (the expression which appears in the Lord's Prayer). The question is whether we can make up for such neglect or offer God satisfactory compensation for such loss. Some debts can be repaid, but others cannot; we can only rely on the creditor's willingness to remit the debt so that it no longer stands between the two parties.

Or sin is like the transgression of law (the Hebrew verb is '*abar*, the Greek noun *parabasis*). God, then, is like a human monarch in his or her capacity as lawmaker or legal authority. This aspect of the monarch's role had great importance in the Middle Eastern world: there the king or queen has responsibility for the making of laws which preserve order in society and safeguard people's rights, especially the rights of the less secure and powerless. Subjects have responsibility for obedience to those laws to that same end. Refusal to obey them counts as 'transgression', the crossing of bounds set by the law; it puts us in the wrong in relation to the law. It makes us guilty and renders us liable to the judgement of the courts and to the penalty which they have authority and power to exact, not least

43

as a way of dissociating monarch and nation from the values expressed in the acts of lawlessness. Normally there is no way to escape that punishment, though in special circumstances the monarch may exercise power of reprieve which restores the guilty person without their undergoing punishment. Similarly God is the lawmaker and legal authority in the world. As is ideally the case with the laws of the state, God's laws reflect the concerns of justice and reflect and buttress the very structure of reality itself. To live by God's laws is to live in obedience to God and in accordance with justice. To decline to acknowledge the just requirements of God's law (for instance by violence towards one's neighbour or by trampling on the rights of the powerless) is to decline to acknowledge God or to know God (see e.g. Hos 4.1–6). It is to become a transgressor: 'Sin is lawlessness' (1 John 3.4). It makes us guilty before God and renders us liable to God's judgement and to the punishment that God has power and authority to exact, which dissociates God from our injustice and lawlessness as well as doing something to restore justice to the violated. In considering reprieve with regard to such penalty, God would have to consider what this said about the unimportance of flouting just laws.

Or sin is like failure to achieve something (the Hebrew term is *chatta't*, the Greek *hamartia*). In secular usage the term suggests missing a target or missing the way (Judg 20.16; Prov 19.2). The most familiar allusion to sin in the entire Bible may be Paul's assertion that 'all have sinned and fall short of the glory of God' (Rom 3.23). It well illustrates how the term 'sin' itself can in Greek as in Hebrew suggest the idea of failure (though we have noted that its regular usage may suggest some more active wrongdoing). The story to which this symbol belongs envisages God as like a parent who lays a possible destiny before a child, a possible role for the child to fulfil, a possible calling for them, and who has the insight and experience to be able to indicate ways for them to realize this destiny. The implication need not be that the child is merely doing what Mother says; they have the opportunity to develop their own insight, make their own decisions, and make that calling their own. They are invited to take up this calling and fulfil their destiny in a way which will bring glory to them and glory to their parent. Sin is like neglect to make that destiny one's own, wilful and stupid failure to realize it. Its wilfulness indicates that we are speaking of more than accidental failure. If the New Testament does use the word *hamartia* with some of the flavour of the Old Testament word for 'rebellion', that reflects how sin involves active resistance to the destiny God sets before us. Its result is disappointment and futility: life has become pointless and meaningless, and the relationship between parent and child is spoiled by sadness, regret, frustration, let-down, and discomfiture. The question for the future is whether parent and child can find a new beginning to the path toward that destiny which the one has in mind for the other. Discipline (God's and the human parent's) will be of importance in encouraging this process!

2 The Extent of Sin

Old and New Testaments use this wide range of symbols to express the nature of sin. How prevalent a problem is it?

In our own parlance we have two ways of speaking of this matter. We can think of humanity as divided into the good, the bad, and the ordinary. The good are the especially generous, open, forgiving people. The bad are the abusers, the oppressors, the deceivers. We locate ourselves and most other people in between these two categories: neither especially good nor especially bad, as we see ourselves as neither especially wise or rich, foolish or poor. At the same time we recognize that whatever may be true of the bad, strangely the good do not see themselves as good, as the wise and rich fail to see themselves as wise or rich. Indeed, paradoxically we would doubt their goodness if they did. They are characteristically aware in themselves of a meanness, a self-centredness, and a resentfulness, even a capacity to abuse, oppress, and deceive, which they share with the so-called ordinary and bad.

Both Old and New Testaments also have these two ways of looking at goodness and badness. On the one hand, they can imply the division into the good, the bad, and the ordinary. Asked what one should do to inherit eternal life, Jesus simply reminds a questioner of the contents of the commandments about human relationships (Mark 10.19). When the questioner declares he has kept these, Jesus responds that this achievement entitles him to an attempt at a higher hurdle. He does not express doubt about the man's claim, directly or indirectly; after all, the commandments were never intended to be some impossibly idealistic standard (see Deut 30.11–14). God gave them to be fulfilled as the condition of staying in a right relationship. In line with that, Old Testament believers sometimes declare that they have indeed fulfilled them – and therefore, for instance, God has no moral reason for letting them be in trouble. Thus Psalm 18 invites the worshipper to declare an astonishing innocence of sin (verses 20–7), while the premise of the debate in Job is that there is such a thing as a person wholly committed to walking in God's way. Israel has its remarkably good, and it also has its remarkably bad: the devastating declaration 'your iniquities have made a separation between you and your God' (Isa 59.2 RSV) is not a general statement about human sinfulness but a pointed critique of a particular group of people in a specific context. NRSV's 'your iniquities have been barriers between you and your God' perhaps gives a truer impression.

The Old Testament also has indications of that other attitude which assumes the universality of sin. In Christian tradition we have been used to associating it with the opening chapters of Genesis; while this is a distinctively Christian understanding of these chapters, not paralleled in Jewish interpretation, it is not foreign to them. One aspect of the chapters' opening emphases is that there was nothing wrong with the world as God created it. The story is expressed in such a way as to set it over against the way other Middle Eastern peoples told the story of the world's beginnings, where the world came about as a result of fear and violent argument among the gods, and humanity itself was formed by the recycling of the corpse of the losing side's champion in this conflict. Conflict and violence antedate creation and permeate the raw material of creation. In Genesis the world and humanity were created good, even if it is odd that the serpent tempter is there in the Garden of Eden. Things go wrong because of human covetous stupidity inside the Garden and human jealous resentment East of Eden. The inclination to invade the divine sphere and the inclination to violence in the human sphere lead God to the gloomy conclusion 'that the wickedness of humankind was great in the earth, and that every inclination of the thoughts of their hearts was only evil continually' (Gen 6.5) – though it needs to be added that in Genesis 6 as in Genesis 2—3 humanity might feel itself a tragic victim of alien pressures as much as a wilful violator of divine love.

Of course that statement of humanity's universal corruption and violence (cf. Gen 6.11–12) might be seen as another contextual statement about a particular generation. Its apparent universalism is in any case compromised by the recognition that Noah does not conform to the rule of sin. Noah, indeed, is a man of justice and integrity, a man whom God likes to take out for company: in effect, the story virtually implies he is without sin. If it does, Noah subsequently manages to prove himself fallible like the rest, unable to contain his drink or control his children (though there is again an element of tragedy as well as of humoured pathos in the account) (Gen 9.20–7). So he is no complete exception to the further gloomy acknowledgement which comes the other side of the flood that in general 'the inclination of the human heart is evil from youth' (Gen 8.21; cf. Jer 17.9). When a psalm invites us to recognize that we were sinners when our mothers conceived us (Ps 51.5) it is only taking that conviction to its logical conclusion. We are sinners from our earliest beginnings. There is no one who does good; all are perverse (Ps 14; cf. 130.3; 143.2; 1 Kings 8.46).

This second side to the Old Testament's convictions about sin also reappears in the attitude of Jesus. He himself reacted negatively to being called 'good'; is the term appropriate to any human being? (Mark 10.18). Of course in truth he was the exception to this rule, but his questioner hardly implied such an awareness. Jesus identifies with the rest of humanity in affirming that in the absolute sense the word does not apply to him. Given that he rejected this description for himself, it is not surprising that faced by people who were committed to a life of goodness, or other people who were inclined to be impressed (or depressed) by them, he attempted to shake the former into a recognition that they had to face questions about what was going on in their inner selves and not be taken in by the outward symbolism of their goodness (Mark 7). These are the people who set the benchmark for goodness and commitment; so Jesus tells his own followers that he expects of them a more spectacular standard of right living (Matt 5). Not that he is romantic about those followers, as if poverty or ordinariness can be equated with goodness. They themselves are 'evil' rather than good (Matt 7.11).

Paul's talk of sin also has those two strands to it. He can (semi-humorously?) mull over the question whether a person might be willing to sacrifice their life for a righteous person or, more plausibly, for a good person (Rom 5.7). But even that hypothesizing is set in the context of a declaration that in the case of the self-sacrifice of Jesus the beneficiaries were ungodly, sinners, enemies of God, a characterization not of a wicked group within humanity but of humanity as a whole. Paul's thinking is indeed dominated by the second of the strands. In that most systematic exposition of his gospel in Romans he begins by setting forth his understanding of the nature and prevalence of sin, for this is the necessary backcloth to his understanding of the gospel.

Its prominence reflects the fact that we are now this side of Jesus's actual death and resurrection. Paradoxically (or perhaps not), sin becomes a problem when it has been dealt with.

Before his confrontation with Christ on the Golan Heights, Paul took the view Jesus encouraged, that his responsibility as a member of the covenant people was to see to his obedience to the commandments and live a life of commitment to God's ways. He recalls the moral and spiritual achievements of that life when he gives us his testimony in Philippians 3. There is no indication that he felt any conscious dissatisfaction with it as he drew near Damascus that day. Then he is overturned by the risen Christ and has to rethink his entire scale of values now he has to view Christ's resurrection as fact and to discover the positive theological significance of Christ's death. Attempting to think through convictions inherent in the account of the gospel he received (1 Cor 15.3), he comes to expound Christ's death as in some way designed to deal with human sin; but that means that the problem of human sin and the nature of real goodness must be more profound than he had realized. It gives him access to that second strand in Old Testament thinking expressed in Genesis, the Psalms, and Isaiah, which he expounds in Romans 1—5.

He sees that by nature we are not merely occasional law-breakers but habitual ones, like teenage joyriders breaking the law for kicks (but no doubt indicating our inner need as we do so), living a life not merely marked by individual transgressions but characterized by inherent lawlessness (*anomia*); against our own better judgement we ignore what the law expects and what we ourselves want (Rom 7). We prefer our own vision of our destiny and our own insight on how to achieve it ('earthly wisdom' rather than the divine grace expressed in the folly of the message of the cross: 2 Cor 1.12), and thus inevitably fail and fall short of the glory of God because that is not the destiny at which we are aiming (Rom 3.23). We are constitutionally rather than periodically rebellious; far from living as in a realm in which God exercises authority, we live under the authority of sin – in a sense by choice, but now unable to declare independence from its power, at least until God acts to take us from that realm into the realm of God's rule (Rom 5.21; 6.12–18). Having once wandered off from that path leading towards provision of grass and water along which the shepherd guides the sheep, we are lost and incapable of finding the way again (Luke 15.3–7). Far from being inclined to reverence God's claim on our lives and our worship, we are characterized by irreverence, impiety, and ungodliness. Our lives are not so much generally clean and pure even if needing cleansing from the occasional dirt which inevitably comes to attach to them, as hopelessly and deeply stained in a way which affects their every layer, quite spoils them, and shames us into hiding from the purity of God. Our infidelity to God as lover, our disloyalty to God as friend, and our ignoring of God as generous father has placed a barrier of conflict, anger, and enmity between us which we as the people in the wrong can hardly begin to attempt to overcome.

It is these realities which are analysed theologically as original sin and total depravity. As the Church of England Articles put it, 'Original sin standeth not in the following of Adam': it is not that we all start afresh and fall for ourselves. We are born into a humanity characterized by realities such as rebellion, lawlessness, and failure, living in a world in which sin has been allowed to exercise some authority. There is a certain inevitability about our being the same sort of people as those among whom we are born, grow, and live; we are bound up in the web of life with them in a way which links us in sin, as well as in other aspects of our being, with humanity as it goes back to its first turning away from God. And even our best deeds are affected by sin ('have the nature of sin': Article 13) because of the context in which they are set in our lives and the stain it gives them.

3   The Consequences of Sin

We have already begun to consider what are the consequences of sin. A prominent theme in theological discussion of this matter, important for our consideration of atonement, is the anger of God (see Campbell 1986).

One can perceive two ways in which Scripture envisages humanity under God's anger, in correspondence to the two ways of seeing the problem of sinfulness which we have considered. In the Old Testament in general, anger is God's response to particular wrong deeds rather than a characteristic attitude for God to take to human beings. Indeed, the Old Testament repeatedly affirms how slow God is to get angry (e.g. Exod 34.6), sometimes to the despair of God's servants who wish God would be a bit quicker (Jonah 4.2). In considering the Bible's symbols for sin we have referred to anger in connection with the friendship-disloyalty-reconciliation family of words. Sometimes a friend or relative or someone else who should have acted otherwise because of their relationship with us lets us down or deceives us or attacks us or imposes unreasonable expectations. It is then that we find we get angry (cf. Gen 27.45; 30.2; 31.36; 34.7; 39.19; 44.18). Anger is a strong feeling associated with jealousy, pain, and grief in the context of a personal relationship.

God's anger thus emerges from a close personal relationship with Israel. Israel is not permanently subject to God's anger, but is so from time to time as a consequence of its unreasonable attitudes which are parallel to the ones we have noted in connection with human relationships (e.g. Num 11.1; 12.9; 22.22; 25.3; 32.10). The motif of Yahweh's anger exercised on Israel from time to time (and on other nations) becomes a prominent one in the prophets (e.g. Isa 10.4, 5, 25). It is noticeably less prominent in contexts where there might be talk of atonement and the propitiation of God's anger.

It is thus questionable whether the Old Testament sees sacrifices as propitiating God's wrath. While anger is an important aspect of God's attitude to humanity in the Bible, there is hardly any book in which it is less prominent than Leviticus. Under the retroactive influence of the New Testament, the question of propitiating God's wrath has had a prominent place in discussion of sacrifice, but this concern has little place in Leviticus itself. The word anger hardly appears. The languages of atonement-propitiation-expiation and of anger do not come together. We have seen in Chapter 1 that the problem with sin in Leviticus is not that sin involves infidelity or disloyalty which makes God angry but that sin pollutes, stains, and spoils, and thus makes people or things repulsive; it is the u-u-u-ugh factor in our relationship with God. The problem that sacrifice thus deals with is not anger but revulsion or rather repulsiveness, a pollutedness of which human beings are as aware as God is. By means of sacrifice God makes it possible for humanity's stain to be dealt with. In this connection sacrifice 'is not something human beings do to God (propitiation) but something which God does for humankind (expiation)' (Fiddes 1989, 71). Sacrifice does not directly relate to anger.

A number of Psalms appeal to God to turn from wrath when no reason for the exercise of wrath is indicated. Christian instinct is to assume that such Psalms implicitly acknowledge that this wrath is a response to human sin; thus Psalm 6 is one of the Christian 'penitential Psalms' despite its offering no expression of penitence. More likely than the presupposition of an implied penitence is a different assumption. Such Psalms presuppose an experience of illness, defeat, or other calamity. They assume that God is responsible for what happens in the world, and is thus responsible for this experience. The event is the kind of thing that happens when someone is angry with you, so it is described as an expression of God's anger even though the Psalmist does not know what might have caused this anger. There is an even more impersonal expression of this way of thinking, when the Old Testament refers simply to wrath coming on someone (see notably 2 Kings 3.27).

The Pauline notion of anger corresponds to the second of the Bible's strands of attitude to the extent of sin. It sees the whole world as lying under God's wrath. This is not an Old Testament way of speaking, though there is an Old Testament equivalent to it. The Old Testament's way of expressing the reality to which Paul is drawing attention is to speak in terms of curse, not in terms of anger. As a result of events related in the opening chapters of Genesis the ground comes to be under God's curse, and so does humanity itself. The curse works itself out in the way in which the ground produces its fruit only at the cost of excessive toil. The idea of such a curse at work is paralleled by the way Paul speaks of God in wrath giving up humanity to the grievous consequences of its own rejection of God, in Romans I. Both indicate awareness of the fact that there is something grievously wrong with human life as we experience it, as a result of decisions made by God to allow (even to encourage) the consequences of human sin to work themselves out in human experience in the world. They do not imply that God's characteristic attitude to humanity is one of glowering anger. They do indicate awareness of that alienation and estrangement which may be the secularized form taken by separation from God in the modern age, not least as reflected in the work of Hegel, Marx, and Freud, and writers such as Camus and Sartre (cf. Dillistone 1968, 2–16, 399–404; Fiddes 1989, 6–12). In both the senses in which Scripture sees humanity as under God's anger (as an occasional and as an ongoing reality), it is something which hangs over us as well as something we experience. The wrath to come threatens to be more fearful than the wrath that has yet fallen upon us or worked out its way in our lives.

God's act of atonement in Christ was designed to deal with the deep and incurable sinfulness of humanity which expresses itself in rebellion against God's authority, infidelity which issues in breakdown of the relationship, disloyalty which has interrupted a friendship, ingratitude which has imperilled love, stain which has rendered humanity repulsive, perversity which has landed us in exile, offensiveness which has put us in debt, lawlessness which has made us guilty, and failure which leaves us far short of our destiny.

4

The Cursed Beloved: A Reconsideration of Penal Substitution

CHRISTINA A. BAXTER

THOUSANDS HAVE BEEN converted through the preaching of the penal substitutionary theory of the cross (though there are questions as to whether it remains a powerful tool in this part of the world in this decade). Have they been converted through a lie? I want to approach this question by looking at three classic expressions of the theory, in John Calvin, Benjamin Warfield, and John Stott. Two main purposes will be served by these expositions: we need to see what they say and we need to be clear on what grounds they affirm the theory. We will then be in a position to look at classical criticisms of penal substitution. We shall need to see if the criticisms address what is actually said or whether our authors as examples of this position have not really been engaged by their opponents. If there are real criticisms to be met, we will then need to think whether they are capable of response from within the model or whether they are of such a kind as to make the model unworkable. Finally we must address the question of what would be lost if we omitted these notions from our preaching.

1 John Calvin (1509–64)

In summary, Calvin teaches that 'all without any exception are defiled at their begetting' (*Institutes* II.1.6) and are 'justly condemned . . . before God' (1.8). Human beings are enslaved by sin and subject to death because in the fall of Adam all have sinned. The penalty or the punishment which we deserve because of sin is death (8.58). In order for that penalty to be averted from us there needed to be a mediator, who is the God-man, and 'we infer he was appointed by God's eternal plan to purge the uncleanness of men; for shedding of blood is the sign of expiation' (12.4). Isaiah 53 is cited as warrant for this necessity of expiation, which involves covering or dealing with sin. Christ 'declared that the reason for his advent was by appeasing God to gather us from death unto life' (12.4). He 'blotted out our own guilt and made satisfaction for our sins' (15.6). This involves more than an act of expiation; Christ went further and propitiated the Father, that is, placated or pleased him, averting his wrath. Thus God's wrath is focused on us without Christ, but the grace of God is made manifest in his sending of Christ who has propitiated the Father. 'For he became a sacrifice for us that "God might not count our trespasses against us"'. He assumed flesh so that he might 'be the propitiation of our sins' (1 John 4.10 AV): commenting on this verse, Calvin insists 'the word "appeasing" [*placatio*] is very important' (17.2).

> As a pure and stainless Mediator he is able by his holiness to reconcile us to God. But God's righteous curse bars our access to him, and God in his capacity as judge is angry toward us. Hence, an expiation must intervene in order that Christ as priest may obtain God's favor for us and appease his wrath' (15.6).

Our acquittal, says Calvin, is in this, that the guilt which made us liable to punishment was transferred to the head of the Son of God, who 'suffered the death that God in his wrath had inflicted upon the wicked' (16.10). The gospel account of Jesus's condemnation by Pontius Pilate is there

> to teach us that the penalty to which we were subject had been imposed upon this righteous man. . . . Thus we shall behold the person of a sinner and evildoer represented in Christ, yet from his shining innocence it will at the same time be obvious that he was burdened with another's sin rather than his own. . . . We must, above all, remember this substitution, lest

we tremble and remain anxious throughout life – as if God's righteous vengeance, which the Son of God has taken upon himself, still hung over us (16.5).

Calvin frequently alludes to Isaiah 53 as specifically referring to the person of Christ (e.g. 12.4; 15.3; 16.5, 6). Moreover,

> the cross was accursed . . . by decree of God's law. . . . Hence, when Christ is hanged upon the cross, he makes himself subject to the curse. It had to happen in this way in order that the whole curse – which on account of our sins awaited us, or rather lay upon us – might be lifted from us, while it was transferred to him. . . . Christ is our only redemption, ransom, and propitiation (16.6).

Because he took it, the sentence no longer threatens us. The sentence is God's anger or God's wrath. Nevertheless

> we do not suggest that God was ever inimical or angry toward him. How could he be angry toward his beloved Son, "in whom his heart reposed" [cf. Matt. 3:17]? How could Christ by his intercession appease the Father toward others, if he were himself hateful to God? This is what we are saying: he bore the weight of divine severity, since he was "stricken and afflicted" [cf. Isa. 53:5] by God's hand, and experienced all the signs of a wrathful and avenging God (16.11).

Jesus is the 'cursed' 'beloved'.

The significance of this event is so far-reaching for Calvin that he suggests, 'we see that our whole salvation and all its parts are comprehended in Christ [Acts 4:12]. We should therefore take care not to derive the least portion of it from anywhere else' (16.19). Christ has done all that is necessary and there is no need for anything to be done anywhere else by anyone else.

Calvin's theory of the atonement does make much of the sacrificial and saving death of Christ, but in discussing the question 'How has Christ abolished sin, banished the separation between us and God, and acquired righteousness to render God favorable and kindly toward us?', he specifically affirms that '*he has achieved this for us by the whole course of his obedience*' (16.5, my emphasis). Indeed, death without resurrection would not be effective:

> Therefore, we divide the substance of our salvation between Christ's death and resurrection as follows: through his death, sin was wiped out and death extinguished; through his resurrection, righteousness was restored and life raised up, so that – thanks to his resurrection – his death manifested its power and efficacy in us (16.13).

Before commenting on this way of looking at the atonement, it may help us to set it in context. R. S. Franks (1962, 135) explains that Anselm (1033–1109) saw the death of Christ in terms of private law: many individuals owed God a debt which could not be repaid, so Christ pays the debt in their place. This does not involve any punishment; it is 'simply' payment of debt. By contrast, Grotius (1583–1645) construes the death of Christ in terms of criminal law, so that Christ bears the wrath or the anger or the punishment of God against sin. It is this context of criminal law which gives rise to the notion of 'penal substitution'. Arguably the seeds of this notion are to be found in Calvin, but he does not spell it out in as much detail, nor does he draw the extreme conclusions which make Franks suggest (1962, 404) that 'Grotius shows himself a true Arminian, and nearer to the Catholic than to the Protestant view'.

This helps us to see how substitution can be understood in differing ways, not all of which are penal. In Anselm's case substitution could be positively evaluated as costly self-offering, though this leaves open the question whether monetary models well describe God's relationship with God's people. Anselm's theory is thus not without problems, but it does describe the atonement in terms of costly self-offering on our behalf and in our place, without resorting to notions of punishment. It therefore does not have the extremely difficult task of showing how the atonement can be the act of one God if it is postulated that the Father punishes the Son. Nevertheless, Anselm's theory does not escape some of the tensions which most explanations of the atonement produce for the doctrine of the Trinity.

Although Anselm's theory is not penal, it is genuinely substitutionary. Modern theology has drawn a distinction between Christ as our representative and Christ as our substitute. Whereas a representative does something for us which we could have done for ourselves, 'Jesus is our substitute because he does for us what we cannot do for ourselves' (Gunton 1988, 165). For Calvin, too, substitution involves Christ's doing for us that which we could not do for ourselves, but he more often casts it in terms of God's wrath against sin, because he finds that language in Scripture, and he therefore highlights our enmity to God. But we must also note with Paul van Buren that Calvin is very careful in the way he explains this substitution of Christ and this bearing of God's wrath on our behalf. He never handles the love and the wrath of God as though they are in direct opposition to one another. They are always understood as being partners in God's relationship to us. 'As seriously as Calvin takes the Fall of man he never for a moment regards it as a Fall out of the realm of God's love' (van Buren 1957, 7). Calvin himself quotes Augustine's comments on John 17.21–3 (*Lectures on St John* CX.6) in this connection: 'The fact that we were reconciled through Christ's death must not be understood as if his Son reconciled us to him that he might now *begin* to love those whom he had hated. Rather, we have already been reconciled to him who loves us, with whom we were enemies on account of sin' (16.4, my emphasis). So it is not the case that God loves us in creating us good, is wrathful to us in the period from the fall to the cross, and now can love us again. Rather, God loves us throughout, even though, while we were yet sinners, we also experienced his wrath because of our enmity against him.

If it is true that for Calvin human beings are both loved of God and subject to God's wrath, this is even more true for Christ. In his commentary on Galatians Calvin observes:

He could not be outside God's grace, and yet He endured His wrath. For how could He reconcile Him to us if He regarded the Father as an enemy and was hated by Him? Again, how could He have freed us from the wrath of God if He had not transferred it from us to Himself? Therefore He was smitten for our sins and knew God as an angry judge' (1965, 55; cf. van Buren 1957, 44).

So Calvin keeps the love and the wrath of God together in the Father, in relationship to us, and in relationship to Christ, in a way which echoes very clearly Paul's pattern of thought; in the gospel 'the righteousness of God is revealed' *and* 'the wrath of God is revealed' (Rom 1.16–18). Although Calvin sets his substitutionary understanding of the atonement in a criminal context, both this trinitarian framework and his notion of incorporation in Christ prevent him from understanding it in impersonal and mechanical ways which would be offensive, because it would make God like a machine which must stamp something and does not much care whether the object passing along the conveyor belt is a letter or a newborn baby. The stamping must happen; it is a matter of indifference what it is that is going to be stamped. It would correspondingly be an impersonal mechanical way of saying there has to be judgement, there has to be wrath, if we said it does not much matter whether this judgement is borne by those who have actually done the evil deed, those who are at enmity, or by someone else. Calvin avoids that problem by presenting the atoning act in a context of relationship. It is the act of the Father with the Son. The Son is acting in obedience to the Father and this is a whole-life activity. It is not just in the death of Christ that we see Christ acting on our behalf but in his life, death, and resurrection. The whole of this is somehow 'on our behalf'. 'The whole of the course of his obedience' was redemptive; 'from the time when he took on the form of a servant, he began to pay the price of liberation in order to redeem us' (16.5).

Another way in which Calvin minimized the problems of setting substitution in a penal context is by taking seriously the New Testament emphasis on incorporation, Christ being in us and we being in Christ (see *Institutes* III). Our being incorporated into Christ is the act of God the Father by the power of the Spirit. 'The Holy Spirit is the bond by which Christ effectually binds us to himself' (1.1). And that act of God is the way in which we receive the benefits of the cross and the resurrection. It is not a mechanical transaction, a legal pronouncement, or a kind of banking arrangement; it is personal and relational. 'So long as we are without Christ and separated from him, nothing which he suffered and did for the salvation of the human race is of the least benefit to us. To communicate to us the blessings which he received from the Father, he must become ours and dwell in us' (1.1). Van Buren suggests that for Calvin 'incorporation means the realisation of substitution' (1957, 97). So relationships within the Trinity are collaborative, the Father, the Son and the Spirit acting together, although in ways which may be differentiated. The relationship between human beings and Christ is equally crucial for us. These perspectives guard Calvin against some of the sharpest criticisms of the penal substitutionary theory. Nevertheless Calvin can still write that our ransom also required Christ 'to undergo the severity of God's vengeance, to appease his wrath and satisfy his just judgment. For this reason, he must also grapple hand to hand with the armies of hell and the dread of everlasting death' (16.10; cf. van Buren 1957, 57).

So although Calvin has a strong trinitarian framework in which he emphasizes that the Father and the Son act together, nevertheless he is not prepared to use it in such a way as to preclude the possibility of distinguishing between Father and Son, nor will he abandon talk about the Son feeling the severity of the divine wrath. The question with which this leaves us is one of language as well as theology. Does it stretch credulity too much to say that the Father simultaneously loved his Son and allowed him to experience the full force of divine wrath?

What are the bases upon which Calvin makes this assertion? First, he says that sin is enmity to God, against which God's wrath is bound to come, and that this wrath comes bearing death. He says this because he believes he finds it in the Old and New Testaments. Second, he affirms that the innocent death of Christ is on our behalf, and again he affirms that because he believes he finds substitution and exchange notions in both

Testaments; he is especially influenced by Isaiah 53 to which he make frequent reference. Third, he assumes fairly readily the notion of criminal punishment as the correct framework in which to understand these two notions. But fourth, he moderates all this by his emphasis on the relational considerations within the Trinity and between God and those who have faith.

2 Benjamin Breckinridge Warfield (1851–1921)

B. B. Warfield was Professor of Didactic and Polemic Theology at Princeton Theological Seminary from 1887 to 1921. He is regarded as a classical exponent of conservative evangelicalism. His collected essays (written on various occasions) on *The Person and Work of Christ* cannot be treated in the same way as the systematic treatments by Calvin or Stott. They include nothing approximating to a chapter on our theme, but Warfield refers to it intermittently as a key issue. What follows is a reconstruction of his thinking from the chief passages.

Warfield remonstrates against some of his contemporaries who present the atonement in what he regards as an inadequate way. First, they are inadequate because they exalt God's benevolence at the expense of God's truthfulness and integrity. We might summarize their view as, 'Of course God will forgive me, that's his job!' By contrast, in scriptural revelation (to use Warfield's terms) God

> is thoroughly honest, a thoroughly conscientious God – a God who deals honestly with Himself and us, who deals conscientiously with Himself and us. And a thoroughly conscientious God, we may be sure, is not a God who can deal with sinners as if they were not sinners. In this fact lies, perhaps, the deepest ground of the necessity of an expiatory atonement (386).

God cannot pretend sinners are not sinners. And that Warfield regards as one of the key problems with other theologies of the atonement.

Second, he suggests that those who are writing in response to the substitutionary theory of the atonement are wrong to suppose that the heart of the problem is how God can induce recalcitrant human beings to repentance, not how a righteous God can forgive sinners while remaining righteous. 'Our modern theorizers are never weary of ringing the changes on this single fundamental idea. God does not need to be moved to forgiveness; or to be enabled to pardon; or even to be enabled to pardon safely. . . . The whole difficulty is to induce men to permit themselves to be pardoned' (384). For these theologians God has no problem forgiving freely, his only problem is getting us in a state of repentance where we can be forgiven.

So third, Warfield says, the problem with this way of seeing things is that it diminishes human sinfulness.

> Nothing, indeed, is more startling in the structure of recent theories of the atonement, than the apparently vanishing sense of sin that underlies them. Surely, it is only where the sense of guilt of sin has grown grievously faint, that men can suppose repentance to be all that is needed to purge it. Surely it is only where the sense of the power of sin has profoundly decayed, that men can fancy that they can at will cast it off from them in a 'revolutionary repentance'. Surely it is only where the sense of the heinousness of sin has practically passed away, that men can imagine that the holy and just God can deal with it lightly. If we have not much to be saved from, why, certainly, a very little atonement will suffice for our needs (387).

Fourth, in some authors he suggests that even moving us to repentance is not absolutely necessary. This makes atonement a human work: all that God requires to restore right relationship to himself is our repentance. Marcus Dods had remarked that the death of Christ 'has made forgiveness possible, because it enables man to repent with an adequate penitence, and because it manifests righteousness and binds men to God' (1900, 187). Warfield comments,

> there is no hint here that man needs anything more to enable him to repent than the presentation of motives calculated power-fully to induce him to repent. That is to say, there is no hint

here of an adequate appreciation of the subjective effects of sin on the human heart, deadening it to the appeal of motives to right action however powerful, and requiring therefore an internal action of the Spirit of God upon it before it can repent: or of the purchase of such a gift of the Spirit by the sacrifice of Christ. As little is there any hint here of the existence of any sense of justice in God, forbidding Him to account the guilty righteous without satisfaction of guilt. All God requires for forgiveness is repentance: all the sinner needs for repentance is a moving inducement. It is all very simple; but we are afraid it does not go to the root of the matter as presented either in Scripture or in the throes of our awakened heart (380).

Fifth, neither does Warfield regard the idea of Christ's vicarious repentance on our behalf as adequate. He berates P. T. Forsyth for teaching what he considers as little more than this.

Christ sympathetically enters into our condition, he tells us, and gives expression to an adequate sense of sin. We, perceiving the effect of this . . . are smitten with horror of the judgment our sin has thus brought on Him. This horror begets in us an adequate repentance of sin: God accepts this repentance as enough; and forgives our sin. Thus forgiveness rests proximately only on our repentance as its ground: but our repentance is produced only by Christ's sufferings: and hence, Dr. Forsyth tells us, Christ's sufferings may be called the ultimate ground of forgiveness (382)

– because they make us repent, but not because they have done something to change our status before God.

In place of this and other defective expressions of the atonement, Warfield goes back to sacrifice and satisfaction as key ideas which cannot be abandoned (368).

Our Lord's redeeming work is at its core a true and perfect sacrifice offered to God, of intrinsic value ample for the expiation of our guilt; and at the same time is a true and perfect righteousness offered to God in fulfillment of the demands of His law; both the one and the other being offered in behalf of His people, and, on being accepted by God, accruing to their benefit; so that by this satisfaction they are relieved at once from the curse of their guilt as breakers of the law, and from the burden of the law as a condition of life; and this by a work of such kind and performed in such a manner, as to carry home to the hearts of men a profound sense of the indefectible righteousness of God and to make to them a perfect revelation of His love; so that, by this one and indivisible work, both God is reconciled to us, and we, under the quickening influence of the Spirit bought for us by it, are reconciled to God, so making peace – external peace between an angry God and sinful men, and internal peace in the response of the human conscience to the restored smile of God.

Warfield acknowledges his debt to Anselm, and to what he regards as the classic notion of the atonement found in the creeds of the universal church. He suggests that it 'reached its complete development only at the hands of the so-called Protestant Scholastics of the seventeenth century' (368). He has outlined for us the chief features of substitution, 'in behalf of His people'; sacrifice, which expiates guilt; satisfaction, 'accruing to their benefit'; such that it obviates the need for works-righteousness (he does not use the actual word justification here, but it is this to which he is referring). This act, Warfield argues, is a revelation both of God's love and of his righteousness. He seems to want to go further than the New Testament in saying not only that God was in Christ reconciling the world to himself, but also that there is a reconciliation of God to the world: the atonement solves not only the problem which sinful human beings have in coming close to God, but also the problem which God has in admitting sinful human beings to his fellowship.

Warfield clearly believes that he bases this summary upon the Scriptures, upon the teaching of the early universal church, and upon classic Protestant statements. He also considers it important that alternative ways of understanding the death of Christ are insufficient. In particular he thinks that repentance on our part is not enough. It is not enough for God, because our sin remains, even though we have repented of it, so God still has to admit sinners to his fellowship. It is not enough for us, because it makes repentance our work, something we have to do, and our 'doing' is clearly problematical – the human record is that our 'doing' always falls short.

Warfield assumes, like Calvin, that human sin produces guilt and that this guilt makes us accursed before God. He, too, assumes that those things are all to be found in the Old and New Testaments. He also assumes, as does Calvin, the New Testament notions of substitution and exchange, that Christ is in our place and that we somehow or other are able to be in his. Unlike Calvin, however, he sets his thinking not in the criminal law court but in the civil law court scene of indebtedness.

3 John R. W. Stott (1921–)

The Cross of Christ (1986) is John Stott's systematic exposition of his understanding of the cross, about which he has written and preached throughout his ministry, and it provides a contemporary example of evangelical understanding of the penal substitutionary theory of the atonement. In discussing why Christ died, Stott emphasizes that Christ 'died for us' (63) 'that he might bring us to God' (64). He 'died for our sins' and he 'died our death' (64). He briefly but clearly relates why substitution must be accompanied by penalty.

> According to Scripture, death is related to sin as its just reward: 'the wages of sin is death' (Rom. 6:23). The Bible everywhere views human death not as a *natural* but as a *penal* event. It is an alien intrusion into God's good world. . . . Throughout Scripture, then, death (both physical and spiritual) is seen as a divine judgment on human disobedience. . . . All this means that the simple New Testament statement 'he died for our sins' implies much more than appears on the surface. It affirms that Jesus Christ, who being sinless had no need to die, died our death, the death our sins had deserved (64–5).

So Stott's argument runs: 'death is the wages of sin'; Christ did not need to pay those wages and therefore took the penalty on our behalf. In a moving passage, Stott argues that it is unthinkable that in Gethsemane Jesus was a coward faced with death, especially since Christian martyrs and martyrs of other faiths go to their death bravely and even cheerfully. Rather Stott attributes this agony to dread of the cup of God's wrath which Christ faced, 'the spiritual agony of bearing the sins of the world, in other words, of enduring the divine judgment which those sins deserved' (76; cf. Calvin, *Institutes* II.16.11–12).

But Stott is always careful not to speak as though this somehow involved division or war within the Godhead, and specifically between the Father and the Son: it was God himself who 'pursued us even to the desolate anguish of the cross, where he bore our sin, guilt, judgment and death' (83). Moreover, 'we must never characterize the Father as Judge and the Son as Saviour. It is one and the same God who through Christ saves us from himself' (140). Elsewhere Stott is even more repudiating of such notions. 'Jesus Christ did indeed bear the penalty of our sins, but God was active in and through Christ doing it, and Christ was freely playing his part' (151). Stott has responded to one of the classic criticisms of this theory, that it so divides the persons of the Trinity as to depict God as un-Christlike. Thus he writes,

> we must not, then, speak of God punishing Jesus or of Jesus persuading God, for to do so is to set them over against each other as if they acted independently of each other or were even in conflict with each other. We must never make Christ the object of God's punishment or God the object of Christ's persuasion, for both God and Christ were subjects not objects, taking the initiative together to save sinners (151).

He underlines this later by affirming that

> the substitute bears the penalty, that we sinners may receive the pardon. Who, then, is the substitute? Certainly not Christ, if he is seen as a third party. Any notion of penal substitution in which three independent actors play a role – the guilty party, the punitive judge and the innocent victim – is to be repudiated

with the utmost vehemence. It would not only be unjust in itself but would also reflect a defective Christology. For Christ is not an independent third person, but the eternal Son of the Father, who is one with the Father in his essential being (158).

This is Stott's version of Barth's 'Judge judged in our place' which puts the judge, not a third party, in the dock.

When Stott explains why a holy and righteous God could not simply let us off our sins and forgive as human beings forgive one another, he writes, 'At the cross in holy love God through Christ paid the full penalty of our disobedience himself. He bore the judgment we deserve in order to bring us the forgiveness we do not deserve' (89). The reason why God acted in this way is expressly not associated by Stott with any necessity external to God. It is not that God is under some external binding force, whether this is to maintain the moral order or to keep his own law, as if there were some external constraint upon God. Rather God acts as the Gospels record, because of God's integrity. What God has prescribed and promised, God fulfils, for God is not capricious. What God wills, God wills. Hence God's words and actions are always integrated and flow uninterrupted from God's inner life (see further 123–8).

Stott goes further in affirming 'we may even dare to say that our sins sent Christ to hell – not to the "hell" (*hades*, the abode of the dead) to which the Creed says he "descended" after death, but to the "hell" (*gehenna*, the place of punishment) to which our sins condemned him before his body died' (79). So he reads the cry from the cross, 'My God, my God, why have you forsaken me?', as revealing that 'an actual and dreadful separation took place between the Father and the Son; it was voluntarily accepted by both the Father and the Son; it was due to our sins and their just reward' (81). Thus he adheres to the notions of satisfaction (123), sacrifice (134), and substitution (149). All these are construed in objective terms: it is not a sympathetic, representative or emotive suffering but a world-changing activity. It changes God's attitude to us and ours to God.

Having examined sacrifice, Passover, and servant songs in

Old Testament thinking, all of which he considers to be consciously related to the death of Christ in the New, he writes,

> we are obliged to conclude that the cross was a substitutionary sacrifice. Christ died for us. Christ died instead of us. Indeed, as Jeremias puts it, this use of sacrificial imagery 'has the intention of expressing the fact that Jesus died without sin in substitution for our sins' (149, quoting Jeremias 1966, 36).

The bases on which Stott is working are as follows. First, he, too, is affirming that sin brought death into the world and that death is a punishment. Second, Christ's fear of death must have a different meaning from other people's fear of death, because it is unthinkable that he was a coward. Third, God's holiness and righteousness mean that God would rather die for us with integrity, than allow us to die, or allow us to remain in sin, or pretend that we are righteous when we are sinful. So God's holiness and righteousness leave God with only one real choice. Refusing the alternatives, God chooses to die for us with his own integrity intact in a way which does not contravene what God intends and what God stands for. Fourth, behind these assertions there is a particular way of reading the Old Testament in relationship to the New, which has features in common with both Calvin and Warfield.

Criticisms of the Penal Substitutionary Theory

Five major criticisms appear in the lines of thought expressed by many different theologians. First, those who stand in the liberal Protestant tradition argue that an ontological act – a changing of our status or being or a real change in the relationship between God and humankind – is not capable of demonstration and raises more problems than it solves. They suggest that a demonstrative or subjective view of the atonement is sufficient, and raises far fewer theological problems.

Second, there are those who argue that the penal substitution understanding of the atonement is unethical. Frances Young (1975, 86) summarizes these critics as suggesting that 'such a picture is immoral, repugnant and sub-Christian. God's justice, they say, is hardly maintained by the immoral punishment of an innocent victim instead of the guilty sinner.'

Third, the penal substitution view is criticized as either un-trinitarian or actually tritheist. Frances Young, again, summarizes this objection (1975, 86): 'It is hardly good Trinitarian theology to envisage a loving Son set over against a wrathful Father as mediator on our behalf.'

Fourth, there are those who argue that the model is self-contradictory. It does not work. We cannot say both that the Father acts with Christ to save the world and that the Father acts against Christ in saving the world. We cannot say that the beloved is also simultaneously cursed. The question here is whether the model involves contradiction or dialectical tension. Is it possible to give any meaning to the two contentions contained in 'God still loves us while he is yet wrathful against us'? Yet that is one of the questions which needs to be addressed if the New Testament makes both propositions.

Fifth, it may be argued that those who hold the penal substitution view misuse the material found in the two Testaments. They assume that if Jesus's death is to be understood in a sacrificial framework, then that in itself implies that it must be understood in terms both of substitution and sin; Chapter 1 of this book has questioned that. They place a disproportionate reliance on Isaiah 53 as the framework for understanding Jesus's death. They rightly emphasize that the New Testament uses substitutionary language, but they take insufficient account of the nuanced ways in which that language is deployed. They recognize that the Epistles especially allude to the wrath of God, but do not note that they always fall short of saying that the Father punished the Son. They pass too quickly from realistic narrative to theological proposition without considering whether the narrative can bear the weight of significance which is being placed upon it. For instance, if Jesus of Nazareth stands in for Jesus Barabbas, does that mean that Jesus of Nazareth is necessarily standing in for everyone else? Is one level of explanation necessarily to be associated with the other? How do we know that this narrative symbolizes that and how might we establish whether it may rightly be deployed this way? When these hermeneutical problems come together, we find that images, models, and analogies offered by the New Testament writers are merged in such a way as not always to allow them to be mutually illumining, and rather sometimes to deny the integrity of the individual pictures (contrast Gunton 1988, 165, where he urges us not to treat the legal metaphor in isolation from others).

Punishment – a Reconsideration

If the penal substitution theory of the atonement really depends on the notion of punishment, then one has to face the question why this punishment is being meted out. In a court of law, people may be punished for a number of reasons. We punish them to reform them, or to give an example to other people, or to make retribution so that things are even again, or to make them suffer beyond what retribution requires (as they would if we required two eyes for an eye), or to protect society. No doubt these motivations can overlap, but they are capable of intellectual separation, and are to a certain extent capable of actual separation. British readers will recognize that different elements are espoused by different political parties. So which (if any) of these notions are being advanced by those who espouse the penal theory?

Clearly the death of Jesus is not reformative, in the normal sense of the word; it does not reform Jesus, but in any case the death penalty is never reformative, and in this case, being without sin, Jesus does not need reforming. Nor is it exemplary in the normal sense of the term, since an innocent person suffering instead of the guilty will not deter the guilty. It might have the opposite effect, as Paul spotted in Romans: we may continue to sin for grace to abound (6.1). It might possibly be a deterrent for people who see what might befall them if they act as it was alleged that Jesus had done; but this is not an idea found in any of the three writers whose work we have examined.

Is the death of Jesus penal in the sense of making him suffer? Often this is the objection of those who oppose the theory of penal substitution, thinking that this lies at its heart. In civilized countries the law does not normally allow punishment which is designed simply to make the guilty party suffer for vindictive reasons. It *would* be sub-Christian to think that the Father could take pleasure in the death of his Son because his justice requires suffering beyond the scope of retribution or putting right what was wrong. Although those who executed Jesus may have believed that they were protecting society, this is not the understanding of penalty appealed to by any of our authors. Society is not to be protected from Jesus, it is to be protected by, or better, saved by, Jesus. So we come to our final category of penalty or punishment, namely retribution.

Is the penal substitutionary theory saying simply that somehow or other God must have his pound of flesh as a kind of retribution? The divine retribution must be exacted against someone; if it is exacted against us, then that would be the end of us, so it is exacted against Christ because then there is the possibility that the innocent sufferer can be raised again; it is not the end of the story.

It important for us to understand that there are at least two situations in which a retributive penalty might be inflicted. The first is where it is possible that the wrong situation can be put right; an example might be the breaking of a window. The second is where the situation cannot be put right; an example might be the permanent blinding of an eye. Retribution can be equal, fair, and proportionate in the first case; the child gives part or the whole of its pocket money to pay for a new window. In the second case retribution is notoriously difficult: hence the nature of Old Testament laws, and the fierce contemporary debate about fair judgements in cases of maiming or rape.

In affirming that the atonement must be understood as penal substitution, is it being asserted that the situation can be put right, or not? All our authors are convinced that that is indeed the gospel. It can be put right. It is therefore misconceived to criticize the penal theory on the grounds that, if blinding a blinder is not equitable, blinding an innocent person for the sake of blinders cannot be equitable. Penal substitution does not imply that God was vindictive. Our authors are arguing that it is like God deciding to pay the bill for the broken window himself. There is penalty. There is cost (the New Testament word!) There is no free lunch at the end of the universe even for God. But the cost of forgiveness is cost to God; the cross is God's declaration and payment of that cost.

Penal ideas can be understood either actively or passively. If I have been offended, I can either be an actor who initiates revenge or I can choose to bear the penalty myself so that it becomes my passion. The penal substitutionary theory of the atonement is not saying that God the Father is an actor who initiates revenge against Jesus his Son, because he does not want to initiate revenge against the true perpetrators. It is saying that God has chosen to carry the penalty himself so that it becomes his passion. A very carefully refined penal idea of the atonement has moved from the image of penalty as punishment to the image of penalty as costliness or debt.

There is a sense in which Anselm's theory handles a thoroughly modern problem. The choice for God is between cost and cost – the cost of seeing humankind die through lack of redemption, and the cost of dying to redeem the human race. Anyone who has had a car broken into knows the choice between cost and cost. Will I pay for the repairs myself now, or will I claim on my insurance and lose my 'no-claims bonus'? Old and New Testaments seem to be telling us that our lives are so bound up with God, that God's life is so bound up with God's people, that there is penalty for sin, either for God or for us. The good news is that God's choice was the costliness of redemption; the cursed beloved were redeemed by the Cursed Beloved.

5

Can One Man Die for
the People?

TOM SMAIL

MY TITLE REFERS to the words put into the mouth of Caiaphas as he tries to justify his plotting of the death of Jesus.
'You do not understand', he says, 'that it is better for you to
have one man die for the people than to have the whole nation
destroyed' (John 11.50). The evangelist immediately proceeds
to add his own comment, 'He did not say this on his own, but
being high priest that year he prophesied that Jesus was about
to die for the nation, and not for the nation only, but to gather
into one the dispersed children of God' (verses 51–2).

Caiaphas was simply expressing the rather cynical opinion
that the death of Jesus was a price worth paying to avoid the
dire consequences with the Roman authorities that might arise
for the Jewish establishment were his ministry to be allowed to
continue, but John uses his statement to emphasize that in the
death of Jesus something decisive was taking place that would
have profound and beneficent consequences not only for Jews,
but for the whole of humanity. His death, in a way that Caiaphas
could never have comprehended, is *huper tou laou*, on behalf of
the people, and my purpose in this chapter is to ask what that
could mean and in what sense it was possible.

There can be no doubt that the phrase is central to the way
that the New Testament writers understand and interpret the
death of Jesus. At the very heart of the good news was the claim
that Paul restates in 1 Corinthians 15.3, not as something that
he has invented but something he has received, 'For I handed
on to you as of first importance what I in turn had received:
that Christ died for our sins (*huper tōn hamartiōn hēmōn*) in
accordance with the Scriptures'. That makes more precise the

Johannine statement, by telling us that what Jesus accomplished on our behalf through his death was effective in dealing with our sins. That again is a common New Testament theme that can make an excellent claim to go right back to Jesus himself and the words with which he shared the bread and wine at the last supper with the disciples, 'This is my body that is for you' (*sōma to huper humōn*) (1 Cor 11.24) and, with the reference to sin even more explicit in Matthew's version of the word over the cup, 'This is my blood of the covenant, which is poured out for many for the forgiveness of sins' (*to peri pollōn ekchunnomenōn eis aphesin tōn hamartiōn*) (26.28).

The prepositions are significant; he dies 'on account of us' (*peri*), 'on behalf of us' (*huper*), and even occasionally 'instead of us' (*anti*) as in Mark 10.45 where the Son of Man is said to have come to give his life 'a ransom for many' (*lutron anti pollōn*). The precise meaning and the theological implications of these prepositions have been the subject of endless discussion over the centuries, but it is enough for me to allude to them as indications of the good biblical foundation for the basic starting-point of this chapter, namely that in dying on the cross Jesus was acting in a vicarious way as our representative on our behalf, or even as our substitute in our stead, doing for us something that on the one hand we were in no position to do for ourselves (*anti hēmōn* – in our place), but something, on the other hand, that was so effective that it involved us deeply and personally, transforming our relationship to God in the present and the future in a far more profound way than any action of our own.

How is it possible for one person to act so decisively on behalf or in place of an unspecified number of other persons in a realm as central and personal as that of atonement, reconciliation and salvation? What is it that this one man can do that is so critical and transforming, not just for his contemporaries but for countless numbers of people far removed from him in time and distance? What by dying can one man do that will make possible and actual a new and reconciled relationship to God for all the people?

Substitution and Evangelical Theology and Preaching

The claim that the death of Jesus has this vicarious element at the heart of it has been very central to the reformed evangelical understanding of the cross, claiming, in my view rightly, that in this it was being faithful to the whole New Testament witness, and especially of course to Paul. One of the main bastions of evangelical orthodoxy, second only in importance to the supreme authority of Scripture, has been the profession of what in the jargon is called a penal substitutionary view of the atonement, that Christ brought us back into reconciled relationship to his Father by bearing on the cross the punishment for sin that was our due.

Now reformed evangelicals are very good at making assertions of that kind and adducing biblical passages that appear to go at least some way in supporting these assertions, but could we really say that many of them have much notion what these assertions mean or know how to justify them to other people? What is it that Jesus did that made all the difference to me and by what right was he able to act on my behalf or in my stead? Questions like that need to be asked and answered, because if they are not, penal substitution remains a theological shibboleth that does not make living contact with real people and the real issues that concern them.

One of the tests that show whether or not we understand our own theology is what happens when we try to preach it. Much contemporary preaching of the cross, whatever the formal theology of the preacher, simply abandons all thought of Christ's having done once for all for us on the cross that which reconciles us to God, and presents the cross as the demonstration in time of God's eternal love for and identification with humanity in its misery and failure. We speak much more with Moltmann of Christ's justifying God to us by sharing on the cross our suffering and God-forsakenness than of Christ's justifying us to God by bearing our sins. The cross becomes much more the justification of an empathizing God to a suffering world than the reconciliation of a sinful world to a holy God. The former approach is to be welcomed but not if it replaces or excludes the latter. No account of the meaning of the cross can claim to be adequate to the New Testament that does not see it in terms of atonement, of the self-giving of Christ once for all on Calvary on behalf of all of us to remove the barriers that sin has created and to bring us into reconciled relationship with his Father.

But that message is very hard to put across in preaching to contemporary Christian congregations, to say nothing of evangelism to our gospel-unfriendly culture, and stories about judges coming down from the bench to pay the fines or even face the death sentences they have imposed on convicted criminals only serve to make the whole process more unreal and indeed unjust.

Part of the trouble is that contemporary society is not interested in the solution because it is not even aware of the problem. How the sinner could be brought back into right relationship with God was a burning question in the sixteenth century: it was the shared starting point of Luther and those who sold indulgences as well as of the people they were addressing, so that they had no difficulty in getting a hearing for their totally different answers to it.

But people nowadays are more worried about their sufferings than about their sins, and modern evangelicals are often more interested in their charismatic experiences than in how Christ (in the words of the Prayer Book) suffered 'death upon the cross for our redemption and made there (by his one oblation of himself once offered) a full, perfect and sufficient sacrifice, oblation and satisfaction for the sins of the whole world'. That is in essence the reformed catholic answer to the question of how God saves us from our sins. Presumably biblically-based Christians still allow the Scriptures to interpret their own situation and their own need to them, so that, whatever others may think, they do know that there is a sin question to be answered and that we are all vitally and personally involved in what that answer might be. There is however good reason to wonder how far they themselves have any clear idea about what it means to say that our situation as sinners was dealt with decisively when Christ died for us on the cross. It might perhaps be just as well that others are not listening if we ourselves do not know what to say.

Problems about Vicariousness

Our problem with understanding Christ's vicarious death, has, I suggest, two main causes. It arises in part from real inadequacies and deficiencies in the theory of penal substitution that we have inherited, but even more from the individualism of the culture that has shaped us, that has dug into it a sense that we are morally autonomous, that we are responsible for ourselves and to ourselves, so that any salvation or moral liberation that might come to us is not something that can come to us from some source outside ourselves, but has to be something each of us achieves for ourselves alone. The moral philosophy that I was taught in Glasgow nearly fifty years ago was totally resistant to all notions of grace, as illegitimate intrusions upon individual freedom, and the specific Christian claim that my salvation depends on Christ's death on my behalf on the cross was indignantly repudiated as immoral and unreal. Whether we know it or not, the individualistic presuppositions that came to expression in that philosophy are hidden not far under the surface in us all and make it hard for us to come to terms with what Christ was doing for us on the cross.

Among the pioneers of the moral individualism that came to its full flower in the culture of the Enlightenment were the Socinians of the sixteenth and seventeenth centuries, who are of special interest to us because they engaged in a critique of reformed theology in precisely the area of our concern. They were unitarians who denied the divinity of Christ and in their soteriology they declared that it was unthinkably unjust for God to punish the innocent Jesus instead of those who had sinned. Pannenberg (1968, 264) quotes D. F. Strauss's summary of the Socinian position on this matter.

> Neither merit nor guilt and punishment . . . is transferable. Not merit, because the law does not demand just good works in general, but also that they be the deed of him who stands under the law. Ethically religious guilt and punishment are not, however, something objective like debts of money – with which the church's orthodox doctrine did not hesitate to compare them –

but something personal, bound to the individual. A debt of money is held to be satisfied when paid, whether by the debtor himself or by another. A moral debt, however, is not paid at all unless it is atoned for by the one who has incurred it.

I react to that rather ambiguously. On the one hand I am dismayed because the last sentence seems to put paid to the whole notion of substitutionary atonement. If it is true, how can I go on saying, 'Behold the lamb of God, who takes away the sins of the world'? And yet, on the other hand, I cannot but assent to the argumentation by which that damaging conclusion is reached. Guilt and punishment are not like fines, things that can be incurred by one person and settled by another. Intrinsically by their very nature, and morally by every rule of justice, they are inseparably attached to the person who, by what he or she does and is, has incurred them. In saying that, am I just conniving with the Socinians in the individualistic prejudices of the culture to which we both belong, or am I sharing with them a valid insight into the way things really are, so that it really is both immoral and impossible for one man to share another's guilt and bear another's punishment?

All this raises profound questions about how people can and do relate to one another. Is the truth about me that I am an isolated individual to whose inner citadels of freedom no one else has access, so that at the end of the day I have to carry a responsibility for myself and my actions that nobody else can take away from me? Or is the truth about me that I only am what I am in relationship to other people, so that responsibility for what I have done and am, what I will do and will become, rests mainly on them and the society to which they belong?

These are the questions that ultimately we have to grapple with if we are going to say anything convincing about vicarious atonement, and here at least we make contact with debates that are of great contemporary interest and relevance in social philosophy, in political debate between the corporatist left and the individualistic right, in penal theory and practice. When there are riots on housing estates in Newcastle and Oxford, are we dealing mainly with villains or mainly with victims, with

78

people who bear responsibility for what they have done, or with people whom other people and society in general have misshapen and betrayed? We shall treat them in very different ways according to how we answer these questions, and they are questions of a similar kind to those that arise as we try to understand the atoning death of Christ.

The Possibility of Vicarious Action

It is interesting that the Old Testament in different contexts affirms both our deep dependence on others and our inalienable personal responsibility in matters connected with our salvation. On the one hand we can think of the marvellous story in Genesis 18 where Abraham is pleading with God to spare the wicked cities of the plain and appeals precisely to the justice of God as the ground on which he should spare the whole city for the sake of ten righteous men, if such can be found in it. 'Shall not the Judge of all the earth do what is just?' (18.25), and his doing what is just will consist precisely in his saving the many on the merits of the few. This is clearly a very different kind of justice than that to which the Socinians so confidently appeal.

And of course, far more centrally, the whole notion of vicarious atonement finds its Old Testament crown in Isaiah 53, 'He was wounded for our transgressions, crushed for our iniquities; upon him was the punishment that made us whole, and by his bruises we are healed. All we like sheep have gone astray; we have all turned to our own way, and the Lord has laid on him the iniquity of us all' (verses 5–6). Penal substitution has always based its case for biblical support on this passage, certainly as far as the Old Testament is concerned.

Ezekiel 14 tells a very different story. 'Mortal, when a land sins against me by acting faithlessly, and I stretch out my hand against it, and break its staff of bread and send famine upon it, and cut off from it human beings and animals, even if Noah, Daniel and Job, these three, were in it, they would save only their own lives by their righteousness, says the Lord God' (verses 13–14). One can almost hear Socinus muttering 'Amen'.

The juxtaposition of these two insights within the Old

Testament tradition may perhaps suggest that it would over-simplify a complex situation to demand a straight choice between them as mutually exclusive alternatives. Our reconcili-ation with God is both something that can and must be done for us, but it is done for us in such a way that we are not excluded from it or deprived of our freedom by it, but rather enabled in real personal response to make it our own. Paul both proclaims a deed done for us and requires us to make our own response to it: 'In Christ God was reconciling the world to himself' is almost immediately followed by 'We entreat you on behalf of Christ, be reconciled to God' (2 Cor 5.19, 20), and our understanding of the vicarious work of Christ must give both what had to be done for us and what could then be done by us their appropriate place. What is done for us and what is done in us and by us are not to be set over against each other. Both are essential elements in our reconciliation with God.

Can we therefore make progress by suggesting that what can be done vicariously for us depends on three factors? First, it depends on the status of the person who is acting on our behalf, how he is related to those on whose behalf he is acting and how he is related to God in whom his action has its source and towards whom it is directed. Second, the possibility of acting vicariously on behalf of others depends on the nature of the action undertaken. If a theory of atonement that understands the cross as Christ's bearing of our guilt and punishment is open to criticism, because the bearing of guilt and punishment is possible only for the person who has committed the sin, might there be other ways of understanding what Christ has done that are not open to these objections? Might it even be that these ways are more faithful to the New Testament witness than some of the orthodox expressions which Socinus credibly rejected? Third, granted that vicarious atonement is something that has to be done for us and that we were incapable of doing it for ourselves, that does not mean that it is done in such a way that we are excluded from it. As R. C. Moberly never tired of saying, an atonement that is done over our heads, that does not reach us, claim us, affect us, involve us, is no atonement at all (see e.g. 1901, ch. 7).

We are going to try to elucidate Christ's vicarious atonement, then, by asking three questions about it. Who was it that did it? What was it that he did? How are we ourselves involved in what has been done on our behalf?

Who Was It that Died for Us?

Who was it that atoned vicariously for us? How did he relate to us so that he could reconcile us to God and how did he relate to God to whom we were to be reconciled? The artificiality and contrivedness that adhere to some Protestant approaches to the atonement stem from their emphasis on forensic imputation rather than incarnational identification. Forensic imputation means that Christ can act for us because by the decree of God our sins are transferred from us to him, so that he can bear them and be punished for them. As the Socinians rightly pointed out, such a view ignores the human and moral realities of the situation. Sins are so personally connected to sinners that you cannot by some legal fiat lift them from one person and land them on another. That is the unreality you end up with if you try to understand atonement in isolation from incarnation, the cross apart from Christmas.

The biblical emphasis, however, is that Christ's relationship to us and our sins is not one of legal imputation but rather one of real and costly identification. He was able to act for us because he became flesh (John 1.14), and became sin for us although he had no sin (2 Cor 5.21). He entered in complete self-giving identification into the human sinful situation. He faced the external and internal pressures that are exerted on fallen people in a fallen world, without himself falling into sin. His qualification to act for us was that he had made himself totally one with us. 'By sending his own Son in the likeness of sinful flesh, and to deal with sin, he condemned sin in the flesh' (Rom 8.3). 'Therefore he had to become like his brothers and sisters in every respect, so that he might be a merciful and faithful high priest in the service of God, to make a sacrifice of atonement for the sins of the people' (Heb 2.17). His solidarity with us in our sinfulness came about, not by some legal fiction or external divine decree, but by his entering our sinful situation and taking upon himself our fallen humanity.

R. C. Moberly suggests that one person can feel and share the shame of another when they are connected by nature or by love, and most of all when they are connected by both, as in the case of a mother and her child, his favourite example (e.g. 1901, 121–6). When my child falls into sin and shame, because I am related to that child as a loving parent, in a very real sense I stand with my child in his shame: his shame becomes mine. That double identification of shared nature and intense love is Christ's qualification to enter and deal with the situation that has been created by our sin.

But the one who acts on our behalf is not only totally one with us. He is also totally one with God. 'In Christ God was reconciling the world to himself.' The agent of atonement, according to the developed Christology towards which that verse is pointing, is not only our fellow human being but the creator God. The one who goes to the cross is God's incarnate Son, 'God from God, Light from Light, true God from true God, begotten not made, of one being with the Father. Through him all things were made.'

The one who acts on our behalf on Calvary is identified with us as our fellow man, but his right to act for us depends on the fact that he is also the Lord our God, as indeed Thomas confessed him to be when the crucified rose again. That means that any attempt to understand God's part in the atonement as being to punish an innocent human individual in place of many guilty human individuals is wide of the mark. He who bears our sins is indeed one with us, but he is also one with God, so that it is God and not just a sinless human individual who hangs and suffers on the cross. God did not substitute an innocent third party between himself and sinful humanity, he substituted himself, he acted as himself and he acted as one of us, as both reconciling God and needing-to-be-reconciled man.

When Athanasius contended with the Arians for the *homoousios*, the identity of being of the Son with the Father, he did so for christological and trinitarian reasons, but also for soteriological reasons. Only God could do for us what Christ has done by his cross and resurrection.

If the Son had been a creature only, man would in no way have been rescued from death, not being united with God. For a creature cannot unite creatures with God, itself needing to be united; nor could a part of creation, itself needing to be saved, be the saving of creation. To avoid this He sent His own Son, who took created flesh . . . that, when all were within the danger of death, He, being other than all, Himself for all might offer His own body to death (*Against the Arians* 2.69).

R. C. Moberly (1901, 352), commenting on this and similar passages in Athanasius, makes the very point we want to make here.

There is a perfectly unique possibility in the Son of God, of representing all mankind, and dying as the representative of all; a possibility which, if it rests in one direction on the verity of His manhood, rests no less on His being the Logos who was with God, and was God, – the Life of life, the Image of the Father, the Creator of all created being; a possibility, therefore, which cannot even be conceived on any other side, or in any other person.

In other words we are not to limit the possibilities of what Christ did for us to what one human creature might be able to do for another human creature. Socinians who were unitarians had no alternative but to do that, because for them Christ was simply another, no doubt exceedingly holy, human creature, and therefore they had to limit what he could do for us to what one creature could do for another.

If, however, the one who dies on Calvary is who the Nicene Creed says he is, God the Son, of one being with the Father, through whom all human creatures were made, then what he can do for us is what the Creator can do for his creation, which is quite different from, although not in contradiction with, what one of us can do for the others. As Moberly says, because of who he is, his possibility of acting on our behalf is 'perfectly unique' and 'cannot even be conceived on any other side, or in any other person'. The only measure we can have of what the

Creator can do when he becomes man on behalf of his creatures is what he actually has done when he came as man in Christ. What he has done will not annul the norms of justice that he himself has established, that are the expressions of the holiness of his own nature, but it will fulfil these norms in a way and to a degree that is impossible and incomprehensible for any of us and that we can comprehend only by looking at what he has done. In the case of God the possibility is measured by the actuality; we know what he could do only from what he did do.

Thus the answer to our question about who it was that acted for us is that it was God incarnate himself. He has a twofold right to act for us, the right of one who has identified himself totally with us as man, and the right of one who has created us as God. He stands totally on the human side with us sinners and totally on the divine side with his Father and it is as such that he can represent us and redeem us in a way that is unique to himself alone.

What Was It that Christ Did for Us on the Cross?

Our second question was, What was it that Christ did in our place? What did the Creator do for his creatures, what did the incarnate Lord do for his people, that far surpassed anything that any of us could do for one another? As we take up that question, we have to emphasize again that his redeeming action on the cross will express and be in accordance with the justice and holiness that are essential to his nature. The demands of his own justice and holiness will be fulfilled in a way that is far beyond our own unaided thinking or imagining, but they will be fulfilled and not annulled in what he does on Calvary. 'Shall not the Judge of all the earth do what is just?' We shall therefore look at some of the ways in which his substitutionary death has been understood in modern reformed theology and ask, Was this something that it could have been both right and saving for God in Christ to do for us?

The typical Protestant answer to that question is that he had to bear on the cross in our stead God's punishment for the sins

84

of the world. God punished Jesus for our sins instead of punishing us, that we might go free. There are all sorts of objections that can and must be raised against this way of viewing the matter.

First, it can be objected that it offers a completely unacceptable view of the relation between the Father and the Son. P. T. Forsyth (1910, 146) asks in what sense it is true that the sacrifice of Christ was penal and goes on, 'Well, it cannot be true in the sense that God punished Christ. That is an absolutely unthinkable thing. How could God punish Him in whom He was always well pleased? The two things are a contradiction in terms.'

Second, by what right or justice can punishment be imposed on anybody except the person who has committed the offence? Is the bearing of punishment not one of those things that cannot be done by one person for another, where the protest on behalf of inalienable individual responsibility made by Ezekiel, echoed by Socinus, must be allowed to stand? Even though I, who am innocent of the offence, should be willing to bear the punishment you have incurred in committing the offence, it would be an unjust judge that would permit let alone organize such an illegitimate transfer.

Third, is it true to the New Testament to say that God's chief concern in the death of Jesus is to exact punishment for sin? Are the sufferings and death of Jesus to be seen primarily as the means of satisfying God's demand for punitive justice? Karl Barth is surely right when he says (1956, 253) that

> The concept of punishment has come into the answer given by Christian theology to this question from Isaiah 53. In the New Testament it does not occur in this connection. . . . We must not make this a main concept as in some of the older presentations of the doctrine of the atonement (especially those which follow Anselm of Canterbury), either in the sense that by his suffering our punishment we are spared from suffering it ourselves, or that in so doing he 'satisfied' or offered satisfaction to the wrath of God. The latter thought is quite foreign to the New Testament.

Indeed, John Goldingay has suggested in Chapter 1 that such thought is even foreign to Isaiah 53.

In a moment we shall see a proper sense in which the death of Christ may be said to be penal, but for now we must allow that the objections to saying that Christ was punished on the cross instead of us are formidable, and not least the one most relevant to our immediate concern, that only the sinner can be justly punished for his sin.

Alternatively, did Christ offer our repentance? Among the reformed theologians who have criticized the understanding of Christ's death we have just been considering is John McLeod Campbell in his *The Nature of the Atonement*. For him sin is dealt with by confession and what Christ was doing on the cross was making a perfect confession of the sins of the world by exposing them in his own body to the judgement of God. McLeod Campbell develops that basic thought in ways that are rich and suggestive but the basic thought itself is highly problematic. To quote Forsyth again, 'How could Christ in any real sense confess a sin, even a racial one, with whose guilt He had nothing in common?' (1910, 148). 'Personal guilt Christ could never confess. There is that in guilt which can only be confessed by the guilty. "I did it." That kind of confession Christ could never make. . . . We alone, the guilty, can make that confession' (1910, 151).

The same criticism can be brought against the approach of R. C. Moberly, who in his great book *Atonement and Personality* sees what Christ did on the cross in terms of vicarious repentance. We ourselves are so blinded and held captive by sin that we are incapable of the required repentance, the turning away from sin and back to God that would deal with sin. But Christ, who is holy and free from sin, makes that vicarious repentance in our place on the cross. But the notion of vicarious repentance carries an inherent contradiction between the adjective and the noun. Only the one who has committed the sin is in a position to repent of it. Like punishment and confession, repentance is something that is inalienably personal to the sinner and cannot justly be transferred from him to one who like Christ has not sinned at all.

If he was not and could not be punished for our sins instead of us, if he did not and could not confess or repent of our sins vicariously on our behalf, what was it that he was doing there for us on the cross? The answer I want to suggest and explore is that he was fulfilling and renewing the covenant that we had broken. That brings us very near Jesus's own statement about his death in the words over the cup according to one tradition of the Matthean version of the words of institution, 'This is my blood of the renewed covenant (*tēs kainēs diathēkēs*), which is poured out for many for the forgiveness of sins' (Matt 26.28; see NRSV margin). God's covenant with Israel is in its frequent Old Testament summary 'I will be your God and you will be my people', and in Jesus that is brought to its ultimate fulfilment on both sides.

The final proof of God's covenant love to Israel is his becoming man, so that he might in our place and on our behalf fulfil the covenant and renew it after it had been broken. As Paul puts it, 'For in him every one of God's promises is a "Yes". For this reason it is through him that we say the "Amen", to the glory of God' (2 Cor 1.20). Christ fulfils the covenant both on God's side and on ours. He is God's ultimate Yes to us, because on our behalf he becomes one of us that he may speak our Yes to God.

The ultimate Yes that God did not hear from the first man Adam, he hears from the ultimate man, Christ. Here in his living and dying, the covenant law of God is fulfilled; here at last is a man who loves the Lord his God with all his heart and soul and mind and strength and his neighbour including his enemy as himself. 'Not my will but yours be done.' 'Father forgive them because they know not what they do.' It is a thought that goes back to Calvin that the atoning thing about Christ is not the amount of his suffering but the quality of his obedience. In his Yes spoken on our behalf the covenant is fulfilled.

That fulfilment involves the cross, because the covenant that Christ fulfils is the covenant that all of us have broken. The humanity which Christ took upon himself was separated from God by a double No, the rebellious No of our sin to him, and the disintegrating No of his righteous judgement upon us. Christ's atoning work was to deal with both these rejections, to turn both these Noes into Yeses, to penetrate into the very heart of the hopeless situation that human sin and God's judgement on it had created, summed up in the cross on Calvary, and from that cross to say Yes to God.

He says Yes to the righteous judgement of God that sinful humanity must die, by taking our sinful humanity down into the death it has brought on itself. Yet he does it in such loving obedience that the cross, the very point where the old sinful humanity is going down to death in God's judgement, becomes the point at which it is gloriously replaced by the new obedient humanity, which says our ultimate Yes to God, and to which three days later God speaks his own ultimate Yes, when Jesus in the power of the new obedient humanity rises from the dead. On the cross, the place of our No to God, he says Yes to God's No to us, and to that ultimate Yes, God responds with his ultimate Yes to Jesus, and all this on our behalf and in our place.

We can now see what P. T. Forsyth means when he says (1910, 147) 'You can therefore say that although Christ was not punished by God, He bore God's penalty upon sin.' Punishment is appropriate only to the offender and Christ had not offended. But he entered in saving love into the pain and horror which is the consequence of human sin and God's judgement upon it, because it was there that his Yes had to be spoken, it was from the midst of the consequences of sin and in utter solidarity with sinners that the saving deed had to be performed.

> The penalty was not lifted even when the Son of God passed through. . . . He did enter the sphere of sin's penalty and the horror of sin's curse, in order that, from the very midst and depth of it, His confession and praise of God's holiness might rise like a spring of fresh water at the bottom of the bitter sea, and sweeten all (Forsyth 1910, 147–8).

Nevertheless, although we can see and indeed affirm what Forsyth intends by his distinction between being punished and bearing a penalty, we may still want to ask how useful this kind of forensic language really is in helping us to understand what God was about in the death of Jesus. Perhaps in the end the biblical concept of righteousness is best understood neither in terms of criminal justice with its concern for appropriate penalty nor in terms of civil justice with its concern for appropriate compensation, but rather in a relational way in terms of the restoration of right relationships between God and his people. That may be why we find Barth's talk of Yes and No more congenial than the older penal language it replaces, or rather translates. Of course the making of our humanity acceptable to God involves the rejection and death of everything in us that defies God, but it is all done, not for the sake of balancing the legal books, but so that we may be brought into the covenant relationship with God for which we were created.

Thus God's purpose in the death of Christ was not the exaction of an equivalent payment for sin – so much sin being balanced by so much suffering – but rather the removal by death of the sinful humanity that had broken the covenant, and its replacement by a new humanity that would keep and fulfil the covenant. 'The death he died, he died to sin, once for all; but the life he lives, he lives to God' (Rom 6.10). The concept of the justice of God that is operating on the cross is thus

> transformational rather than punitive or distributive. That is to say, it accepts human responsibility and culpability for the breach of the universal order which results from rebellion against God, but holds that justice is done not by the imposition of equivalent suffering . . . but by a process of transformation in which the reconciliation of persons enables the acknowledged evil of the past to become the basis for present and future good (Gunton 1988, 188).

If we see it like that, then this was a fit work for God in Christ to do on our behalf and in our place. Punishment, confession, repentance are inalienably attached to those who have committed the relevant offences. But Christ entered in love into the sinful situation that was beyond our coping and the fallen nature that was beyond our curing, to execute his transformational justice upon it, so that in the very act by which the old humanity went down to death there was a new creation of a new humanity that was in right relation to God.

Only sinners can be punished for their sin, can confess it and repent of it, but only the sinless can take our sinful nature down into death without himself perishing, only the Creator can re-create in himself the humanity that has rebelled against its God into the humanity in which God's covenant is at last fulfilled. This is a work that only he could do but that he has done in our place and in our stead.

How Are We Involved?

How are we involved in what has been done by Christ on our behalf? Gunton is again helpful here (1988, 165–6).

> We have to say that Jesus is our substitute because he does for us what we cannot do for ourselves. That includes undergoing the judgement of God, because were we to undergo it without him, it would mean our destruction. Therefore the 'for us' of the cross and resurrection must *include*, though it is not exhausted by, an 'instead of'. . . . [But] the centre of the doctrine of the atonement is that Christ is not only our substitute . . . but that by the substitution he frees us to be ourselves. . . . He goes, as man, where we cannot go. . . . [But] he does so as God and as our representative, so that he enables us to go there after him. . . . We need both substitution and representation to begin to do justice to the implications of the decisive events with which we are concerned.

What Christ does he does instead of us (substitution) but he does it on our behalf (representation) so that, because he has done it, we may enter into the good of it, so that in him we die to sin and rise into a relation of new life with God. Pannenberg speaks at this point (1968, 263–4) of an inclusive substitution, of his dying to sin and rising to God in the way that was possible only for him, so that we might be set free to die to sin and rise to God in him.

The whole purpose of the atonement was that, in union with him, we should be delivered from the old humanity that died in him in order that we might rise to the new humanity that was re-created to new life in him. What he did *for* us and *without* us on the cross has its whole goal in what he will do *in* us by joining us in union with himself by his Spirit, so that we are reconciled to God in him and are enabled to participate in his fulfilment of our covenant with God.

The work of the atonement where Christ alone gives himself for us cannot be isolated from the work of the Spirit in which we are incorporated into his life and all that is his becomes ours. That is what Paul is expounding in Romans 6, 'Do you not know that all of us who have been baptized into Christ Jesus were baptized into his death? Therefore we have been buried with him by baptism into death, so that, just as Christ was raised from the dead by the glory of the Father, so we too might walk in newness of life' (6.3–4).

Or, as Moberly puts it (1901, 152),

> Christ is crucified first and risen before our eyes; that Christ crucified and risen may be the secret love of our hearts. Calvary without Pentecost, would not be an atonement to us. But Pentecost could not be without Calvary. Calvary is the possibility of Pentecost: and Pentecost is the realization, in human spirits, of Calvary.

Thus on the cross we are excluded only that we might then be included, substitution is for the sake of participation, the atonement has its goal in our incorporation through Christ in the new humanity he has created for us in order to share with us.

So, can one man die for the people? He can if that man is the incarnate Creator come to re-create his people by fulfilling the covenant that they broke and could not fulfil, by taking the old humanity down to death and in the doing of it raising a new humanity to life in which by his Spirit we might all share. 'It is expedient that one man should die for the people and also for the scattered children of God to bring them together and to make them one in him.'

6

'With, through, and in' Christ:
A Eucharistic Approach to Atonement

JENNY SANKEY

FOR A WORKING definition of atonement let the following suffice: atonement (at-one-ment) refers to the saving work of the Holy Trinity on behalf of all creation; through the focus of the ministry, death, and resurrection of our Lord Jesus Christ; to the end that all might be united in responsive praise of God the Father. It involves a dynamic moving out from the trinitarian God and returning back to the trinitarian God. I want to explore this trinitarian focus on the person and work of Christ through an analysis of the eucharist.

It was the eucharist which Christ left behind to serve as a regular communal focus for his life and ministry.

> Undoubtedly it was our Lord's own interpretation of his passion, perpetuated in the eucharistic liturgy, that constantly nourished the early Church's understanding of atonement. We recall particularly the words Jesus spoke to his disciples toward the end of their last journey up to Jerusalem, and at the institution of the Holy Supper on the night in which he was handed over, for in them he gave his supreme revelation of the meaning of his life and death, and provided the Church with a permanent centre of reference to which it could return in proclaiming his death until he returned (Torrance 1988, 168–9).

The eucharist is the permanent centre of reference for Christ's own interpretation of his passion. The sacraments actually draw us and others deeper into the ministry of Jesus.

The whole of Christ's ministry, death, and resurrection form a dynamic continuity. In his ministry he declares that 'the Son of Man has authority on earth to forgive sins' (Mark 2.10), so already there was some basis for forgiveness. Salvation involves not just his death, but his ongoing life: 'For if while we were enemies, we were reconciled to God through the death of his Son, much more surely, having been reconciled, will we be saved by his life' (Rom 5.10). This ongoing life involves the life of the risen and glorified Christ and also the person and work of the Spirit of Christ. There is a continuity of Christ's life through death. That continuity of life through death is provided by the resurrection and the gifting of the Spirit.

Atonement embraces not demanded death but life freely offered through death. The notion of sacrifice provides a continuity between death and the life that is offered: 'The statement that Jesus is *the* sacrificial victim, therefore, actually serves to emphasise the story by which he came to suffer that death.' The notion of sacrifice throws the life and ministry of Jesus into sharp relief. Jesus freely offered up what he did not owe. In this way he is both priest and victim in the eucharistic liturgy: 'The concept of suffering implicit in sacrifice is rendered as *self*-offering. Jesus is not a victim only, he is the offerant' (Sykes 1991, 294). God's offering to us in Christ solicits our offering of ourselves to the Father 'with, through, and in' Christ. Christian sacrifice involves the voluntary oblation of self. This is enacted for Christians in eucharistic worship and life.

Jesus offered to the Father the completeness of his life and ministry, an offering from the human side, an offering of life through death. The limitations of death were then exceeded by the life that Jesus received back from the Father in the Spirit of holiness at the resurrection. A pathway through death was opened up for us to be progressed along through being baptized and incorporated into the eucharistic community. As Christians grow deeper into the eucharistic community they communicate to those outside what they value enough to live and die for.

Despite its central focus in a completed action in the past, the dynamic of atonement is forward-looking. Its object is that all might unite in praise of God the Father. Atonement has a teleological or purposive aspect. At the human level, it is a 'from, by, for' movement: from the life of sinfulness, by the

atoning work of the Holy Trinity in Christ, for a life of thankfulness and celebration.

Although atonement focuses on humanity, on account of
human responsibility for the fall, it has repercussions for the
whole of creation. Atonement focused in Christ enables creation
to point more fully than before to the Creator. The bread and
wine, intentionally left by Christ for our use, point beyond
themselves at the eucharist, encouraging all creation to praise
God the Father. 'I asked the whole mass of the universe about
my God, and it replied "I am not God, God is he who made
me"' (Augustine, *Confessions* 10.6, using Rom 1.20).

The Three P's: Evil as Perversion, Privation, and Power

Presentations of atonement are technically 'parasitic' upon presentations of evil. The most persuasive theories of atonement are
those which can change their shape with the change in shape
of perceived evil.

> Theories of atonement are somewhat like lymphocytes in the
> body: they are solutions going around looking for a problem,
> and taking the shape of the problem as it is identified. . . .
> [They] are simply applications of the cure (the death and resur-
> rection of Christ) to the problem of sin or mortality however it
> is identified (Bowker 1991, 97–8).

There are at least three traditional ways of discussing the character of evil: evil as perversion of the good, as privation or withdrawal of the good (Augustine's *privatio boni*: see Evans 1982),
and as power battling the good.

Evil as perversion involves something good which is either
out of alignment, and so manifests itself as evil, or something
good which persists in putting itself in a context wherein there
is a strong compulsion to sin. It involves a badly aligned or a
weak will. Susan Howatch notes of one of her characters: 'He
sinned because he was not aligned properly with God, and once
a proper alignment had been established then the disastrous

95

compulsion to sin receded' (quoted in *Christian* 1993/2, 4). Idolatry is the classic biblical example of evil as perversion of the
good; it is worship directed away from God.

A simple example of evil as privation is to define sin as 'the
absence or withdrawal of praise'. Salvation on that simple
example is then the 'restoration of praise' (Mowry LaCugna and
McDonnell 1988, 195). Another is to use 'forgetting' as the
absence or withdrawal of remembering: it is not so much that
humans are antagonistic towards the Father on this view, but
rather that they are prone to forgetfulness (cf. Schmemann 1988,
ch. 6). Gregory of Nyssa in *The Making of Humanity* makes use
of the privation theory to envisage the genesis of evil as the withdrawal of the beautiful and good. Jesus himself articulated the
desolation of the cross as the absence or withdrawal of God's loving concern. It is evil as privation of presence. The terminology
of God-forsakenness speaks powerfully of privation. At the cross
Jesus did not say 'Satan, Satan, why are you persecuting me?' but
'My God, my God, why have you forsaken me?'

Regarding evil as the privation of good involves regarding
evil as having no abiding substance. Evil on this view lacks
abiding qualities. It is no independent principle, despite its
present effects. This view encourages Christians to 'fill the gap
with good', which is achieved with the Spirit's help drawing us
into the pattern of Christ (the moral aspect of atonement). A
Jewish example of evil as privation is seen within the Noahide
commandments, one of which is the command to set up courts
of law; the lack of a judiciary system encourages evil.

The analysis of evil as an attractive power goes further than
the image of evil as a perversion or privation. The subtlety and
subterfuge of evil is to be powerfully attractive without having
any substance to satisfy should we succumb to its attractiveness.
Evil as a power is a common New Testament theme, especially
prominent in Colossians and Ephesians (see Aulén 1970; and
on the similarities with the Palestinian Judaism of Paul's day,
Sanders 1977). In the context of life in the Spirit, holiness is
also an attractive power overcoming the seductive power of evil
and the desire of human beings to sin.

The 'sinlessness' of Christ means that in the context of temptation Jesus experienced the attraction of sin, and overcame the power of attraction, without having initially fallen for it. Jesus knew that sin had no substance to satisfy and he correctly judged the situation without giving in to the power of attraction. To be able to come alongside us in our situations of sin or temptation, Jesus need not have committed sin or even have been tempted by every single sin it is possible to commit. In judging, he overcame, and in participating in his judgement, we too can overcome. Jesus enables our effective repentance, our co-operation with the power of holiness which overcomes the attraction of sin at the human level – our cooperation with the will of the Father for our life with, through, and in Christ. Christians demonstrate the power of overcoming evil by praising God that he has broken the power of evil's attraction in Christ. Praise is a powerful action, for both praiser and praisee, as any psychologist will testify.

At baptism, Christians have committed themselves in cooperation with God to turn from evil in its various guises. The eucharist retains the strict expectation of self-involvement in setting our lives right with God and humanity. It presents opportunities to make real our repentance in renewed fellowship with the eucharistic community. And going further than merely demonstrating that the power of sin is broken for us, the eucharist opens us up to the power of righteousness and holiness. The righteousness of God is the power of God. The eucharist emphasizes what atonement is for: for holiness of life in thankfulness to the Father, that 'in him we might become the righteousness of God' (2 Cor 5.21). We experience the attraction of the holy towards the good which alone can satisfy: that is God alone. We turn from sin, a powerful attraction which cannot satisfy, towards holiness, a powerful attraction which has substance and does satisfy. The theme of satisfaction will recur later.

Clues from the Synoptic Jesus:
Evil as a Power

In recognizing the ambiguous form of evil it is significant to examine the activity of the Jesus of the synoptic Gospels as he responds to its manifestations. These Gospels present a Jesus who embraces popular talk about demonology. Jesus engages in activities such as exorcisms and dramatic healings. Such activities are also engaged in by other Jewish wonder-workers (as Matt 12.27 implies) such as Honi the Circle-drawer.

Jesus always provides checks on how people envisage the relationship of God to the demonic, notably with those searching questions which never lose their power: 'Who do people say I am?' and 'Who do you say I am?' Rather than dwelling on evil in its various guises, he points to himself in relationship to the Spirit of God his Father. 'If it is by the Spirit of God that I cast out demons, then the kingdom of God has come to you' (Matt 12.28). It is the Spirit of God who drives Jesus into the desert and permits the devil to tempt him. He is tempted to deny the Father by word and action. The interrelationship between Son and Spirit is essential here; indeed, all three persons are significant.

The evil realm is handled most effectively by a trinitarian theology. A narrow monotheism will often encourage the denial of the reality of evil (God is good and there is none beside him, so evil has no reality), or encourage the portrayal of an almost 'demonic' character in God (God is the creator of evil and God is one so God is evil). Christian writers on atonement have to be able to distance themselves from 'demonic' notions of divinity, those that too closely associate God with evil. Where they have been successful they have generally been so by the sophistication of the trinitarian doctrine of God. For instance, the Spirit drives the Son into situations where he will be tested, but the Son aided by the Spirit never denies the Father's active love by word or action. This is a realistic model of human life into which Christians are invited to grow as they try it on for size.

By making use of a systematic Christian framework, it is possible to see the following pattern emerging in the Christian relationship to evil; God uses evil but is not compromised by it.

1 A movement *with* the Son: resistance to evil powers and working to overcome them in God's strength.
2 A movement *through* the God-human: claiming the victory

over evil powers through Christ's person – largely at cross and resurrection.

3 A movement *in* the Spirit of the Father and Son: the Spirit may drive us to the place where evil appears most attractive but will help us not to sin by denying God in word or action.

Sacrament as Christian Self-Involvement in Christ's Ministry

Atonement is a dynamic, forward-looking movement. The motive of atonement is towards the formation of a holy people articulating thankfulness to the Father. Christians continue Christ's ministry in the Spirit of Christ as they are formed into a holy (read 'charismatically attractive') people. In the time between Christ's ascension and his return, the eucharist incorporates Christians into atoning extensions of the incarnation. The sacraments are set up as a help to communicate the gospel and to encourage us into the holiness of life which carries on communicating the gospel.

In both baptism and eucharist there is a progressive threefold movement – one-off for baptism, repeated, iterative cycles for eucharistic life. It is this threefold movement which recurs in this chapter and which is linked with the Holy Trinity. The link with the Trinity is not any simple pattern of here Father, then Son, and now Spirit; it is a profound involvement of all three persons with, through, and in the human condition. It depends on the *perichorēsis* or interplay between the three persons together. That interplay has a particular focus in Christ's humanity, for it is there that atonement is effected for us and for all creation.

The threefold 'with–through/by–in' pattern is suggested by the doxology of the ASB Rite A eucharistic prayers which sum up our movement of praise 'by, with, and in' our Lord Jesus Christ.

It is precisely there, at the Cross, that the risen and ascended Lord comes to meet us that we, united with him through communion in his body and blood, may be lifted up with him into the highest in the power of the resurrection and exaltation, and worship the Father with, in and through him (Torrance 1976, 8).

There is no hard and fast rule as to which way round these prepositions come; the point is rather to emphasize our distinction from, yet intimate involvement with, Christ.

The threefold pattern of baptism is:

1   We have died *with* Christ (to sin and its power of attraction).
2   We have been saved *through* Christ (by the atoning work of the Holy Trinity).
3   We are enabled to live *in* Christ (by the power of the Spirit of Christ).

The threefold pattern of eucharist is:

1   We praise the Father *with* Christ.
2   We praise the Father *through* Christ.
3   We praise the Father as we live *in* Christ by the Spirit.

Every eucharist is a recollection of our inseparable link with Christ in baptism. The eucharist is extended into a way of life as each Christian lives out his or her baptismal vocation in the world.

The Orthodox theologian John Zizioulas (1985, 220–1) speaks of a double movement: a baptismal movement which renders the church 'dead to the world', especially to the presence and work of the devil, and a eucharistic movement of referring the world to God as 'anaphora/offering'. The Roman Catholic Rite of Christian Initiation of Adults (1969) gives as one of its baptismal options:

Do you reject Satan?	I do.
And all his works?	I do.
And all his empty promises?	I do.

Here is the recognition of the need to reject the work of Satan. It carries deep insights into evil as perversion of the good ('empty promises') and into evil as lack of substance.

Christ died and was raised by his God and Father so that Christians might live in him, our Saviour and Lord. The 'in him' signifies 'in the risen and glorified Christ', the humanity that inclusively transcends race, culture, class, and sex. That resurrection life has been opened up for all through what he alone – as the God-human – was able to achieve. What he achieved is to open up 'the gate of glory', the phrase used in the ASB post-communion prayer (and cf. Carey 1986).

Christians anticipate in this life the glory that will be more fully revealed in the life to come. Baptismal turning to Christ, repenting of sins, and renouncing evil is a 'three in one' unified activity. Their unity across time is held together through the original one-off turning and the regular discipline of repentance. The test of repentance is to be able to be in the same context and situation again and to resist the temptation to repeat the sin. This proves that evil has lost its power of attraction.

Sacraments and Mission: Involving Others

The research commissioned for the Decade of Evangelism has shown that for most people growth in faith is a gradual movement over some years (see Finney 1992). This research notes the largely untapped potential of the sacraments for communicating the gospel, speaking of baptism and eucharist as evangelistic services. To invite confirmation candidates to give some voluntary testimony to God's working in their lives would be an example of this in practice.

A deeper understanding of the pneumatological dimension of atonement should help illuminate evangelism. The Spirit transforms Christians into a charismatically drawing and attractive community through the power of holiness. And that is particularly the case with eucharistic worship: it is evangelistic. Such an understanding encourages us to invite all comers to eucharistic services (perhaps holding eucharistic guest services?) Hearing the story proclaimed in word and action and walking up to the front for a blessing can be a profoundly moving event.

The sacraments and the associated Gospel narratives draw our attention to Jesus's hands, face, and body – to his full humanity. Their continuing significance relies on his divine activity as the Son of God. So the sacraments encourage a balance of the humanity as well as the divinity of Christ. It is essential to preserve that balance in missionary presentations of Christ. It is all too easy to exalt the divinity of Christ and bypass Christ as the human role model for us to grow into.

Ray Anderson (1982) has written of the significance of Christian rituals for the understanding of what it means to be human. He speaks of the eucharist as 'liturgical evangelism'. It was the sacraments of baptism and eucharist which focused the mission and ministry of the early 'Jesus-movement'. In the early centuries a rigorous catechumenate ensured the appropriation of the gospel traditions, and strict church discipline ensured that repentance retained its intimate connection with eucharistic life.

Self-Involvement in Christ's Ministry as the Realization of Atonement

Linking atonement to the sacramental life is not to suggest that people automatically become Christians through baptism. After the one-off commitment, made public in baptism, there is a gradual deepening of faith associated with growth in eucharistic thankfulness and celebration, in which the atonement won for us comes to be truly realized in our lives. In ordinary usage, 'to realize' is taken as an autonomous human intellectual act. In the Christian context, realization is the work of the Holy Spirit in our whole lives.

> For the New Testament the cross is unique – but not isolated. The redemption once for all effected there is real-ised in the process of human history through the education of the Spirit. Redemption does not happen over the heads of the creatures but involves them, assumes them into responsibility and it does so by creating a subversive movement, a solidarity in redemption. This does not mean that people are their own saviours or

liberators – here is the disanalogy – but it means that God's work of redemption is effected through the toil of human history, by treating human beings as 'fellow workers' (1 Cor 3.9) (Gorringe 1986, 67).

The sacraments are regular reminders of our responsibilities to co-operate with the God who has acted savingly towards us.

Human involvement, in a self-involving active response, completes the realization of atonement. Once protected from compromising the once-for-all sacrificial oblation on the cross, and from turning Christians into their own liberators, the eucharist can harness this dramatic encouragement to self-involvement. It can send us out to live and work for justice, peace, and the integrity of creation. There have always been those who draw a close connection between eucharistic doctrine and social ethics, notably William Temple (and cf. Suggate 1991). It is more than appropriate to link human working for justice and peace, and human passing judgement on sin, with atonement; otherwise a portrayal of atonement would be open to charges of political naiveté and unconnectedness. There is a close interconnection between the sin of anti-Judaism and many Christian portrayals of atonement (see Sankey 1993, ch. 8; and John Kelly's chapter in this book). This strengthens the case for Christian repentance in realizing peace between the religions. It is important to be challenged by seeing the cross through the eyes of modern Jews (as Littel 1975). There is need to repent of the Christian 'teaching of contempt' for Judaism (Jules Isaac 1964, 1965). At the stage of the formation of Christian identity the Jewish people and religion were plundered of their riches: their Scriptures, their God, their election, their corporate self-understanding as Israel, were all appropriated for Christianity (Ruether 1974). Through such repentance will come involvement in Christ's ministry of justice and peace to religions and to nations.

Incorporation into Christ as Substitution and Participation

I shall concentrate on a movement which is 'with, through, and in' Christ. This may be similar to what is figuratively expressed when John's Gospel describes Jesus as 'the way, the truth, and the life'. The way is the 'with' movement, the truth the 'through' movement, and the life the 'in' movement. It would need to be addressed how far this needs to continue to be interpreted exclusively with respect to other religions, especially Judaism (see Schoneveld 1990).

'With him' is the stage where we can live alongside Christ for he is in complete solidarity with us; despite being the way or the path, he is also a fellow-walker on the path beside us. 'Through him' indicates the stage where Christ takes us where we cannot go ourselves, and he does with us what we as sinful humans cannot do; he conforms to a sinful nature which is not his own. 'In him' indicates the stage where we are conformed to Christ's resurrection body which bears the imprints of the cross. At this stage we cannot speak of two separate individuals, for the only existence we have is intimately linked to his. 'I have been crucified with Christ; and it is no longer I who live, but it is Christ who lives in me' (Gal 2.19–20). Incorporation in Christ then becomes a way of life. Our minds and bodies have become living sacrifices offered daily to God in Christ.

The use of a restricted 'through' sense indicates an acceptance of a substitutionary role for Christ, and it seems essential for this to include a penal aspect. But difficulties arise if we wish to count the whole of humanity legally culpable for what they have not voluntarily undertaken. There has to be a combination of 'original sin', some tendency which is ours by nature, and 'committed sin', that which each of us commits individually and holds us individually culpable. Both appear in Romans 5.12: 'Sin came into the world through one man, and death came through sin, and so death spread to all because all have sinned.' Penal substitution coheres better with sins against a voluntarily undertaken code than with general tendencies to an inauthentic life.

Talk of substitution implies a strong interpretation of the mediatorial role of Christ. 'There is one God; there is also one mediator between God and humankind, Christ Jesus, himself human, who gave himself a ransom for all' (1 Tim 2.5–6). The mediation is effected in his humanity. The use of an 'in' form in association with the 'through' form indicates that the substitution is followed by participation in Christ. Such an understanding of participation after substitution is particularly associated with Calvinist theology with its strong doctrine of the Spirit (see Hart 1989). Our subsequent participation reduces the risk of substitution degenerating into alienation, the lack of personal involvement.

The same 'with, through, and in' movement is expressed in the eucharistic prayers, themselves a movement of praise 'with, through, and in' our Lord Jesus Christ. The liturgy of the eucharist and an academic understanding of atonement need the same 'with, through, and in' shape. In his study of links between *The Atonement and the Sacraments*, Robert Paul maintains, for example, that 'in the sacraments the Risen Christ takes us to the centre of his redeeming act and reveals its meaning in the act of sacred drama'. As well as speaking of drama as enacted meaning, he makes much of the Hebrew *zākar*, with its making present of past events, as the background to the eucharistic 'do this in remembrance of me', 'the action of bringing an event *out* of the past *into* the present' (1961, 360, 369). 'The whole sacramental system means nothing else than personal identification, of the Church and all her members, in the region and method of Spirit, with Christ' (Moberly 1901, xxvi, and see further ch. 10; also Torrance 1976; Cocksworth 1993). The gospel will be more readily communicated when the essentially eucharistic character of the Christian life is recognized. The aim of atonement is that all creation should be united in praise of God the Father. Humanity is restored through the self-offering of Christ to participate in his praise of the Father. Humanity does not offer creation to God, but we do, with Christ, offer the praise of creation, returning to God our 'eucharistic stewardship of creation' (Stamps 1986, 463). We give thanks and we celebrate what God has done for us in Christ and calls us to in the Spirit of Christ. The eucharistic prayer is articulated by the president, to whom the bishop has delegated authority to preside in his absence, and to whom the priestly people gladly submit in the obedience of Christ, but it is a communal, 'we' prayer.

A Dynamic Trinitarian Christology

The movement 'with, through, and in' is a trinitarian movement in the context of a two-nature Christology. It concerns our incorporation into Christ. It is dependent on a dynamic 'two-nature' Christology, a so-called 'modern Chalcedonian' Christology. It is Chalcedonian because of the two-nature talk of the Chalcedonian Definition (451 CE), modern because of the sense of dynamism which was lacking in that Definition. That dynamic aspect needs to be there in an approach to the unfolding of Jesus's life and ministry. It is particularly the resurrection which focuses this dynamism. The New Testament is written from the perspective of faith in the resurrection and the implications for Christology of resurrection faith.

This link between dynamism and God is sufficient to extend the classical Hellenistic idea of the unchangeability (*apatheia*) of God. It is the central thrust of Moltmann's *The Crucified God* that the classical Hellenistic doctrine of God (omniscient, omnipresent, impeccable, apathetic) should be modified by a close reading of Scripture, notably the story of the cross (see also Song 1982). In accepting the need to modify the Hellenistic idea of the unchangeability of God, however, I seek a solution more integrated with Christian worship as incorporation into the life of Christ.

Our assumed sinful nature was dealt with once-for-all by a fully co-ordinated self-offering of God and human together in the humanity of Jesus. Let it be emphasized that it was in the humanity of Jesus where this all had to be achieved, in the humanity wherein the problem was seen to lie. This is what separates out an incarnational faith from any other: it works out the solution from the inside out, rather than from the outside in. Jesus is the one to whom Christians look to express fully a life of obedience offered to the Father. He is also the one in whom we see the Father's self-offering to us. At the resurrection, Christ was released from the *limitations* of bodily existence, while still retaining a bodily form. The atonement is dynamically self-involving of both God and humanity in mutual self-giving.

Christ needs to be more than a static 'God-human'. There has to be some dynamism to the presentation of Christ, showing how he opened up more fully to God's working in his humanity as that humanity 'increased in wisdom and stature' (Luke 2.52). The use of Wisdom categories in Christology is growing in importance (see e.g. Schüssler Fiorenza 1983). Wisdom categories provide a creation-oriented context and one which throws into sharp relief the dynamism behind the co-operation of divine and human wills. It is the decision of Christ to resist the powerful attraction of evil that proves the central locus of atonement. Having emphasized his humanity as the centre of atonement, I am now in a position to qualify this further. What really matters in Christ's humanity is his will, which meets, agrees, and co-operates with the will of God. It was for this reason that early Christian doctrine had to refine its understanding of Christ's humanity. He was not just the divine Word replacing the human will in a human body; he was fully human with a human will.

God's Wisdom sought co-operation from the human will. Christ provided a perfect, fully responsive will. Wisdom's seeking and Christ's growth into mature cooperation involve dynamic movement on both sides. It is into that mature co-operation that Christians are assumed as they grow in wisdom and in holiness. Christian liturgy is largely about the formation of the Christian will: it concerns attitudes and values but also a mature co-operation of the adult child with the Father for the good of the whole creation.

What is seen in Christ is the opening up of a human individual to being filled with the very nature of God in a way which does not prevent Jesus from being a human individual. It is this 'opening up' of humanity to the Spirit of God into which Christians are drawn. Becoming more alive to God does not overthrow our humanity; it completes and crowns our humanity by refining our mind and will. It makes our humanity more charismatic, endowing it with the power of attraction.

That movement in Christ's ministry on behalf of all creation due to his openness to the Spirit becomes real in Christian lives. All the baptized are called to become ministers of Christ on behalf of all creation. The interplay of Son and Spirit before the Father in the earthly ministry of Jesus is essential to provide the pattern of co-operation with the Spirit of God and the will of the Father. As Christians participate in Christ they have access to the means of their glorified charismatic humanity, even as the Spirit draws them into conformity with Christ. Christians move from being *with* Christ in his human praise of the Father, to being set free *through* the God-human act of atonement, to being alive *in* Christ as they open up to the Spirit's promptings. Thus they are conformed more and more to the risen and glorified Christ. This demonstrates itself in the attraction of people wholly at peace with themselves because their will is voluntarily aligned with the will of God for themselves. Such people can empty their relationships of self to such a degree that they can effectively minister to others. This emptying (*kenōsis*) is achieved not through self-abnegation but through self-fulfilment, knowing the self enough to offer the human will by aligning it to God's will for that self.

Satisfaction Theories of Atonement Revisited

Anselm of Canterbury in the twelfth century offered a satisfaction theory of atonement. It is based in a dynamic 'two-nature' Christology. In his work *Cur Deus Homo?* (*Why Did God Become a Human Being?* or *Why the God-human?*) he highlights how both God and humanity must concur in a united response from within humanity.

Anselm is able to maintain the significance of the human self-offering, co-ordinated with the divine self-offering, by the provision of a satisfaction for sin. The notion of satisfaction is one which can be used in a liturgical context as well as in more reflectively analytical writing. The Book of Common Prayer thus speaks in the Holy Communion of atonement in terms of the three interlinked notions of sacrifice, oblation, and satisfaction for the sins of the world.

Humanity has offended God by holding back from honouring God and must make satisfaction for this dishonour to God, but it is unable to offer anything of sufficient worth. So God must make this satisfaction as a human. Hence God must become a human and offer satisfaction as the God-human. Such an offering for sins which are not his own receives its just reward, pardon for all those who approach the Father in Christ's name. Anselm makes it easy to see that the work of atonement is accomplished in Christ's humanity, itself the locus of both problem and solution. Indeed focusing on honouring and on a voluntary offering from the human side acknowledges the human will as the locus of atonement.

With Anselm it is very clear that atonement takes place in the humanity of Christ, and with a quite self-aware humanity, not just a semi-conscious receptacle of the divine work. The human will is self-aware and co-operates with God's will for it. This provides a balance between the two natures. It is based partly on an understanding of evil as a privation of good (sin as the lack of honouring), partly on evil as a perversion of the good (a response of honouring, but honouring one who is less than God), and partly on evil as a power (active rebellion, dishonouring God). This concept of honour interlinks evil as privation, perversion, and power, and goes far beyond the commonly accepted feudal definitions of satisfaction.

Anselm's prayerful theological method and his *Meditation on Human Redemption*, with its eucharistic overtones, demonstrates the application of this dynamic side of Chalcedonian Christology to Christian spirituality. To honour God as a way of life is the aim of all the baptized. Regular attendance at the eucharist encourages Christians to honour God by a life of sacrificial ministry. They are incorporated into the satisfaction offered to God as they offer themselves, and particularly their wills, 'with, through, and in' Christ. This way of life is the satisfaction of right honouring; it is also the power of holiness and righteousness. Getting to grips with evil as a power is rare in such analytically coherent material. It demonstrates that Anselm's writing is imbued with a life's reflections on, and formation by, the church's liturgical tradition as well as deep personal encounter with God in intimate prayer.

There is much to learn from a satisfaction theory, even if it means moving beyond Anselm. To satisfy another is to know their will for themselves and to co-operate fully with what they will. In common parlance one speaks of satisfying customers or examiners. You do not satisfy another by offering what you think they want or what you think they ought to have. You must find out their will for themselves and align yourself to it. It is somehow deeper even than the notion of reconciliation for personal relationships. Satisfaction requires the one who has committed the offence to enter imaginatively into the mind of the one offended and explore a suitable recompense, a recompense which will bring not just reparation and restored relationship but pure delight. This ability to enter into the mind and heart of another depends on the transcendence of oneself and is a mark of the Holy Spirit. Satisfaction is the fruit of one who can know two selves so completely that his or her own self can effectively be harnessed in meeting the will and inner desires of the other. To learn what it takes sexually to satisfy another human being is very close to learning what is appropriate to satisfy God. It goes further than recognizing the pain of human sinfulness to God. It means finding out what gives God pure delight and fulfilment-in-relationship.

The depth of God's delight in relationship with humanity in Christ is greater than any delight he might achieve without us. Here is the reason for the incarnation. It also compels us to look behind the mythology of what God wants: do we accept the standard glib answers regarding what God wants in the way of delight or are we willing to ask God what he really wants? We may sometimes be taken aback by the answers. Satisfaction is the fruit of a growth in wisdom, in self-knowledge and self-assurance, and in reaching out to God and to others. The challenging question with which we are left is, Does our eucharistic worship and self-offering in Christ satisfy God?

7

The Cross, Our Worship
and Our Living

CHRISTOPHER COCKSWORTH

THE TASK OF this chapter is to consider the way the cross relates to our worship and to our living. To engage in this sort of analysis is an important and demanding task and it is one which needs to be undertaken. Nevertheless it is equally important to acknowledge the limitations of the analytical method when dealing with such profound issues. My hardest thinking, reading and discussing about the cross has often felt like a scene from one of G. K. Chesterton's 'Father Brown' detective stories. As Father Brown gazes on what he knows to be the key piece of evidence, he declares 'We've found the truth and the truth makes no sense' (Chesterton 1992, 107). For him the clue to the solution of his mystery lay in the body of a dead Scottish aristocrat. For us, the solution to the mystery of our faith lies in the dying of a Palestinian Jew. We know that in this dying lies the truth about God and humanity and the truth about our worship and our living. But the meaning of this truth so easily evades us. Just at the moment when we think we have grasped it, we lose it. Little wonder really, for here we are dealing not with the wisdom of the wise but with the foolishness of God. This is not to say that the cross confronts us with irrationality and demands that we suspend all critical judgements; it is simply to say that the categories, the definitions and even the words of our philosophy are too crude, too anthropological, to handle this reality. The reality is so new and so transcendent to human experience that it needs to be allowed to create its own categories, definitions and even words – its own mode of understanding.

Of course any Christian theology worthy of the name will be

allowing the event of the cross to inform its analysis at every stage, by way of forming the categories with which it is working. But this in itself is not enough. Perhaps the Orthodox tradition would point to the neglect of the primacy of worship in the theological process as one of the reasons for the dryness of so much discussion of the atonement in the Western church. Certainly liberation theologians would want to say that we have so often arrived at an intellectual impasse in our doctrine of the atonement because we have failed to realize that the meaning of the cross can only be understood by engaging in Christian practice. I am not suggesting we put this book down and start worshipping or working, but rather that we should recognize that the Christian way of knowing involves the modes of adoration and action as well as analysis and that the adoration and action must be allowed to inform the analysis, just as the analysis must inform the adoration and action.

The Letter to the Hebrews provides a good example of the interpenetration of the modes of our knowing. Its subtle and sophisticated doctrine of the atonement is developed from a reflection upon and comparison between Jewish and Christian worship. But this is neither ivory tower nor other-worldly theology, because it is written for those who are experiencing the harsh realities of Christian living. Indeed, although its understanding of worship appears to centre on narrowly cultic concerns, its definition of worship is, as we will see, none other than the definition of Christian life. The rest of this chapter is simply an attempt to see what the writer to the Hebrews' application of liturgical theology to the event of the cross can teach us about the truth of the cross for our own lives.

The Place of Worship

The God of Hebrews is 'a consuming fire' (12.29) into whose hands 'it is a fearful thing to fall' (10.31). The awful holiness of God requires distance between God and people, a cultic separation. Wolfhart Pannenberg points out that such separation was necessary in Hebrew thought not in order to protect the holy from defilement but to protect the profane from 'the threat of the holy' (1991, 400, referring to von Rad). The Israelites in the wilderness 'kept their distance' from the holy one revealing himself in the darkness of the cloud (Exod 20.20–1). The Philistines who captured the ark eventually learnt the cost of treating the holy God of Israel as a Canaanite idol and cried out 'Who is able to stand before the Lord, this holy God?' (1 Sam 6.20). And when the Lord inhabited the temple, the priests dared not, could not enter 'because the glory of the Lord filled the Lord's house' (2 Chron 7.2).

Here is the basic liturgical dilemma: only the holy can bear the presence of the holy God (Heb 12.14). Hebrews goes to intricate lengths to show how Jewish ritual embodied this principle – particularly the rites of the Day of Atonement. Perhaps the beginning of the atonement narrative in Leviticus was in the writer's mind, which recalls Aaron's sons being consumed by the fire of God's holiness because they tried to offer an unauthorized sacrifice (Lev 16.1; 10.1–3). Hebrews goes on to describe the tent with its two sections. The priests had right of entry into the first; but with the second it was a different matter, for this was the holy of holies in which the ark of the Lord was placed. Here only the high priest was allowed to tread and only once a year and then only bearing the blood of sacrifice in his hands. And all this was only a 'symbol' of the reality (Heb 9.9). Its role was to be descriptive, educative of the reality, it was not itself the reality. The reality is not the cloth of a tent or the bricks of a temple. It is 'nothing known to the senses: not a blazing fire, or gloom or total darkness, or a storm; or trumpet-blast or the sound of a voice speaking which made everyone that heard it beg that no more should be said to them' (12.18–19). It is 'the most holy place' of God's presence (10.19).

Just as the tent and temple could be no more than a symbol of God's presence being the place of true worship, so the sacrifices could be little more than a statement about the need to be pure in the presence of God. Although the sacrifices of the law had an effect on the external, by establishing 'bodily purity', they were not able to produce the internal transformative effect on the character of the person which is needed to establish moral purity.

These assumptions about the holiness of God and the sin-fulness of humanity are the basic assumptions of the Judeo-Christian liturgical tradition without which we will make little sense of the doctrine of the atonement in anything like its tra-ditional form. They are examples of categories which have been formed by the dealings of God with his people and which there-fore need to inform any attempt to think theologically about the cross. But they are also categories which still relate to human experience because they capture something of what it feels like to be a human being. They may need to be enculturized by using different words and images but this is not an impossible task. For example, the problem of pollution immediately evokes strong and passionate feelings of horror at the spoiling of beauty, the need for the earth to be cleansed and the causes of pollution overcome. Similarly, news of moral atrocities still has the capacity to cause a widespread sense of moral outrage which may include a sense of defilement, a yearning for cleansing and a concern for justice to be done as well as for forgiveness and healing to be found. Here is the language of sin, purity and perhaps even sacrifice.

The Promise of Perfection

As well as reflecting the priestly concept that the *place* of true worship is none other than the holy presence of God, Hebrews is framed within the prophetic hope of the presence of God being the *destiny* of the people of God. According to the promise, there would come a time when, in Pannenberg's words (1990, 400), 'the holiness of God . . . enters the profane world, penetrates it and makes it holy'. The time will be eschato-logical time: the time of the fulfilment of the promise and the welcoming of God's people into the sabbath of God's pres-ence (4.1–11). For the writer, this time has begun in Christ (9.26). The one who is 'the reflection of God's glory' (1.3) is the one who shared equally in our human nature (2.14) and who learnt obedience through suffering. The holy presence of God was at work in an individual human life, fashioning it into the perfection which he both desires and requires. The fashioning, renewing, reconstituting and recreating of human nature in Jesus happens throughout his life as he faces the trauma of temptation and yet does not give way (4.15), as he wrestles in prayer with 'loud cries and tears' and yet submits himself to the will of God with reverence and devotion (5.7) and as he learns obedience through the giving of himself to death (10.4–10) and through his experience of death (2.9).

It is at the cross that Hebrews sees the process by which Christ is perfected coming to its critical point. It puts the psalmist's words on to the lips of Jesus: 'Here I am! I am coming to do your will' (10.9). The will – the plan, the purpose, the promise of God – is for us to be made holy 'through the offering of the body of Jesus Christ once for all' (10.10). This decision of Jesus to pour out his life for others was not made lightly or easily. It was forged out of a deep and dark struggle in which he wrestled with 'the one who had the power to save him from death'. Jesus was gripped by the same fear of death which Hebrews sees us all sharing (2.15). It was a fear rooted in the recognition of death as the 'place of expulsion and of God-forsakenness' (Brandenburger 1969, 217; quoted by Peterson 1982, 89). But Jesus did not give way to the fear. He faced it and found a way through it and so 'learnt obedience' (5.8) as he freely, though painfully, submitted himself to death, so that by God's grace his experience of death should benefit all humanity (2.9). Here we see Jesus reversing the pattern of Adam. Adam fails to live in obedience to his calling. Jesus succeeds. Though subject to the limitations of Adam (5.2), he chooses to obey the will of God and in so doing re-forms the humanity he shares with us so that in him God's creative intention for humanity is fulfilled as, after his death, he is crowned with the glory and honour which God destined for all the children of Adam (2.6–9).

This reference to the ascension is one of many which indicate that although the cross is the *critical* point in the perfecting of Jesus, the *climactic* moment happens as the crucified but risen Jesus of Nazareth 'enters heaven itself', the sanctuary of God's presence, the holy sabbath rest of the fulfilment of God's purpose for all that he has made. He enters as the pioneer who goes before us (3.1; 12.2) and as a priest to 'appear in the presence of God on our behalf' (9.24). This is the beginning of eschatological time. The cross is thus the pivotal moment of creation, for it happens 'at the end of the age' (9.26) and is consummated by the risen Christ ascending into God's presence in the coming city (13.14) of the world to come (2.5).

The Priest of the New Covenant

The writer uses some of the boldest incarnational language in the New Testament in order to define the identity of Jesus as the Son of the Father, but at the same time maintains a radical emphasis on his humanity. His reason for demonstrating the latter is to establish the right of Jesus to be the high priest or mediator of the new covenant. The role of the priest was to act on behalf of the people in relation to the holy presence of God. In order to represent the people, the priest had to be both one of the people and chosen by God to fulfil this role. Jesus qualified on both grounds, as our brother (2.11) and as God's Son (5.5).

Hebrews sees Jesus not as part of the old, Levitical order of priests, but as part of the eternal and transcendent order of Melchizedek and as the mediator of the new covenant. In this sense Jesus is the eschatological priest, the one who comes at the climax of God's purposes to fulfil God's promise to perfect his people so that they may enter the place of his presence and offer there the worship which is pure and acceptable. Hebrews claims both that human nature has been perfected in the person of Jesus Christ and that the perfection which has been formed in Christ is not merely of particular significance for the human being Jesus, but is of universal significance for the whole human race. It is of universal significance because Christ has been appointed to be the high priest who represents us and in so doing gives us access to all that he has achieved.

Hence, for Hebrews, the particular form of Christ's calling is to fulfil the role of the people's priest. There is therefore a double aspect to his perfecting. There is in Christ the perfecting or fulfilling of what it means to be a human being and there is the particular point of Christ's perfection or the particular character of Christ's calling which is to to be the people's priest – and, more specifically, to be the priest who offers the sacrifice for sin. The way in which he is called to obey God is thus by fulfilling the role of the priest. But the way in which he is called to fulfil the role of priest is not just by making the sacrifice for sin, but by making himself available *as the sacrifice*, as the victim, as the one who will bear the sins of many and bear them away, as the one whose self-giving will create the conditions for the forgiving of others. And Jesus not only offers to do this but actually does it: he experiences the event of God's contradiction of sin and alienation of the sinner. He does so not as the passive victim of the old covenant but as the active victim who is at the same time the priest of the new covenant. Hence, as Colin Gunton suggests (1988, 154), in his sacrifice Christ not only experiences the judgement of God, he exercises the judgement of God by willingly taking sin to the place where all its destructive tendencies are outworked.

It is at the point of his death that the two aspects of Christ's perfecting come together. His obedience to the will of God for the good of others is that which makes Christ's sacrifice *both* the expression of the perfect human attitude – because here God finds a complete and pure self-giving of a human being to his will for the good of others – *and* the efficacious action of expiation – because Jesus bears the defilement of the people's sin before the judgement of the holy God and suffers the consequence, the death, which comes as the two meet:

> Christ's death was atoning not simply because it was sacrifice unto death, but because it was sacrifice unto holy and radical judgement. There is something much more than being obedient unto death. Plenty of men can be obedient unto death; but the core of Christianity is Christ's being obedient unto judgement, and unto the final judgement of holiness (Forsyth 1910, 89).

Through this perfect offering of the perfect priest a new possibility for all is created. On the basis of his offering Jesus enters heaven. He enters as the perfected human being, the pioneer or leader of our faith. His presence in heaven means that the humanity which he shares with us has been redeemed and made holy – and as Barth said (1956, 351), the fact that there is room for Jesus means that there is room for us. However, he enters heaven not just as the pioneer but as the priest who has offered the perfect sacrifice and has become the Saviour ('the source of eternal salvation for all who obey him': 5.9), the one who 'is able for all time to save those who approach God through him, since he always lives to make intercession for them' (7.25).

The new possibility created by the priestly ministry of Jesus is that through him we may enter into the sanctuary, the place of God's holy presence:

> Therefore, my friends, since we have confidence to enter the sanctuary by the blood of Jesus, by the new and living way that he opened for us through the curtain (that is, through his flesh), and since we have a great priest over the house of God, let us approach . . . (10.19–21).

Here is the climax of the writer's argument. Through the living, dying, and ascending of Christ, we can enter the sanctuary. We can stand in the holy presence of God and offer an unending sacrifice of praise (13.15). This is the joy, the delight and the reality of Christian *worship*: it takes place in the presence of God through the priesthood of Christ. This is why Calvin could say that Christ is our altar on whom we lay our oblations (*Institutes* IV.8.17) and also, commenting on Hebrews 2.12, that 'Christ leads our songs, and is the chief composer of our hymns' (1853, 67). It is also here, within the sanctuary, that our whole life is lived as a sacrificial giving to God. This is the joy, the delight, the reality of Christian *living*: it is life lived in the presence of God through the priesthood of Christ. To be in the presence of God is the reality of Christian worship and living, because Christ has opened up for us a 'new way' (10.20) through all that would divide us from God's presence; and this way is nothing else but himself. Following Westcott's construction of 10.20, we have 'a way through the veil, that is, a way consisting in His flesh, His true human nature' (1903, 322).

Daniel Hardy and David Ford (1984, 63–4) describe the connections in Martin Luther's mind between the cross, the presence of God and the character of Christian praise and practice in a way which summarizes where Hebrews has led us so far, and points to where we need to go next:

> The key to the whole of existence is to live *coram Deo*, in the presence, before the face of God, and this God is identified through the cross. Luther's way of bringing together the cross and the *coram Deo* precisely defines the distinctiveness for him of Christian praise. Praise is simply faith being freely itself before God.

Our Participation in the Perfection of Christ

The next task is to indicate how the general relationship which we have with Christ's person and his work through his participation in our humanity and his appointment as our priest is translated into a personal experience in the particularity of individual human lives. To do so, we need to refer to Hebrews' understanding of holiness or righteousness as an eschatological reality.

When we come to the writer's fascinating and moving catalogue of Old Testament characters in Hebrews 11, it is easy to feel that we have come to the end of his argument and that, after the complexities of the comparison between Jewish and Christian worship, we are being treated to a poetic piece of narrative to inspire us along the way. However, the chapter actually plays a vital part in the whole argument. Hebrews shows that although the great forebears displayed the sort of faith by which they 'received approval as righteous' and 'were commended for their faith' (11.4, 39), their actual perfection had to wait until the fulfilment of the promise (11.39–40). We may say therefore that their holiness or perfection was a potential one; it still lay in the realm of the promise.

We have seen that for Hebrews this promise has been fulfilled in Christ. The eschatological hope for the holiness of humanity, and of all creation, is fulfilled and established in Christ. In Christ and through his death, humanity has been renewed, reconstituted and re-created. The perfection which was promised is now present in the ascended Christ – as Paul says, he has been made *our sanctification* (1 Cor 1.30). He is the one who has entered the heavenly or the eschatological place which is the presence of God. He goes there, as Luther says in his comment on Hebrews 10.19–22 (1968, 226), as the 'ferryman', the one whose role it is to take others with him. He takes us with him as we participate in the eschatological righteousness which is nothing less than the holiness of God (12.10) and which has been formed in him and is his gift to share with those for whom he died as the sacrifice and now lives as the priest.

The ground of this participation is always the racial relationship we have with Christ through the giving and revealing of God and the liturgical relationship we have with Christ through God's choice of him as the priest who represents us, but this relationship takes particular and personal form through the process of initiation involving (at the least) faith and baptism (10.22). By faith and through baptism we participate in Christ and therefore in his eschatological righteousness and holiness by our identification with and acceptance of his priestly identity and work. We simply accept that we are *made holy* not through the blood of bulls and goats, not through the sweat of our religious ritual and moral toil, but by the offering of Christ's body, the self-giving of God. In this acceptance we have passed from darkness into light and have 'shared in the Holy Spirit' (6.4). This is an eschatological experience, it is a taste of the gift from heaven (6.4). We might call it a relative holiness, in that it is only relative to Christ and is not actually formed in us, but it is a real holiness, for our sins have been forgiven, our consciences have been cleansed, and we have the confidence to be in the presence of God.

Hebrews does not see a conclusion to the matter in the person's initiation – indeed, it demands that its readers go beyond the fundamental doctrines of faith and baptism (6.1–2). It defines Christian existence in the dynamic terms of pressing on to the goal which is ahead. It calls for perseverance, self-sacrifice, hope, good works, commitment to the assembly and a life of worship lived in the presence of God. In this developmental experience there is a participation in the eschatological righteousness and holiness of Christ through sharing more deeply in the life of Christ, following more truly in the way of Christ, and believing more fully in the truth of Christ. It is the process which Paul describes as being moulded by God to the pattern of his Son, so that he should be the oldest of many brothers (Rom 8.29). As we develop in the life of Christ, through our share in the Spirit and through the praying (Heb 7.25) and pastoring (4.15–16) of Christ our priest, so his holiness is formed within us. We may call this the beginnings of an actual holiness as we are consecrated by our communion with the consecrator (2.10).

Although we participate in the promise and have a share in the righteousness of Christ, we too are waiting to enter into the fullness of our inheritance. This will happen when Christ 'will appear a second time' (9.28), bringing the salvation which we have tasted and welcoming us into the city for which we have been looking, where we will rest in the sabbath of God's new creation, the sabbath which by God's blessing though Christ is made holy (Gen 2.3). Then our holiness will be complete and the promise fulfilled:

> Blessed be the Lord, the God of Israel,
> for he has come to his people and set them free.
> He has raised up for us a mighty Saviour,
> born of the house of his servant, David.
> Through his holy prophets he promised of old
> that he would save us from our enemies,
> from the hands of all who hate us.
> He promised to show mercy to our forebears
> and to remember his holy covenant.
> This was the oath he swore to our father Abraham:
> to set us free from the fear of our enemies,
> *free to worship him without fear,*
> *holy and righteous in his sight,*
> *all the days of our life.*

Particular Consequences

David Peterson claims that Hebrews was written in order to overcome 'a general spiritual lethargy, involving loss of zeal, lack of confidence and faltering hope' within a Christian community facing the reality of persecution for its faith. The writer's 'method was to present a vision of Christ perfected through suffering and opening "the new and living way" for mankind into the sanctuary of heaven' (1982, 185). For much of the time our worship and living display the same sort of lethargy and lack of zeal, confidence, and hope which Peterson finds amongst the first readers of Hebrews. The task of these final sections therefore is to draw out some of the particular consequences of Christ's perfection for our worship and living so that we, like them, may be inspired by the vision of Hebrews.

Worship

To be in the holy presence of God and to worship God there, is to experience eschatological salvation, for it is a participation in the new humanity perfected through Christ's ministry. In order for us to enter this place there needs to be *anamnesis* – a calling to mind. Hebrews spends a good deal of time referring its readers back to the cross in order that the significance of the cross may fully register in them. Although the event of the cross is past and although it was the physical and historical experience of one person, its significance endures as an eternal reality for all people of all time. The significance is to be found in the presence of Christ in heaven as our pioneer and as our priest. *Anamnesis* of the cross therefore involves becoming more fully aware of all that Christ's presence in heaven means for us and of all that Christ is doing for us now on the basis of his sacrifice. As our pioneer he is the one who has gone before us to prepare the way into God's presence. As our priest he is the one through whose mediation we can enter the new covenant of the heavenly Jerusalem (12.22–4).

As well as *anamnesis* there needs to be *epiclesis* – calling on the Holy Spirit. Hebrews does not have a developed doctrine of the Spirit, but even so, the Spirit is seen as the witnessing Spirit who speaks through the Scriptures of Christ (3.7; 9.8), and as the eschatological Spirit who comes to us with the life of the world to come (6.4). As the perfection wrought in and by Christ is seen by Hebrews as the eschatological reality in which we may participate, we do not have to step far to arrive at Calvin's definition of the Spirit as the bond of our communion with Christ. It is through our communion with the ascended Christ in the Spirit that his work of consecration has contact with us and brings us into the changes implicit in the new covenant relations with God.

The *anamnesis* by which we call to mind the significance of Christ's sacrifice and the *epiclesis* by which we have communion with Christ's ascended presence are rooted in the corporate worshipping life of the church – most visibly in its celebrations of baptism and eucharist. Hebrews refers to our bodies being 'washed with pure water' (9.22) and intimately relates this to the cleansing of our consciences. Almost all commentators see this as a reference to baptism, so that in one sense the whole of Hebrews can be seen as a post-baptismal exhortation. Because we have been baptized, immersed into Christ, we truly participate in the new, perfected humanity which has been formed in Christ through his life, death and entry into heaven. In Christ and through him, our pioneer and priest, we come before God's presence and offer an unending sacrifice of praise (13.15). Although our baptism assures us of our participation in Christ and of our entry into the place of God's presence, in order to receive all that our baptism involves, we must be continually taking hold of our right of entry. As Calvin said, 'Christ is not simply united to us by an indissoluble bond of union but from day to day is increasingly knitted with us into one Body until he becomes utterly at one with us' (*Institutes* III.2.24). And the way Hebrews sees our ever-deeper participation in the life of Christ happening is through our taking every opportunity to join in the worshipping life of the church. The *anamnesis* calls to mind all that has been made available for us and so evokes a sense of thanksgiving which propels us further into the worship of God (12.28) in the full confidence of our faith in the blood of Christ and the living way of his flesh (10.19–22).

In all this it is difficult not to see allusions to the eucharist in which we share in the body and blood of Christ (1 Cor 10.15–20) and so celebrate the reality of the new covenant relations with God. Although it is a matter of debate whether Hebrews itself makes explicit connections with the eucharist, its implicit connections have been enough to make it a quarry for eucharistic hymnody and liturgy. Its picture of our entering the holy presence of God through the body and blood of Christ, and offering there the sacrifice of praise, applies to all Christian worship, but it is particularly descriptive of the eucharistic action. Christians of all sorts, including those on the mantelpiece of evangelical honour, have found the eucharist to be the place where we enter into a depth of communion with Christ and an intensity of worshipping experience, so much so that, in time, we are changed by the encounter. In a brilliant piece of Anglican apologetics, Richard Hooker turned the sixteenth-century debates about transubstantiation on their heads by arguing that the function of the eucharistic elements is to be a means, by God's appointment, through which we participate in Christ and, in so doing, become changed into his likeness:

> to us they are thereby made instruments as mystically yet truly, invisibly yet really work our communion or fellowship with the person of Jesus Christ . . . whereupon there ensueth a kind of transubstantiation in us, a true change both of soul and body, an alteration from death to life (*Ecclesiastical Polity* V.67.11).

Hence we can say that as we participate in the life of the ascended Christ in all our worship and most specifically in the eucharist, the perfection which has been formed in him for us penetrates more deeply into the moral and spiritual fabric of our lives so that we become more fully that which we are declared to be. From a full trinitarian perspective we can go on to say that all this happens as we pray the *epiclesis*, as we seek the witnessing Spirit who speaks to us of Christ and as we receive the eschatological Spirit who brings us into communion with the ascended Christ. From this trinitarian perspective we can add that our worship through the ascended Christ happens not just *in* the presence of God but *within* the presence of God, as the Son prays and praises the Father through the eternal Spirit. No wonder we are to worship in reverence and awe (12.28).

Living

For Hebrews, Christian worship does not just include those times when the assembly comes together to offer the sacrifice of praise through Christ. It pervades the whole of the life of the community, so that, through mutual sharing and good works, we live the sacrificial lifestyle which is pleasing to God (13.15–16). The new covenant relations with God involve not just the cleansing of our consciences from the guilt which keeps us from God's presence, but the changing of our character so that our consciences are refined and retuned to God's will for his church and his world. It is about the law being written on our hearts because we 'know the Lord' (8.11) and live each moment of each day in his presence.

The new covenant has begun, our consciences have been cleansed, because through Christ's priestly ministry our perfection has been forged and through our faith in God's promises we truly participate in his perfection. However, this eschatological perfection can only be formed in us here and now as we persevere in our faith, that is, as we continue in the confidence of our confession of Christ (in our approach to worship) and as we continue confidently to confess him (in the words and works of our lives). The perseverance which Hebrews calls for in our living requires *anamnesis* and *epiclesis* just as it does in our worshipping. It requires *anamnesis* in the sense of calling to mind that God is not ashamed to be called our God or for us to be called his children (11.16; 12.7). This covenant of fatherly love and filial trust is an ongoing relationship in which God hones us into his holiness (12.5–10). It is a process which involves a real 'struggle against sin' (12.4) – and not just the sins of personal life, but the sins of believers which may disrupt the community's peace, and the sin of those in the world who are seeking to destroy the community's existence. The *anamnesis* also involves the calling to mind of the example of Christ (12.2). Jesus fought with sin in the sense of struggling with the weakness of humanity and with the temptation to give way to the forces which drive us from obedience to God. Jesus grappled in the garden of Gethsemane with the full implications of God's demands and chose to endure the cross for the sake of the joy which lay ahead of him (12.2). Just at the point where the readers of Hebrews find themselves – giving up in the face of persecution – Jesus perseveres and so becomes the pioneer of our faith and the pattern we can follow.

The pattern is one of dying and ascending. The first readers of Hebrews faced this reality in its harshest form. They were called to follow Christ to the point of bloodshed (12.4), to bear his humiliation – execution as a social outcast and religious heretic (13.13). Many readers of the letter since them have faced the same fate and looked forward to the same vision of 'the permanent city' where they shall ascend with Christ. Although other readers of Hebrews may not have to replicate the literal pattern of Christ's death, the same rhythm of dying in the fight against sin and ascending into the presence of God with Christ remains the distinctive pattern of Christian existence. Through this discipline, this training, the crooked paths of our lives are made straight and our injured limbs are healed (12.7–13). It is not that this process earns us the right to be in God's presence; that has already been secured in Christ. It is rather that as we follow in the way of Christ we find that his determined resistance to sin and his dedicated obedience to God become actualized in our lives as we share in his life.

Hence, as we saw earlier, the *anamnesis* is not just a recollection of the historical experience of Jesus, but a realization that Christ now stands in the presence of God as the priest in and through whom we have access to God. The *anamnesis*, therefore, leads to the *epiclesis* – the invocation of the Spirit who is the bond of our communion with Christ. The Spirit we have received (6.4) is the one through whom God perfected the humanity of Christ and the one through whom God forms

Christ's perfection in us as we participate by the Spirit in the ascended life of Christ. The Spirit is the one through whom Christ offered himself to the Father (9.14) and so the Spirit is the one through whom Christ now offers to the Father our praise and prayer, our confession of him and our commitment to his way, as we bring them to him, our priest who, through a life of obedience, leading to the sacrifice for sin, has become for all who obey him 'the source of eternal salvation' (5.9).

Part Two

Focusing on the
Contemporary
World

8

Jesus the Man and Women's Salvation

CHRISTINA A. BAXTER

THE NEW TESTAMENT is famous for its universalism, which sits awkwardly alongside its exclusivism. 'God so loved the world,' we are told, 'that he gave his only Son, so that everyone who believes in him may not perish but may have eternal life.' That nestles closely in the same Gospel as Jesus's claim 'No one comes to the Father except through me.' Such exclusivism has never been thought to exclude women because they were women. Rather the newness of the Christian claim is often described as its insistence on God's universal intentions, which include women as well as men. So what, in this century, has made women even raise the question which this paper addresses? I can identify five motifs amongst those who write in this area, which I will look at briefly before I consider a sixth, which particularly concerns me.

Does Jesus Save Women?

Many women ask whether we can credibly claim that Jesus saves women, when their experience of the church of Jesus Christ has been one of oppression and exploitation rather than liberation and honour. In the early part of this century the Church of England flatly refused to allow some women with land rights to vote alongside men for members of their Parochial Church Council. They were not seeking to stand in the election, simply to vote, but they were refused. We live in a country whose culture has been based on Christian teaching and thinking, but one where we are only now celebrating seventy-five years of female suffrage (see further Storkey 1985). What is the meaning of salvation for women, if it has meant being saved into all the freedoms and responsibilities of a minor child, while men are saved into the adult decision-making of business, politics and church? What kind of salvation was this? What can women expect from the salvation which Christ has achieved, and which it is claimed is available to them in the church?

The second motif which we find in those who write about this subject is epitomized in an article by Reta Halteman Finger (1988) where she asks whether any of the three main classic theories of the atonement, which she terms the theories of substitution, moral influence, and *Christus Victor*, will encourage healthy characteristics in women who are being saved, or whether they will keep women in positions where salvation does not materially change them. So she explores the effects of these models of the atonement on women in their everyday experience. She implies that both the model of substitution and that of moral influence reinforce women in patterns of submission to injustice, in the name of love. If Jesus hung innocent or wrongly accused, for instance, women might be persuaded to continue to suffer injustice without protest in the imitation of Christ.

In preferring the *Christus Victor* model, she suggests it exposes the systemic evils of oppression, patriarchy, militarism, and materialism, but concludes by asking,

> Can we feminists trust in Christ to deliver us from evil? Can we believe that this man Jesus stripped himself of whatever male rights and privileges a sexist society gave him, and engaged in mortal combat with the powers of patriarchy? Can we trust that His resurrection in the power of God's Spirit is the beginning of the end of patriarchal oppression? (1988, 18).

She answers her question 'I believe we can.' But I want to explore her query in a little more depth before I draw that conclusion.

I focus here on her assertion that the *Christus Victor* model could be saving or liberating for women because it shows the vulnerable overcoming the powerful. Christ is victor over the powers of death and evil on the cross. Even this, however, could reinforce women's susceptibility to suffer, rather than initiate change. It could reinforce their felt vulnerability, in the face of male physical, political and ecclesiastical power. It could reinforce their tendency to self-offering in a way which leaves little room for reciprocal self-sacrifice. If this model is not to be abused as a means of keeping women suffering, vulnerable and self-giving, we need to understand the dialectic in Jesus's own act as *Christus Victor*. Jesus goes willingly to the cross, but he is self-determining. Those who are vulnerable need to know that they can choose this or not, and those who are powerful need to hear that they can choose to suffer or not. The vulnerable need to hear about the possibility of self-determination, and the self-determining need to hear about the possibility of suffering. If this does not happen there is no salvation for the powerful or the weak; each is reinforced in the prison of their own making. This is important, because there are major differences between Jesus's sufferings and those of women today. He did not claim his rights, though he had them. But he overcame evil by letting it do its worst on him, not for himself, but for others. He knew he did not deserve it, but he chose it.

Contrast the case of a woman exploited because of her sex, perhaps discriminated against at work by male colleagues. She does not suffer this for others. She suffers it because of others. She has mixed feelings. She knows herself a mixture of good and bad, deserving praise and blame. She does not deserve this kind of treatment, perhaps, but other kinds of reproof might be appropriate. There is a twist in non-innocent suffering, and all human suffering other than Jesus's is non-innocent. This woman has not chosen suffering. The beneficiaries of her suffering are not people she has chosen, but people who have stolen her rights from her. She questions whether her suffering, if it is dumb like the sheep before the shearers, will achieve any victory over evil. Indeed, she wonders if it does not encourage the continuance of wicked practices. So the models of atonement may not be experienced as saving experiences for women. They may at best reinforce the marginalized position of women in society, or at worse legitimize male patterns of oppression. This is the danger to which Reta Halteman Finger alerts us. The agenda her article imposes is that we discover how to avoid this happening.

In particular, if we take seriously the challenge of liberation theology, we need to ask 'Have we checked both sets of criteria?' – the criteria of thought, doctrine, and right speech, as well as those of practice, behaviour, and right living. One might sharpen this question by asking whether the death of Christ as an exemplary pattern is a dangerous tool which should not be deployed against individuals or the powerless, which perhaps should not be used at all, or should only be used corporately in community, and then chiefly among the powerful. Ironically, it may be the case that the proponents of the exemplary model, who are so quick to suggest that substitutionary atonement is morally offensive, may not realize how morally offensive the exemplary model can turn out to be. Mutual deference is a very different matter from preaching the self-giving love of Jesus as the example which reinforces the giving of some in order to maintain the taking of others. So Halteman Finger is making us ask questions about whether the ways in which we understand the atonement are really liberating or saving in the experience of women. (I am not excluding the possibility that these remarks may not also be applicable to the experience of some poor marginalized men, but at the moment my prime attention has to be given to women, because that is the point of this chapter.)

The third motif to be found amongst feminist writers who examine the text of the New Testament, especially the Gospels, is the question whether a male Jesus can save women at his death when his life is so ambivalent. Is Jesus sexist? For instance, he only chose men to be among the Twelve. There is much evidence on both sides of this debate, so here I offer a few examples to sharpen our thinking. Some women have claimed that Jesus shows remarkably positive attitudes to women, attitudes out of step with his time. He encourages the Samaritan woman, for instance, to dialogue with him about theology. Susan Thistlethwaite (1990), however, warns us against being so confident in this regard. She suggests that this way of reading

Jesus's attitude depends on an anti-Semitic hermeneutic, which attributes all that is worse in patriarchal society to the Judaism of Jesus's day. Feminists, she suggests, who themselves have suffered at the hands of men, who stereotype them in order to demean and reject them, should beware of espousing the same mechanisms against the Jews. Perhaps we have to admit that there is a genuine ambiguity in the New Testament texts about this matter. If Jesus was a Jewish reformer, we should not be surprised if his teaching and practice highlighted aspects of Judaism which needed reform. But until we can be sure what were the prevailing attitudes of Jesus's contemporaries, it is difficult to judge how radical Jesus was, and there remains the possibility that Jesus was not as radical about women's issues as Western white women in this decade would like him to be have been. If this is so, if he is to save them, it might have to be from liberalism or radicalism into the conservative or conventional role models of the past. To some women this may not feel much like salvation. And that raises another set of issues which need to be addressed.

Does salvation have to be *experienced* as salvation for it to be considered salvation? Do I need as a women to feel freed or saved in order to be saved, or may I be saved even though my experience of it feels something rather different? There may be biblical warrant for arguing that it is not necessarily the case that we have to feel saved, or feel better, for salvation to have occurred. The people of Israel, for instance, found the hot wilderness of wanderings hard, pined for the fleshpots of Egypt, considering the security of slavery preferable to the risks of freedom. Were they or were they not saved? Beyond the question which only women can answer, whether they experience relationship with Jesus as in any sense salvation, there is the further question as to what constitutes salvation, and who defines it.

The fourth area in current literature, where questions are raised regarding the possibility of a male Jesus saving women, comes in the discussion of the correct gender of the president of the eucharist. Although such discussions are not intended to raise soteriological issues, they do so implicitly. Claims that only a male person can represent Christ as the president of the eucharist imply that there is more significance in the fact that God became incarnate as male man than in the fact that God became human person, since at this key service to celebrate our salvation it is the former and not the latter which needs somehow to be highlighted by the president. Since incarnation is for salvation, and the eucharist is closely linked to that salvation, such assertions raise these questions in sharp form. T. F. Torrance answers them equally sharply: to 'obtrude anything of ourselves' into the eucharist calls into question the

> unique unrepeatable and completely sufficient nature of the sacrifice of Christ on the cross. . . . To insist that only a man, or a male, can rightly celebrate the Eucharist on the ground that only a male can represent Christ, would be to sin against the blood of Christ, for it would discount the substitutionary aspect of the atonement. At the altar the minister or priest acts faithfully in the name of Christ, the incarnate Saviour, only as he lets himself be displaced by Christ, and so fulfils his proper ministerial representation of Christ at the Eucharist in the form of a relation 'not I but Christ', in which his own self, let alone his male nature, does not come into the reckoning at all (1992, 12).

This is another way of saying, from a Reformed perspective, that the eucharist is Christ given to his church, to which we contribute nothing, and least of all do we contribute our male or our female natures, for that would be to make this sign of our salvation dependent upon us, and not upon God. Thus in raising this question at all, issues of salvation have been directly brought into view, and it is only by appealing to soteriological criteria that Torrance can combat them.

Debaters appeal both to the creation narratives and to the incarnation itself to justify their conflicting positions. The reason that neither creation nor incarnation can be a sufficient answer to this problem is that both are ambiguous. The Genesis texts about the creation of humankind, taken in the context of the New Testament, can be read both ways. Capable scholars argue supporting the notion that women as well as men are in the image of God, so that if the president of the eucharist is in any sense imaging God that president may be either male or female, but those texts are also capable of being understood to imply that male man is in the image of God and that female is in the image of man, so that male man more clearly images God, and therefore properly presides at the eucharist.

Incarnation is ambiguous, because it is gender-specific. It is male, and we have yet to discern whether its particularity in this respect is exclusive or inclusive. Briefly, if it is read exclusively, it may be warrant for only male presidents being appropriate at the eucharist. If it is read inclusively, it points to the possibility that any human being might preside at the eucharist because the maleness signifies to us real humanity. The question which we need to pose to those who argue for exclusivity at this point and suggest that only men should preside at the eucharist is whether they can with integrity claim the maleness of Jesus as the basis for exclusive claims in relation to church order whilst at the same time claiming the figure of Jesus as the basis for inclusive claims in relation to salvation. No one who argues for male-only presidency at the eucharist is also arguing that only men are saved. So they are using the same person, the same event in two different ways, both exclusively and inclusively. That practice needs to be defended. Upon what criteria does it work? Or is Scripture being twisted like the waxen nose of which Reformation figures such as Johann Geiler spoke, to suit any face?

What is Not Assumed is Not Redeemed?

Parallel to this last issue is a fifth motif in theology which implicitly raises the question of this chapter. It is sometimes argued that certain ways of talking about God put the salvation of women in question – for instance, it may be suggested that there is a correspondence between the male human Jesus and the divine Son of God, or God himself, such that male gender may be attributed to the Son or to the Father or to the Godhead. In other words, there is a way of arguing in theology which suggests that because the incarnate one is male, that tells us something about the maleness of the divine Word, or the maleness of the Father, or the maleness of the Godhead taken as a totality. Two problems may follow, one experiential, the other theological. Women who have suffered sexual abuse at the hands of men may find it impossible to receive salvation from God when God is conceived as male. Theologically, all talk of salvation which appeals to recapitulation, identification, or substitution may be at risk.

Clearly there is a theological issue which needs to be addressed here, if the assertion that salvation is of God implies the assertion that salvation is available only from the male. Christian theology has both traditionally and recently said that God is spirit and is beyond gender, and that the fact that men and women are created together in the image of God means that God is not more like one than the other. But behind both the fourth and the fifth debates, concerning presidency at the eucharist and concerning gender in God, there lies a dictum of the church which requires that we take these questions very seriously. It is a dictum which gives force to these arguments, and in lesser measure to the other three. It is one which has often been applied in Christology and soteriology: 'What is not assumed is not redeemed.' If the church is right to deploy this assumption in building its theology, then it must show how female humanity has been assumed, or how it has been redeemed, that principle notwithstanding. It is to this contention to which I now turn, because I think it is crucial in the question as to whether a male Saviour can save women.

We must first establish whether it is true that what is not assumed is not redeemed. If it is true, is it the case that as Jesus has not assumed female humanity, therefore female humanity is not redeemed?

This little phrase was much appealed to in the early church in its defence against heretics, and it seems at first sight to be a useful and helpful summary of the truth about the person and salvation of Christ. Its truthfulness was most clear when it was applied to inadequate understandings of the person of Christ. Initially it seems a credible and a helpful way of approaching that question. But it highlights the contemporary problem of an increasing divide between men and women which has been a feature of the latter part of this century in the Western world. We have begun to understand how we often see men as the norm and then regard women as the abnorm. We do this in our laws, social benefits, modes of employment, and other realms. Sometimes this manifests itself in the ways we talk about ourselves. It has led me to some odd reflections. Because I have a very highly developed sense of my own normality, I catch myself thinking as I hear someone speaking in a way which implies that the male is the norm, 'Well, I am normal, so that must mean I'm male! No, no, that can't be right! I am not male, but I am normal, so how does that fit with what is being said at this particular point?' As the distinctions and divisions between men and women have increased, the question under discussion has increasingly become a tension point. Can we continue to hold that 'what is not assumed is not redeemed' if it is crucially important that the assumption of the human nature by the divine Word is male?

In an article on this subject Maurice Wiles reminds us that this phrase 'the unassumed is the unhealed' 'comes from Gregory Nazianzen's Epistle 101 and sums up an important aspect of his case against Apollinarius' (1969, 47). Whilst this argument does not directly touch on our question with respect to women, Wiles's exploration of what the phrase meant and might mean can give structure to our thought. In the early church it was used in the debate about the full humanity of Christ, and it focused the soteriological impetus to affirm that anything less than full humanity would not or could not save us. In traditional soteriology the 'double *homoousios*', the conviction that Christ was of the same nature as God and of the same nature as human beings, has been a cornerstone of the gospel. It was God in Christ reconciling the world to himself, so salvation is secure, because this God was acting to secure it. God really is like Jesus because in Jesus God is with us. When Jesus reproves evil, invites repentance, or offers forgiveness, we hear God reproving, inviting, and offering forgiveness. Any alienation, separation, or enmity has been overcome in the reconciling act of incarnation which is for crucifixion and resurrection. Reconciliation is the completed work of Christ, something anticipated in the incarnation but completed in the ascension. The contention that this really is God saving is an important aspect of classic Christology.

It is the other side of the double solidarity that was being highlighted by the early church in the statement that what is not assumed is not redeemed. Clearly the New Testament tells us that 'the word became flesh', he was 'born of a woman', he was 'like us, sin excepted'. The New Testament falls short of precisely affirming that this is a real human being just like one of us; those actual words do not appear in the New Testament text, though it labours the reality of this humanity, especially in the Johannine literature.

So why did the early church espouse this tag, 'what is not assumed is not redeemed', which could give rise to so much heart-searching amongst women? It wanted to affirm that this person was really human. In order to do so, it devised a simple soteriological test to apply to any Christology to see if it would work. It concluded, probably on the basis of the theory of recapitulation, that what has not been assumed has not been redeemed. If the divine Son or Word was the medicine of God for the healing of all human ills, one can see that unless the medicine has been applied all over (to coin a phrase), we cannot be sure that the body is healed all over. Behind the theory lay ideas to which our world no longer adheres, about the solidarity of the human race and about the possibility of one acting for all.

Now the tag appears to be an *a priori*, something which is self-evidently true, but it was actually, I believe, an *a posteriori* inference which paraded as an *a priori* argument and convinced enough people to become commonplace. Wiles helps us to see this. He suggests (1969, 48) that anyone convinced of one side of the equation (for instance, that there really is salvation) can on its basis be helped to affirm the other side. Most people were convinced that Jesus had saved them; this helped them to see that he must have assumed a whole man or real humanity. Others who were sure that Jesus was fully human could be helped to see that this implied the full availability of salvation to everyone. Neither side of the equation could be demonstrated; the argument was simply an invitation to exploration and to faith.

If the dictum is therefore not self-evident one can ask whether it can be substantiated. I do not think it can be. We simply become involved in a circular argument about the nature of the incarnation which cannot be settled by appealing to any principles such as we could know outside of this unique act. Perhaps, then, the tag itself is helpful, but incapable of universal demonstration. In a more moderate form Wiles suggests that we might express this principle today as 'You can't do anything effective about something without entering into that kind of relationship with it which is appropriate to your intended objective.' This is a kind of statement of the obvious. 'If you want to enable someone to stand on his own feet', Wiles goes on, 'you can't do it by entering into that kind of relationship with him which is constituted by carrying him on your shoulders' (1969, 52). Wiles is making us ask a question to which we cannot know the answer in advance regarding what God must do in order to save the whole of humankind; into what kind of relationship with humanity God must enter. Obviously we cannot know that in advance, because only God knows what it will take to save the human race. It may be known only after the event, and then its appropriateness can be reflected upon. We can say after the event, 'How appropriate that God saved humankind by becoming fully human' or 'How appropriate that God saved humankind by entering male particularity', and perhaps we need to say both, but we cannot thereby demonstrate that it had to be so.

Some further questions are raised by this. First, the New Testament is clear that what Christ has done has universal significance for the whole created order, which extends far beyond humankind. How does incarnation in a male human being effect such universal consequences if what is not assumed is not redeemed? Clearly the theory cannot work by the simple medicine analogy. Indeed, we need to go back to the beginning, where we see the initial act of Eve, copied by Adam, has consequences which extend far beyond humankind into the created order –

because of God's fiat, because God says so. Some such parallel understanding may be assumed in relationship to the single act of salvation, even if we appeal to the notion that because human beings had been appointed stewards over creation their actions were capable of influencing everything else.

Second, even if we were able to demonstrate that the tag 'What is not assumed is not redeemed' applies in principle to human salvation, it clearly does not apply to all the possible categories in which we might think. The church wanted to assert that Jesus was not without soul, mind, spirit, or flesh; that is, they wanted to assert that Jesus possessed all that was necessary for Jesus to be truly human. But they did not extend these categories to nationality, age, handicap – or gender. Strictly speaking, if the tag worked at all it would need to apply to all the conditions of being human. No one suggests that anyone over thirty cannot be saved by this person because he only lived until he was thirty, nor for long did they suggest that anyone who is not Jewish cannot be saved by this Jewish person. So perhaps we must abandon the tag and reckon that in principle it is possible that this person could have saved, or does save, people whose humanity is not identical to his. This, of course, could include women. We cannot in advance of God's unique action set up principles which need to be fulfilled for salvation to be accomplished. We can only think after the event about what its consequences may be.

So why a male Saviour? When we ask this question, we may need to begin by accepting the particularity which makes Jesus universally available. Richard Bauckham and Rowan Williams (1987) make a point of importance in this context. When God became human there was a choice; human beings are either male or female. If this was to be a genuine human being that was a straight choice. Of course God was free because God is sovereign; we cannot say that God could only have become incarnate in a male, since that would be to limit God. So we have to view incarnation in this male person as a way of guaranteeing the genuine humanity of Jesus and his universal availability to us, precisely on the basis of his being really human and human in a particular kind of way. I do not want to specu-

late about why it might be that God became incarnate in the
male and not in the female because I think it is speculation of
an unhelpful kind. But I do think it important to understand
that the particularity of Jesus's humanity functions precisely to
emphasize the reality of that humanity and its universal availability. That helps us to understand that the male particularity
is not exclusive but is actually an aspect of the inclusive act of
God in salvation. It was in order that God might be universally
available that God took the risk of becoming human. The particularity of the maleness of Jesus is a guarantee of his genuine
humanity and not an expression of the superiority of males in
general.

Jesus as Saviour in Women's Experience

When we turn to the question of women's experience of Jesus
as Saviour, I have to be personal; I cannot speak for other
people. Does Jesus as a matter of fact save women, even though
he is a man? Has he saved women? Does he save this woman?

In the New Testament there are aspects of salvation in which
women certainly seem to participate. For instance, they are
taken from sickness to health (the woman with the issue of
blood), they are taken from ignominy to apostleship (the
Samaritan woman), they are taken from sin to freedom (the
woman taken in adultery). The answer of countless women
through subsequent generations, often known to us chiefly
through their hymnody, has certainly been that their experience
of encounter with Jesus has been a saving one. But the answer
has to be given by each one of these women. One of the questions which I think needs to be asked is 'Does it mean something
different for women to be saved by Jesus from what it means
for men to be saved by Jesus?' I will only be able to answer
that question in dialogue with men, and that dialogue is only
just beginning.

So how does Jesus save me? I believe there are four moments
in my salvation. The first is the cross-resurrection event, the
second is the moment of preaching when I hear the news of
that and make a response, the third is the 'now' and every

143

subsequent 'now' of my life, and the fourth comes at the end time when Christ saves me fully and it is demonstrated that that is the case. Now if I look at the models of atonement and salvation, I have to ask myself whether they engage with me as a woman in the kind of way in which the church has affirmed that they can engage with everyone.

I begin with the model of sacrifice. I am not in a position as of now to establish scientifically that Christ is a full, perfect, and sufficient sacrifice for my sins, let alone for the sins of the whole world, because I am not in possession of a machine which might prove that this is the case. That statement about Christ is made by faith; it is not universally demonstrable. I know that Jesus lived self-sacrificially, I believe he died for me, my experience is that my guilt and sin when entrusted to him is dealt with; my experience is that the guilt and sin of others that I have counselled really can be handled by this person and that his sacrifice seems to avail for them as for me.

As far as justification is concerned, I find myself in a new covenant relationship with God because of Jesus. Now this covenant relationship is stronger in Jesus than it is in his church. Many women's groups have affirmed that their relationship with God through Jesus when they are amongst other women is often more saving, more wholesome, more healthy, more health-giving, than they found it to be in a mixed church. This raises a number of questions for the church. In my own life, I find that the points at which the church excludes me are often the points at which Jesus accepts me, as seems to have been the case in the narratives of the New Testament. At the point at which women were excluded, Jesus accepted. The story of the women with the issue of blood illustrates the point. Excluded by society, she is touched by Jesus. Jesus's companions try to exclude the woman who comes to anoint Jesus, but she is included by Jesus. Thus the experience of justification is that we find ourselves in a new relationship with God because of Jesus, and often we are most clear about that at the point at which society and the church seem to be excluding us.

Third, the model of redemption brings to me the knowledge that I am bought with a price which gives me a sense of worth and value which diminishes the praise of those around me and draws the sting of their condemnation. Redeemed by God, redeemed into this new relationship with God through Jesus Christ, women are enabled to have a sense of worth which is not always given to them by the society in which they live.

Although victory matters to me as a concept which helps me to understand the atonement, it feels less significant as part of a past act accomplished than as part of the continuing activity of God in my life.

Reconciliation, like redemption, is an ongoing metaphor, one which extends into my relationships with other people. Having this new relationship with God makes it possible for me to call into question some of the attitudes which we experience or accept for ourselves.

So how does Jesus save me now? In some ways my experience of salvation becomes more powerful as the years go on. It broadens its scope and it deepens into interpersonal relationships and into other places. The experience of Jesus saving is heightened at the points where the structures and the attitudes of other people, in particular those of the church, seem to be denying it. There are two further themes which I want to draw out of this. The first is that the Jesus who saves only saves, or effectively saves, those who allow themselves to be saved by him. The model of that for me is the story of the foot-washing in John's Gospel. Second, the scandal of the Jesus event is not that here God has become male but that here God has become human. It is that scandal from which we must not escape if we are ever to plumb the depths of this salvation.

Now can we go on from that to reaffirm that Jesus really does save women, and do so in a way which can radically transform our experiences today and can address some of the questions which we have as Christians in the context of the church? One issue we need to begin to address is our understanding of ourselves as men and women in relationship to God and in relationship to one another. We may begin to see the way forward in the way that Barth talks about the Trinity reflected in humankind, which was highlighted for me by reading a thesis by Gary Deddo (1990). He outlines the way that Barth uses this image in ethical issues. Male and female differentiation is differentiation in unity, as God's differentiation is differentiation in unity. We can begin to understand ourselves as not only separable and different but also united, and we must learn not to emphasize the one as if the other were not also true. We are different, as men and women, and we need to affirm our differences, but only in the context of our common humanity.

We then need to go on to see that our unity in differences must be expressed in deference one to another, because it is that deference which allows our unity to be expressed. Such uniting deference to one another in love is at the heart of the salvation which Christ has made available for us. That is a principle behind the household codes in the New Testament, which are based on the salvation which Christ has achieved on our behalf; it is the spur to our new patterns of behaviour as Christian people. It challenged first-century patterns of behaviour, challenged the way in which husbands and wives had hitherto related to each other, and encouraged them in mutual love and unity to defer to one another, to love one another, and to give way to one another. It challenged ways in which parents had domineered over children, or masters had domineered over slaves, by reminding them of their unity in Christ and by encouraging them to defer to one another, to give way to one another, to love one another.

Similarly, if the assertion that Jesus saves, that Jesus the man saves women, is to cut any ice in this generation, then the church has to show it to be working. The church needs to be the place where it is clear that women are of equal value to men, where women are equally saved as men, and where women and men together can be united in action, different in action, and deferring to one another in action, in a way which is mutually saving, mutually enriching, and mutually up-building. And I think one of the reasons why some of these issues have been raised in such a hard form in this generation, and one of the reasons perhaps why I struggle with the question myself, is that the church is not always the place where that differentiated unity and deference to one another's differences is actually very evident.

Finally, I should say something regarding one other question. What comfort is there, if any, and what theological significance is there, if any, in the fact that when the Gospels explain to us the way of the cross for Jesus, they are consistent in highlighting that this destiny is always at the hands of men and never at the hands of women. Women warn Jesus of his death, they anoint him, they stand with him at the foot of the cross, Pilate's wife tries to avert it, women are there at the resurrection. They are not betrayers, they are not deny-ers, they are not flee-ers. Is there something here which may help our understanding? Can it be pondered in a way which does not portray women as all-good and men as all-bad, which would be the mirror image of the teaching of some Christian leaders in the past? Women's guilt, or their participation in the death of Jesus, may need to be expressed in some other kind of way. If it remains a faith-statement that Jesus the man saves women, it also remains a fact-statement that the women could not save Jesus the man.

9

Sin and Atonement in Feminist Perspective

SALLY ALSFORD

Sin and Salvation

ACCORDING TO WILLIAM LAW, the doctrines of sin and salvation, fall and redemption are the two pillars on which 'the whole nature of the Christian religion stands' (see Coates 1951, v; cf. Berkouwer 1971, 12; Milne 1975, 3). Most, if not all, belief systems include both an analysis of the human situation as problematic, as needing change, and proposals for how such change should or will come about. As Jenny Sankey noted in Chapter 6, there is likely to be a reciprocal relationship between an understanding of the problem and of the solution, particular expositions of the nature of salvation depending on particular conceptions of the nature of sin.

It will also follow that if our view of sin is inadequate, distorted, or in need of change, then our view of salvation may be correspondingly inadequate, distorted or needing change. And Christian – specifically Western – views of sin have indeed been subject to a range of criticisms in recent years.

In this chapter I focus particularly on criticisms from the perspective of feminist theology. Feminist critiques have become increasingly familiar in our society over recent decades, raising questions about the way Christian theology can or should respond to the concerns of contemporary society. Criticisms of Christian feminism frequently suggest that Christianity is in this respect being wrongly influenced by secular movements of thought (e.g. Oddie 1984, 152). In response one might argue that there are resources within Christianity for feminist ideas; the influence or source is not 'secular', not an intrusion into authentic Christianity. One might also argue that it is not only inevitable but also necessary that Christian theology develops through dialogue and interaction with contemporary ideas.

Further, asserting the truth of Christianity surely involves asserting that Christianity is true to the way things are. Some theological formulations may not do justice to the reality of our human experience (see S. Alsford 1987, 211–28, on Pannenberg's theological anthropology). Now our understanding of sin or fallenness is presented as truth about our human situation without or in need of salvation. Christian theology must take very seriously any challenges which claim that our theological formulations are not true to the experience of certain people or groups of people. Only on the basis of a true understanding of moral evil can we understand 'that transformation or *metanoia*, that healing, which constitutes our salvation'; we need to ground 'soteriology in an anthropology via a phenomenology of moral evil' (Surin 1982, 135).

The broad consensus of the Christian tradition has been that human nature and existence are affected in every part by sin. This consensus has arisen from the common conviction that we are saved totally in Christ, and therefore that the need from which we are saved was total. But definitions of sin have been shaped by different kinds of dualism which have influenced Christian theology down the centuries, and by different anthropological presuppositions. Is it the physical – expressed above all in sexuality – which is the true locus of fallenness, of the propagation and power of sin? There are well-known critiques of this particular dualism and of corresponding views of salvation as essentially spiritual, but it is a deeply ingrained and persistent way of thinking. Before God are we essentially individual souls and minds fallen and in need of salvation? Or is humanity essentially relational, and should we understand sin and salvation in a relational way?

I assume that sin and salvation may have to do with every part and facet of human nature, and so criticisms that a view excludes part of human experience must therefore be taken seriously. Humanity is a complex totality, not easily divisible into components such as mind or spirit or soul. There must be a breadth in our view of sin which corresponds to the breadth of human beings and their situations and to the breadth of salvation which includes all of this. Further, a complex range or cluster of meanings may necessarily be associated with the idea of sin (cf. Chapter 3 above). In his analysis of symbol and metaphor, Paul Ricoeur describes words as 'tensive' entities, resisting restriction to a limited range of possible meanings and involved in a process of innovation (cf. van Leeuwen 1981, 93). Sin is such a tensive symbol which has a range of meanings, some opaque and paradoxical, as our human experience is frequently opaque and paradoxical.

Concern that sin may be treated in too limited or narrow a way has been expressed by a range of people writing from different perspectives (see Menninger 1973; Morris 1974; O'Shea 1968; Thelen 1946; Trigg 1984). Such writers are concerned lest sin be limited to the individual rather than the corporate, to the active rather than the passive, to the negative rather than the positive, to action rather than essence. Feminist theology, like other forms of liberation theology, is concerned with human experiences of oppression, exclusion, suffering – and thus with sin, the invading of the tragedy into the lives of human beings (to use Surin's expression). Considering some of the particular concerns of feminist theologians may deepen our understanding of sin in specific ways, which may enable us to grasp more of the 'tensive' nature of sin, and contribute to a deeper understanding of atonement.

Male Sin/Female Sin

In 1960 Valerie Saiving Goldstein suggested that the widespread tendency of contemporary theology to identify sin as separateness and anxiety leading to self-assertion and pride was a specifically male perspective. Such a view of sin – seen in Nygren and Niebuhr – reflects the male experience of the need for differentiation from the mother, an experience which provokes much anxiety and which requires active self-assertion.

The man's sense of his own masculinity, then, is throughout characterized by uncertainty, challenge, and the feeling that he must again and again prove himself a man. It also calls for a kind of objective achievement and a greater degree of self-differentiation and self-development than are required of the woman as woman. In a sense, masculinity is an endless process of becoming, while in femininity the emphasis is on being. Another way of putting the distinction is that woman is more closely bound to nature than is man (Saiving Goldstein 1960, 105; see further Chodorow 1978; Gilligan 1982; both referred to by Hampson 1988).

These characteristics of anxiety and active self-assertion are seen by Saiving Goldstein in the masculine role in the reproductive process and in modern Western culture which emphasizes and encourages external achievement, self-differentiation, and separation from nature. The exposition of the human situation in terms of anxiety and estrangement and the identification of sin as 'pride, will-to-power, exploitation, self-assertiveness, and the treatment of others as objects rather than persons' is an exposition which reflects and is relevant to male experiences and perspectives on the world. It is also an exposition which is matched by an understanding of redemption as restoration of the I-Thou relationship which is lacking, as the primacy of the personal and as characterized by love as self-giving rather than self-assertive.

Saiving Goldstein is not simplistic about this analysis of male and female experiences. She recognizes that there is no 'impassable gulf' between male and female perspectives, and that women's experience has changed significantly in the modern era; there is thus some ambiguity over how far the differentiation of roles is innate and how far socialized (and how far it is good or bad). Women may also believe in values of self-differentiation, challenge and adventure. She does believe that there are specific, innate differences, seen in the 'deep need of almost every woman . . . to surrender her self-identity and be included in another's "power of being"' (1960, 108). The female experience is much more a continuous process of development and passive acceptance. Achievement of the 'feminine role' is relatively easy for women and finds its fulfilment overwhelmingly in the service of others.

The conclusions which Saiving Goldstein draws from this analysis are that the temptations and sins of woman as woman are not the same as those of man as man. 'The specifically feminine dilemma is, in fact, precisely the opposite of the masculine', and the contemporary theology which is shaped by male experience and understanding is therefore not adequate to the universal human situation.

More specifically she suggests that a list of specifically feminine temptations and sins could include triviality, distractibility, diffuseness, dependence on others for one's self-definition, tolerance at the expense of standards of excellence – 'in short, underdevelopment or negation of the self'. Just as 'male' sins are destructive outworkings of male experience and potentiality, so 'female' sins are destructive outworkings of female experience and potentiality. Not surprisingly, the view of redemption as self-sacrificial love is also seen to be inadequate. Women are now increasingly able and likely to want to develop as individuals (rather than being defined solely by their 'feminine role'), to want to assert themselves, but the male perspective which speaks of self-assertion as sin may cause women to strangle such desires as in conflict with their calling to love and service of others.

Saiving Goldstein concludes her article by arguing that whereas Western society has been shaped by male priorities and expectations in the past, its orientation is now changing to a 'feminine' one in which openness, co-operativeness, and relationality are increasingly important – more important, even, than individual identity (1960, 110–11, referring to Riesman 1950 and Arendt 1958). In a sense she is here arguing against any tendency to marginalize her thesis as relevant only to women. It is relevant to human society and experience in general. Her influential article, one of the first to apply feminist thinking in this area, brings out something of the complex range of issues which impact on our conceptions of sin and salvation. This feminist critique makes clear how our anthropology will be crucial, and must address the question of the nature of differentiation between men and women.

In 1980 Judith Plaskow applied and developed some of Saiving Goldstein's argument with a study of the conceptions of sin in Reinhold Niebuhr and Paul Tillich. While Plaskow wants to focus on cultural rather than innate/biological factors as shaping women's identity and experience, she concurs with the understanding of women's sin as failure to take responsibility for self-actualization. She finds Niebuhr and Tillich lacking awareness of women's experience in their formulations of sin as anxiety and pride. Although Niebuhr isolates two abuses of freedom – its exaltation or its abdication – he only talks about the first, and fails to take account of women's experience. Seeing the struggle to achieve independent selfhood as sinful reinforces women's servitude. Tillich, Plaskow argues, although concerned with self-actualization, often equates it with estrangement on an ontological level (i.e. actualized being *is* estranged being) so that self-actualization cannot be seen as having positive value. Tillich's overall concern with 'monistic ontology', reunion with the divine ground, means that the finite self tends to be lost or negated.

Plaskow's conclusion is that neither Niebuhr nor Tillich defines sin in fundamentally social ways whereas the women's movement is especially aware of the social nature of sin, of sin as defining structure. She is also critical that although sin has a number of different meanings for both Niebuhr and Tillich (not all these meanings being in the same realm of discourse) there are problems with the universality of the claims they make on behalf of the particular.

The focus of these critiques is thus on ways in which the view of sin may be limited by the perspective within which it is formulated and on ways in which limited views of sin may presuppose or imply limited views of salvation. The alternative or additional perspective on sin which Saiving Goldstein and Plaskow suggest (sin as failure to take responsibility, failure of self-actualization) seems a valid interpretation insofar as Scripture describes sin not only as rebellion but as falling short, missing the mark. It involves not only what we have done but what we have failed to do.

Sexism as Sin

Another line of feminist argument concerning sin urges that sexism and the tendency to polarization should itself be recognized as sinful. First, there is the feminist critique which focuses on ways in which women have been associated with characteristics or aspects of human existence which are identified as the realm or root of sin (e.g. physical existence itself, sexuality, nature as opposed to spirit or culture, and irrationality), and on the harmful effects this has had on women (e.g. Scanzoni and Hardesty 1974; Dowell and Hurcombe 1981; Ruether 1983; Noddings 1989). This argument is part of a broad critique of sexism as wrongfully assuming and propagating a view of women as not only different but inferior and in some sense to blame for sin.

Second, many feminists have gone on from analyses of this kind of differentiation to argue that such sexism should itself be identified as sin. 'Women cannot neglect the basic theological insight that humanity has become alienated from its true relationship to itself, to nature, and to God. Not sex, but sexism . . . is central to the origin and transmission of this alienated, fallen condition' (Ruether 1983, 37). Ruether argues that feminism in itself presupposes a radical concept of sin, as it claims that the most basic relation of human community has been distorted into an oppressive power structure (see also Ruether 1973). René Padilla speaks similarly: 'As a result of the fall woman ceases to be *'ishah* (bone of his bone, flesh of his flesh) and becomes *Eva* (living). Now Adam sees her not as a companion who shares his life, but as the "mother of all living" (Gen 3:20), a means of reaching a goal linked to feminine biology' (Padilla 1983, 21, as quoted by Kirk 1987, 27; cf. also Spencer 1985).

In their analyses of sexism as sin, feminist theologians – like liberation theologians in general – concentrate on the collective nature of sin, on sin as corporate and situational, as involving deeply ingrained attitudes and assumptions which are part of the process of socialization (cf. Moltmann-Wendel 1986, 69); '*oppression* is itself viewed as a symbol of the social reality of sin' (Russell 1974, 111; cf. Berry 1978). Such emphasis on sin as corporate has also characterized Roman Catholic explorations of original sin in recent years. Piet Schoonenberg (1965), for example, talks of original sin as 'being situated' within the sin of the world which determines or conditions individual freedom (cf. also Betty 1970; Vandervelde 1981).

Schoonenberg, Russell and others who focus on sin as collective do stress that individual freedom and responsibility must also be maintained, and here we have an application of what Ricoeur (1967, xx) calls the 'servile will', 'a free will which is bound and which always finds itself already bound'. Arguably our assumptions about the different roles *and values* of women and men are largely a matter of socialization and are thus beyond our control; the oppressive situation of many women is largely beyond their control. Yet human freedom and responsibility must play a part unless we are to speak in terms of fate rather than sin – to say that individual human beings are not to blame.

Polarization as Sin

Some feminist theologians develop this critique further. They are concerned not solely with the dualism of female and male but with the very process of differentiation, with the tendency to polarization.

W. W. Berry discusses images of sin and salvation in Ruether, Daly and Russell. Ruether, in particular, she describes (1978, 27) as having a 'central picture for understanding human existence and its hope [which] is "dualism" moving toward "unification"'. Ruether is primarily concerned with the specific dualisms of sexism, 'the most basic duality', but in liberation theology – which has a broader agenda – she identifies sin as 'a loss of the unit(ies) of human existence through the development of a consciousness which perceives and shapes reality in terms of "false polarities"', as a habitual polarization of the qualities of our experience (Berry 1978, 28). Berry discusses at some length the ambiguity regarding whether the dualities/differentiation in itself is the root of the problem or whether the problem arises when these dualities become 'false polarities' expressed

in terms of domination. There is correspondingly some ambiva-
lence over whether salvation is unification (overcoming of differentiation) or reconciliation and mutuality. This discussion
indicates one of the great divides within feminism in general.
It also illustrates the interdependence or symmetry between
understandings of sin and of salvation. Our formulation of the
implications of atonement for women will significantly depend
on our analysis and understanding of the nature of sexism.

Daphne Hampson, too, is concerned not only with the
oppression of women but with the 'seeming universality of this
male propensity to dichotomise', though again her major concern is with the specific polarization which accords a secondary
and inferior place to women.

> A transcendent monotheism . . . would seem to be tied into a
> dichotomous understanding of reality. . . . Nor does it help that
> there is also present a certain understanding of kenosis or of
> sacrifice . . . such that God in Christ is seen to come as a humble
> man, or human beings are told that sin is hubris and love an
> agapeistic self-emptying on behalf of others. They do nothing
> to help those whose problem is lack of power, whose need is
> for the justification of legitimate self-assertion (1991, 5, 8).

Hampson thus brings together a critique similar in some
respects to that of Saiving Goldstein and Plaskow with the
approach taken by Ruether. Her vision of salvation is also similar to Ruether's, a vision of 'connectedness'. In her exploration
of salvation we see a further emphasis which feminist theologians frequently share with one another and with 'creation'
theologians such as Matthew Fox (1983) who argues that 'original blessing' should be more basic to our understanding of ourselves than original sin.

Hampson argues that the 'male' view of sin goes with a view
of conversion as a 'breaking of the self' in order to be present
to others and to God in service. A once-born model is more
suited to women's experience than this twice-born, life-out-of-
death model. Salvation is rather a 'coming to self', healing,
empowerment to be. 'Themes of kenosis or of sacrifice have no

priority over those of a rightful self-assertion, or the empowerment of persons' (1991, 11). Salvation is redemption of what is present rather than violent revolution.

Mary Grey (1989, also 1990) is also concerned with the relationship between what she classes as 'Greek' and 'Latin' doctrines of the atonement and with feminist critiques of the Latin doctrine. She judges some feminist critiques as overreactions to distortions of the Latin view, but does herself find problems with certain elements in this tradition, especially with its focus on Jesus as victim, on death and destruction (cf. also Primavesi 1991). Her 're-imaging' of atonement in terms of re-creation and birth reflects a similar desire to emphasize atonement as the positive validation of humanity, as self-affirmation. She is arguing for creation and redemption to be seen as a unified process (cf. Williams 1982; Kelsey 1982).

While feminist critiques may want to urge models of salvation and sin which stress continuity – a process of healing, coming to self – rather than the radical discontinuity of the traditional creation-fall-redemption scheme, they do also want to indict sexism, and the breakdown of mutuality, as sin of the most serious kind. Any view which emphasizes sin but de-emphasizes the fall raises the question of theodicy, the question of the origins of sin and evil, of freedom and necessity. This leads us on to a problematic area of feminist theology (indeed of feminism in general): 'Who is to blame?'

Sin and Responsibility

Feminist critiques raise questions not only about the nature of sin and the nature of sexism as sin, but also questions about the location of this phenomenology within a broader systematic view of the relationships between God and human beings, between human beings and one another, and between creation and redemption.

Berry notes that whereas atonement doctrines are classically concerned with the subjective and objective dimensions of sin, feminist critique is chiefly concerned with the objective and collective, and not much with the subjective, with personal responsibility and guilt. Of course some feminist critiques are concerned with personal responsibility and guilt as specifically male. Hampson (1988, 246) emphasizes the male tendency to polarize, to dominate, or to go in for 'a self-abasement which is equally destructive of community'. Mary Daly's blaming of men is notorious and is accompanied by the assertion that salvation will be through women.

Even less extreme or explicit feminist critiques which designate men or male perspectives specifically as the source of sin risk the danger of stressing the objective nature of sin as sexism in such a way that women are seen solely as passive victims. Necessity is stressed and freedom and responsibility are lost. Christian theology must avoid any formulation whereby sin becomes identified as unavoidable fate. There may be elements of tragedy in the Christian view of the world and sin (as Ricoeur notes) but it is not ultimately a tragic world-view and the very notion of sin implies personal responsibility at some level.

This question of freedom and responsibility is at the heart of Christian debates about sin and salvation. It relates especially to the concept of original sin, focusing as this does on sin as something congenital and beyond our direct control.

The idea of original sin has a history of 'strenuous, emotional debate . . . waged throughout the entire history of the Church and her theology' (Berkouwer 1971, 424). It is widely accepted that original sin is both an extremely problematic concept and an extremely important one. Even Tillich (1957, 2:64, 67), who suggests that the doctrines of original and hereditary sin should be dropped completely because 'they seem to be beyond salvation', wants to retain something of their meaning, replacing them by 'an existential description of the universal and tragic character of estrangement'. Sin, which involves the idea of personal responsibility, is also tragically inevitable (cf. Niebuhr 1941, 1:278; Ricoeur 1967, 239; 1978, 51, 52; Surin 1982, 141). Maintaining this tension between inevitability and freedom is, of course, no easy task, and is an area where the interrelationships between sin and salvation come into particularly sharp focus (see S. Alsford 1987).

Original Sin and Sexism

Feminist analyses of sexism offer us insight into the nature of sin as tensive, as a complex of concepts, history, and reality which determine our lives (as women and as men) structurally, on a pre-conceptual and pre-conscious level, but in which we are also clearly implicated. It is a complex where, as Niebuhr says, perhaps the relation between fate and freedom cannot be fully rationalized. It may be helpful to think of sexism as an element of original sin in that it is there as a collective, structural reality before we contribute to or protest against it. Sexism seems to be a flaw woven into the very fabric of human history, yet it is not a reality which can be separated from human lives and human responsibility (Hampson 1988, 237).

From the point of view of feminist critique, then, there may be a need to develop an understanding of the relationships and situations of men and women which does more justice to the ways in which our lives are made up of complex interrelationships between our context and socialization, and the freedom with which we appropriate and react to those determinants and influences. 'Individuals bring about societies even as societies bring about individuals' (Berry 1978, 50). In her formulation of eco-feminism, Primavesi (1991, 325) talks of the need to develop an 'uncommon perception' of sin, a view of sin as structural in ecological terms, but one which also considers 'the mechanics which turn us into unwitting co-authors of this sin. It is not just outside us, we are part of it: we are its accomplices.' If we want not to take the route of blaming men rather than women for sexism (a route which seems both simplistic and dangerously reinforcing of polarization) but to avoid seeing sexism as unavoidable fate, detached from human agency, then we need to consider further the relationship between structural, collective, 'pre-existent' sin and individual responsibility and involvement – in traditional, dogmatic terms the relationship between original sin and sins.

Feminist theology does sometimes open itself to criticism, in the course of which some of its insights may be lost; criticizing traditional formulations as too narrow or limited, it can itself end up presenting too narrow or limited a view. To be fair, we should note that much (if not most) feminist theology is quite explicitly particular in its aims and claims. It begins from a concern with women's experience and directs its attention to women's experience, not generally claiming the status of a systematic theology. Berry (1978, 50) talks of the methodological contribution which feminists bring to theology: theologians 'must preserve a methodological doubt about any of their claims to grasp that which is absolute and universal in human experience'. The result of this contribution may be 'to recall theology to a more consistently dialectical view of the human self, its sickness and health' – which may be close to what we have here called a tensive view of sin, encompassing both determination and responsibility.

If this is the case, then particularity (the particularity of women's experience) may, as Plaskow argues, represent possibility not just limit in our understanding of sin. She quotes J. L. Segundo: 'The possibilities of a wide extent of universality depend . . . not on an impossible horizontal impartiality, so to speak, but on the human depth of a definite commitment' (Plaskow 1980, 209, quoting a Harvard seminar paper by Segundo).

What pointers for an understanding of atonement emerge from this analysis?

Theology and Anthropology

Some of the arguments above might be summed up in Rahner's assertion that theology must be anthropology. Our theology of the atonement, like our theology of sin, must be related to the lived experience of human beings in the world. If sin is seen and experienced in terms of concrete social structures, stereotypes, and expectations, as corporate as well as individual, then salvation must have a genuine relationship to this experience. To put this point another way, the claim to a salvation with universal relevance must take account of the particularity of human experience – not only as including women's experience, but also as including the experience of the servile will, the experience of personal sin and of the 'already there' of sin.

To say that theology must be anthropology begs the question of what comprises our anthropology. To draw out just one point from the above analysis, is it, in fact, the case that the nature of sin may be rather different for women and for men? How particular must our theology be? And if our theology does relate to all these particularities, then what/where is the continuity? Women's experience of the world (in general) is surely likely to be different from that of men (in general); whether such differences are due to nature or nurture does not affect our argument at this point. This being so, then surely sin, as a disjunction between what is and what ought to be, will be experienced in different ways. If sin can be seen as (or as including) dysfunction in relationships, in one's sense of identity and self-development, then sin is likely to take some different forms for men and for women. There will be some continuity in our understanding of sin as disjunction between what is and what should be and in our insight that in any situation there is likely to be the tension between the sin we commit and the sin which pre-empts us, but sin will be experienced by different people, in different situations, as taking different forms (cf. Coakley 1990, with her emphasis on the link between different notions of creatureliness and differentiated views of sin).

This becomes a vital consideration where universal claims are being made on behalf of the particular. If theology has been written largely by men and if women's experience has been excluded or invisible, there is clearly a need to redress this situation. It is important to take very seriously the point which Saiving Goldstein stresses, that the particular forms of sin which may be seen as developing out of women's situations and experiences are not forms of sin which are necessarily confined to women. Neither should we expect them to be true to the experience of every woman. This would be an unhelpful universalizing of particularity and would suggest a prescriptive polarization.

This line of thought must also have outworkings in our understanding of salvation; if such an analysis of sin is accepted, then there must be corollaries for our exposition of the atonement. Theology must be anthropology. Our theology of the atonement must be addressed not only to universals (and specifically not to particulars treated as universals) but must also relate to the particularities and complexities of human existence. It must address both the objective and the subjective dimensions of sin and human need, both the individual and particular and that communal, precognitive, unrationalizable level of experience which is included in the meaning of original sin.

Sin and Atonement

Within the Judeo-Christian framework, the identification of sexism as sin is hopeful because that framework can suggest a solution in salvation. To be a real answer or antidote to the problem of sin, to provide hope in the face of this complex, tensive, at times tragic reality, salvation must also be tensive. In our understanding of atonement we must allow for a range or cluster of possible meanings which may be more or less related to the particular and to the individual, to the subjective and to the objective.

In terms of the feminist critiques outlined above, this may involve a re-evaluation of the Western emphasis on sacrificial imagery and language in conceptualizing atonement, for this is only one image/model/metaphor among many within Christian Scripture and tradition, even if it has in practice been a dominant one. When combined with the complex processes and forces of sexism, a primary or sole emphasis on the death of Jesus, understood as a sacrifice, has been perceived historically and in practice as negative and harmful to many women.

A more tensive view of atonement could include increased emphasis on Jesus's whole life, death, and resurrection as salvific, and could take up and develop themes suggested by feminist theologians, such as wholeness, healing, reconciliation, creation, and birth, and the acceptance and vindication of the oppressed and suffering which we see in Jesus's life, death, and resurrection taken as a whole. Where the history of Jesus may convey a message of the need for humility and self-giving for some, a tensive view of salvation can also encompass a message of liberation of the enslaved, of life and freedom, overcoming of suffering and oppression.

Christianity could well claim to have been consistent and universal in preaching a message of self-sacrifice as the central, core meaning of (and response to) salvation. Feminists might grant that claim but argue that the implications and outcomes of this message have been very different for women and for men (Bushnell [1869] famously argued that women's greater affinity for the gospel emphasis on self-sacrifice made them less well equipped for leadership and public office). The interpretation and application of the message of self-sacrifice has been closely linked with particular social and anthropological presuppositions so that a supposedly universal meaning has been applied in very particular ways.

Atonement and Sacrifice

I have suggested that our view of atonement needs to be tensive and to allow room for a range of meanings and images, but Christina Baxter and I have also argued that self-sacrifice is not a helpful image for women. Should we then abandon this language and imagery which has been dominant in the West and is for many virtually synonymous with Christianity (see e.g. Wallace 1981, 56)? Should we perhaps retain it only for the benefit of men (as some of the feminist analysis might seem to suggest)?

Women may indeed be more likely to need empowering and self-development, need to find and assert themselves rather than to give themselves up. But what is the aim of this empowerment? If the aim is one of reciprocity, with God and with other human beings, then there must be some level of self-giving. But what has often been described as self-giving and self-sacrifice for women has not in fact been a self-giving on the part of the women, but has been a taking by individuals or by systems. For many women this false 'self-sacrifice' has been structural rather than personal. It has been an expectation regarding their role which social, political, and economic structures have virtually enforced, so that women have often had little or no element of self-awareness or choice (for choice involves alternative options).

This does not necessarily mean that true self-giving (rather than giving up of self or self-negation) cannot be a helpful and even empowering model for women as well as for men. It does mean that true self-giving is genuinely a choice, and it presupposes prior possession of that which is given. Self-giving can then be an act of self-assertion. Relationship, community, and reciprocity require personhood and individuality in order for there to be genuine response and mutuality. I find myself hesitant in advancing this line of thought, because such language has so often been abused, and because women have been deeply damaged by the misuse. But if our talk of the atonement omits any use of sacrificial, self-giving imagery, then that may also result in a limitation of the tensive scope of the atonement, and a limitation of the options available for women. Is this element of women's experience (also that of other oppressed groups) thus excluded from our theology of the atonement?

If Jesus is seen not exclusively as a model of the victim who finds themself already given and powerless but as a model of a giving of self as a choice (cf. Walker 1993), on the basis of self-knowledge and self-possession, of personhood, a self-giving aimed at mutual giving and reciprocity, then we may have the basis for a model which illuminates the meaning of the atonement, the truth of the human situation, and the nature of mutuality in a way which can be helpful for both women and men. Jesus was taken, handed over, given as a victim by human beings; we can see here an identification with the oppressed which in no way suggests the prescription of such misuse as normative or good. This aspect of the passion is subverted by the ultimate victory of the resurrection and the vindication of Jesus; in the language of liberation theology this fulfils the pattern highlighted by Phyllis Trible (1984), whereby even in the most awful stories of the abuse of women, God is on the side of the oppressed. But it is also subverted by Jesus's own appropriation of his own death, so that we speak of the crucifixion as his *self*-giving, the aim and result of which is not a hierarchical relationship of oppression but a relationship of mutuality (on which see Grey 1990).

Diakonia summarizes the whole ministry of Jesus, who does

not subordinate and enslave others in the manner of Gentile rulers, but is the suffering servant who liberates and elevates them from servitude (Schüssler Fiorenza 1983, 320).

In the life, death, and resurrection of Jesus of Nazareth, the whole of our predicament is focused so that we have not only a perspective on life in all its humanizing and dehumanizing aspects but also a possibility of hope against hope (Russell 1974, 136).

10

The Cross, the Church, and the Jewish People

JOHN G. KELLY

TOM SMAIL BEGAN Chapter 5 by reminding us that, even in that most difficult of Gospels for the Jewish-Christian dialogue, John makes a remarkable comment about the meaning of Jesus's death on the cross. Whether or not Caiaphas actually said or meant that Jesus's death was in some sense on behalf of the nation of Israel, it is John's editorial comment on the incident which repays careful reflection (John 11.50–2). In a Gospel that for many is the tap root of Christian anti-Judaism, supersessionism, and even anti-Semitism, John, with his distinctive use of irony, adds the clarification that Caiaphas, wittingly or unwittingly, has struck at the heart of the meaning of Jesus's death on the cross. For John the route to the universal significance of the cross is by a full recognition that the death of Messiah Jesus is explicitly and self-consciously for Israel not against Israel, is on Israel's behalf before it is on behalf of others; crucially that Israel is at the heart of the intended beneficial scope and reach of this event before others.

This most universalist of Gospels whose salvific horizons stretch as wide as the dizzy heights of its Christology cannot escape the fact that Israel was uppermost in the mind of Messiah Jesus precisely at the point of his deepest abandonment on the cross. Indeed, that this priority of Israel comes from a writer who avers so high a Christology points to an interpretation and understanding of the cross that sees here God's deepest reaching out in love to and unshakeable solidarity with his people Israel.

If the church has developed an interpretation of the cross that sees it as the point of God's rejection of Israel, of Israel's rejection of Jesus, of the loss of Israel's inheritance, and of its transference to the church, then it must reckon with the fact that Jesus died for the Jewish nation before he died for the scattered children of God beyond Israel's boundaries.

Further, John makes it clear in a final rider that one of the purposes of Jesus's death on the cross was to embrace in love both Israel and those outside of Israel in order that they might be brought together into a profound unity, or as he puts it 'to gather [them] into one'. The ultimate effect was destined to be the reconciliation of Israel and the Gentiles, the ending of their hostility in a unity Jesus would willingly pay for with his life. In addition, it should be noted that John sets this 'prophecy' in a context intended to show clearly both the increasing popularity of Jesus among the Jewish people of the time and the feared political consequences of his popularity, consequences seen by some in positions of responsibility in the Jewish community in terms of the destruction by the Romans of both the Jewish people and the temple (John 11.45–8). Jesus is portrayed here in the midst of his people and inextricably bound up with their future and the realities of their political situation under Roman rule, paradigmatically in his death.

The Flawed Symbol of the Cross

In the identity-shaping history of Jewish-Christian communication, the cross and interpretations of it have played a decisive role. The cross operates as one of the central symbols of Christian discourse and action. This is true both within the Christian communities, and in its operation as the defining symbol of Christianity for those like the Jewish people who stand outside institutional Christianity. For Jewish people, of course, the cross can be far from a symbol of Christian love. It may be an image of hostility, denigration, verbal and physical attack, pogrom and even perhaps holocaust (see e.g. Flannery 1985; Littel 1986; Cohn-Sherbok 1991; Blumenthal 1986, 32; quoted in Lodahl 1989–90, 332).

Of course to speak of the cross as symbol is to raise the question of the hermeneutics which have accompanied interaction with the symbol in various times and at various places.

The theological interpretations of the cross which have accompanied it have provided the concepts and categories for its reception, interpretation, and appropriation. It is these interpretations which have then formed part of the justification for the painful history of Christian relationships with Jewish people.

Christianity and Judaism had contemporaneous formative periods which involved not only interaction but also the self-definition of the one by contrast with the other (see Schiffmann 1981; Dunn 1991b). In addition, the sense of identity which inheres in the adherents of the respective traditions is rooted in the radical separation and hostility which their histories and therefore their doctrine and theologies have bequeathed.

It can be argued that the resulting relationships and therefore identities have been shaped less by the event of the cross than by certain institutionally legitimated and sanctioned interpretations of the event of the cross, notably those consonant with supersessionist ideologies of Christian identity. It is the contention of this chapter that this has resulted in a distortion of Christian identity, in the destruction of the possibility of real community between Christians and Jewish people, and consequently has diminished Jewish identity also. The processes at work here must be subverted in the interests of the emancipation of both communities, an emancipation that has as its goal both real community between them (what one might call a community of communities) and also relationships of freedom and mutuality. The extent to which Jewish and Christian perceptions of the cross differ so radically, and the historical developments which have generated such divergent responses, have been made clear for many in the extended process of reflection on the event of the holocaust which is now under way in both Jewish and Christian circles.

Judaism and Christianity after the Holocaust

There has been a slow but increasingly influential recognition that the theology and doctrine of the churches in the West played a significant, even if not decisive, part in producing the context in which the holocaust became not merely thinkable but achievable (see e.g. Ruether 1974; Klein 1978; Rubenstein and Roth 1987; Eckardt and Eckardt 1988). For many the roots of this anti-Semitism are clearly to be seen in the New Testament writings themselves, which provide the theological support for the church's 'teaching of contempt' in respect of Jews and Judaism (Isaac 1964; 1971). The literature in this area is vast; there are particularly acute historical and sociological observations in Katz's *From Prejudice to Destruction* (see also Wistrich 1992).

For 'the Church made the Jewish people a symbol of unredeemed humanity; it painted a picture of the Jews as a blind, stubborn, carnal and perverse people' (G. Baum, 'Introduction' to Ruether 1974, 6). Where possible it converted this image into social and political measures which set the Jews apart in dress, manner of work, and place of abode. It developed the myth of the 'wandering Jew', homeless as a result of divine punishment for the killing of Christ on the cross. Holy Week of all times became the period when, with the passion narratives fresh in Christian minds, Christian-inspired pogroms were the lot of Jewish people. Along with this charge of deicide came allegations of ritual murder. All this on top of a theology which had the church supersede Israel completely in the divine plan of salvation. Israel's role of being a light to the nations, a role in which it had allegedly failed, was now held to be the property of the church.

It has been concluded that 'the holocaust was the culmination, in great part, of Christian teachings about Jews, of misinterpreted and erroneous theology' (Cargas 1990, 8). Of course it is an overstatement to assert a simple linear relationship between Christian teaching about Judaism and the holocaust. The situation is one of real complexity. This is so not least because the nineteenth century saw the translation of the religiously motivated 'anti-Judaism' of earlier periods into a secularly inspired and racially based 'anti-Semitism' in a surprising way. The term anti-Semitism was coined in Germany at the end of the 1870s and came tragically and ironically in the wake of Jewish emancipation. Those behind the new anti-Semitic movement were at pains to stress that they were not merely carrying over the attitudes of the past and that they were rejecting former attitudes to Jews and Judaism. The new vocabulary of 'anti-Semitism' was designed to reflect this shift in emphasis which came at a time when ecclesiastical influence was ebbing under the pull of secularizing forces. The diminishing power and credibility of the church and of theologically inspired reasoning in the nineteenth century ought to have freed emancipated Jewry from the religiously inspired prejudices they had suffered for so long. There were to be new political motives for prejudice against Jewry, however, which required a new and credible ideology as legitimation. Accordingly, 'the adoption of the name "anti-Semite" rather than anti-Jew was meant to suggest that it was not the Jewishness, that is, the religion, of the Jews that aroused opposition, but some aspects of their character that found expression in their behaviour' (Katz 1980, 4). The anti-Semites would in fact turn increasingly to forms of social Darwinism, and combine these with views of history indebted to Hegel (see Steinberg 1990).

None of this implies any lessening of Christian responsibility for the holocaust. The secular ideology which inspired the holocaust may well have been as profoundly anti-Christian as it was anti-Judaic, but the plausibility of the ideology depended upon the web of beliefs and stereotypes about Jewish people inherited from the Christian past, even if in the process this amounted to a subversion of Christianity from within (see Wistrich 1992, 69). Christian interpretations of the cross had in effect contributed to the 'matrix of values' which legitimated the holocaust. Jewish 'responsibility' for the rejection and death of Jesus formed a key element in this inheritance from the churches.

It was the image of the Jew that was inherited from Christianity that determined the secular perception of the Jew. The difference was that on the cognitive level this perception had to be supported by reasoning derived from the newly evolved systems of thought. It was this composite character of modern anti-Semitism – an absolute archaic image covered by a layer of justifications – that made it an irrational phenomenon inaccessible to overt, logically oriented argumentation (Katz 1980, 320).

The formation of that 'image' was a process extending over centuries in a combination of theological and sociological factors, but a process whose roots can be seen in the New Testament's narrative presentation of the conflict of Jesus with Jewish authorities of his day, his trial, and the events leading up to his death. Whether or not the New Testament writings are in fact anti-Semitic is a matter of debate (see Gager 1983; Johnson 1989), as is the appropriateness of using a nineteenth-century racial and political term such as 'anti-Semitism' in respect of religious literature of the early years of the Common Era. But 'whether the New Testament is anti-Semitic or not, there is no dispute that it was read in an anti-Semitic way by some in the Church, especially by some of the early Fathers' and then in the 1930s (McGarry 1977, 4; cf. Davies 1969, 70). The 'effective history' of the narrative of Jesus of Nazareth as instantiated in a given historical context operated to generate and empower social forces beyond the confines of the church. The tragic results of this have generated a call for a wholesale renewal of Christian hermeneutics and theology (see especially Tracy and Schüssler Fiorenza 1984).

One result of reflection on the holocaust may be its making Christians aware of the extent to which understandings of the death of Jesus and of the people behind his death operated to generate this climate of hostility. The related but equally important point is the way traditional interpretations of Jesus's life and death were further unable to generate action in solidarity with Jewish people at the time of their destruction. Christians can of course point to some of their number such as Dietrich Bonhoeffer and Corrie Ten Boom who courageously acted to save Jewish people and to stand with them against National Socialism (though many of the 'righteous Gentiles' were not necessarily Christians at all). One must of course acknowledge the incredible pressures and difficulties of Christians under a totalitarian regime such as National Socialism. But even those in the Confessing Church are open to the charge that their concern was primarily for the freedom of the church from state interference and secondarily for the Jewish-Christians (see now Barnett 1992). The plight of Jewish people as Jewish people did not evoke a praxis of solidarity. If the tradition failed in its generation of hostility it also failed to generate solidarity in action. It failed at the one point that mattered at that moment (cf. Hall 1985, 183, with his quotation from Luther).

In short, it can be said that the holocaust has profoundly challenged Christian theological formulations in at least three crucial areas. First, the work of Ruether and others has led to discussions of the link between christological formulations and Christian anti-Judaism and anti-Semitism; 'anti-Judaism is the left hand of Christology'. Second, the magnitude and nature of the suffering of Jewish people and others during the holocaust has challenged Christian notions of the cross as an unassailable and effective event of redemptive suffering. Third, it has laid bare the connection between interpretations of the cross which have produced contempt for Jewish people and legitimated their persecution, especially when ecclesiastical and state power have been combined, and which have been a building block in the assessment of Jewish people as under the judgement and wrath of God as killers of the Christ of God. It has also shown that such traditions of the cross have failed to operate as criticism of political oppression or to legitimate resistance in solidarity with the oppressed, particularly Israel. The present chapter can only begin to address the third of these issues. In doing so, however, it is striking at the heart of the issues involved in the other two categories in a way that also seeks to provide fresh resources for theological renewal in those areas.

The Great Reversal

It was for Israel that Jesus died (John 11.50-2). In the end the Christian tradition turned the cross into an event against Israel, one which was the basis not of Israel's salvation but of her rejection and even destruction. The effective history of the event of the cross has turned the foundation narrative on its head. In the same act it has also provided the justification for actions by

Christians which undermine the intent of the action of Jesus in giving his life for his people.

The centrality of the cross in Christian life and worship, instantiated in both word and sacrament and reinforced in hymnody, places it at a strategic position in the Christian tradition, the church's 'corporate memory' which provides the framework for the individual's perceptions and experiences (cf. Thiselton 1981, 44). Personal belief and actions towards others, individual judgements and the corporate memory and testimony of the community, are dialectically related. So the community's understanding of the meaning of the death of Jesus in relation to Israel forms part of the community's corporate memory which is transmitted by means of the reading of scripture, preaching, liturgy and hymnody. A popular hymn, for instance, contains lines such as 'Then "Crucify" is all their breath, and for his death they thirst and cry'. Such means of transmission provide the inevitable context within which individual Christian reflection and action in relation to Israel take place.

This instance points to the way in which the tradition can be a source of oppression and falsehood as well as of truth. A critical hermeneutic is required that does not merely understand the tradition but is also free to call it to account. 'In order to liberate Christian theologies . . . critical theology uncovers and criticizes Christian traditions and theologies that have stimulated and perpetuated violence, alienation, and oppression. Critical theology thus has as its methodological presupposition the Christian community's constant need for renewal' (Schüssler Fiorenza 1993, 63; quoted in Ackermann 1993, 32).

There is clearly a glaring contradiction between a theological tradition which sets the cross against Israel and uses it to justify setting the Christian community against Israel when the event at the foundation of the tradition was an event for Israel and one which had as its purpose the uniting in reconciliation and fellowship of Jew and Gentile, the nation and the dispersed children of God. What is required is a critical theology, able both to call the tradition to account for its failures in respect of Israel and also to generate a renewed perspective. Ironically, it may only be a true theology of the cross that has both the critical and reformatory power to achieve this.

The holocaust has had a revelatory significance in its laying bare the extent to which the theological tradition has fallen into error and deviated from its dominically sanctioned roots. The remedying of such a contradiction, however, must come from within the theological tradition itself by means of the resources already to hand within the foundation narrative. Otherwise the exercise would not amount to theological renewal but to replacement. There would be an element of eccentricity about the enterprise which would legitimate claims that it depended not on the 'faith once delivered to the saints' but on guilt-ridden and guilt-driven responses to Christian failures. In this way, the renewed theological tradition can remain recognizably Christian and orthodox even if profoundly changed by a fresh engagement with the critical power of the cross.

The need to respect the requirement of 'orthodoxy' has two important dimensions. First, it militates against the production of theologies for the Jewish-Christian dialogue that are so far removed from the concerns of the mainstream that they are unable to function as catalysts for change within the tradition they purport to represent. Second, it operates to maintain and revitalize the link between belief and action and opens the way to orthopraxis. 'What is at issue is the maintenance of that degree of continuity which is necessary for Christian *identity* and more especially for participation in *patterns of behaviour which have been instituted and prescribed* by those events on which the community itself has been founded' (Thiselton 1981, 64).

An appropriation of the socio-political dimensions of the cross must be one that recognizes the practical dimensions of a theology of the cross as a doctrine for battle that goes beyond ecclesiastical criticism to social criticism (Moltmann 1974, 72–3). Yet if solidarity is a leading motif on such a view, there is a case for saying that such a theology of the cross must also go beyond the pursuit of solidarity and direct Christian thought and action in the direction of a hoped-for reconciliation (see Simpson 1989, 536–8). It will be a reconciliation based in a relationship of Jew and Gentile free from distortion and oppression, a relationship envisaged as the ultimate result of Jesus's death in the Johannine narrative, which exhibits precisely the same scheme of solidarity resulting in reconciliation (see John 11.50–2). Beliefs, attitudes, and practices which hold together can be reshaped together to lead to fresh involvement in the actions which reformed beliefs about Jesus's solidarity with Israel may be held to require. The first stage of such a theological renewal and reconstruction comes in the recognition of the implications of the Jewishness of Jesus.

Jesus, Israel and the Cross

In the history of Christian scholarship there is a clear tendency towards abstraction and away from the Jewish identity of Jesus (see e.g. Gunton 1991, 69–71; Osborn 1990, 218–20; Hebblethwaite 1989). Indeed, G. B. Caird expressed the view that 'we have failed in the quest for the historical Jesus precisely because we have left out of consideration all those factors which would enable us to see him as a genuinely historical figure' (quoted in Borg 1987, 208). This will include his Jewishness.

The historical actions and intentions of Jesus in the social and political context of his time are easily lost or misinterpreted in reconstructions which move too quickly to seek continuity between the historical Jesus and later dogmatic understandings of him. One area where this is the case is in the tendency, only recently challenged successfully, to paint a picture of the Judaism of Jesus's time as a uniform entity which was the natural and inevitable precursor of later rabbinic Judaism, so providing clear-cut Jewish opponents of Jesus for a church that needed to see and present the Judaism of its own day as a clear-cut opponent.

Rather, the first century was one of a radical pluriformity, and it may well be more accurate to talk of the 'Judaisms' of the first century (so e.g. Theissen 1978; Dunn 1991b). Indeed, the movement around Jesus was one of a number of such movements for renewal within the Jewish people. It was a time of competing visions of the shape and future of Israel, a struggle for the hearts and minds of the Jewish people in which political and religious factors were intertwined and in which Jesus and his followers were actively engaged (cf. Borg 1987, 209–10).

For historical reasons Caird (see 1965; 1982; 1983) sees both Mark and John as grounding a belief in the solidarity of Jesus with all humanity in his solidarity with the Jewish people. He notes that the Gospel tradition contains a significant amount of material which is not obviously related to the life or needs of the early church but which nevertheless links Jesus positively with the history, politics and aspirations of the Jewish people. Even after the Christian message has been universalized and the Jewish people have come to be perceived as opponents of the gospel, the Gospel tradition nevertheless retains within it evidence of Jesus's solidarity with his people as it was expressed in his ministry.

The first element of this material is the traditions regarding John the Baptist and his baptism of Jesus. In the context of the Baptist's message to Israel of impending judgement and his call to renewal of life within the people of God, the baptism functions as a proleptic symbol of admission to this renewed or reconstituted Israel. Despite embarrassment in the early church as to why a sinless Jesus needed to be baptized, and the implied subordination of Jesus to John at this point, the tradition was retained. *The point of the baptism, however, was solidarity, not sin*:

> Jesus recognized the national character of John's summons to repentance and accepted his own involvement in the national life of his people. But this is to say that at the outset of his ministry Jesus was concerned with questions of national policy: What does it mean to be the Chosen Nation of God? How can Israel preserve her character as the holy nation in a world overrun and controlled by pagans? What must Israel do if at God's winnowing she is to prove wheat and not chaff? (Caird 1965, 7).

It was not possible for a faithful Israelite like Jesus to do other than identify with such a movement for national renewal. Indeed, the period of Jesus's ministry was broadly one in which the plurality of 'Judaisms' and factions within the people exhibited competing visions for the nature, future and destiny of what it meant to be the people of God.

If John expected salvation to extend only to a remnant within Israel, he did so in the manner of the prophets, and with the crucial proviso that the remnant community was avowedly open to all Israel. His remnant, unlike contemporary remnant groups such as the Essenes or the Therapeutae, did not exist as a separate, organized, and closed community. 'In this respect as in others the key to the distinctiveness of John's movement lay in its genuine openness to all Israel. . . . Other remnant groups were closed. The Johannine remnant was open' (Meyer 1979, 120).

If Jesus accepted John's basic prophetic framework, it is interesting to note two implications of this. First, in Jesus the stress on judgement is replaced by an increasing stress on the reign or kingdom of God. Second, national renewal via an open remnant community comes to be exemplified in the ministry of Jesus as he reaches out to all the lost sheep of the house of Israel, clean and unclean, pure and impure, welcoming them into the renewal of the people of God in an open and inclusive manner. 'The proclamation of God's reign bore immediately on the restoration of Israel and the concomitant salvation of the nations' (Meyer 1979, 129). Thus the Saviour is always found with a saved Israel, and a Messiah with a messianic Israel. If the nations were to be included in this salvation, as clearly they were, it was in effect to be via the salvation wrought by God for the primary beneficiaries, namely Israel (Meyer 1979, 33–5).

If Jesus's ministry began in a baptism of solidarity with Israel and continued in a proclamation of Israel's salvation from the coming judgement of God by means of the renewal of life he offered openly to all Israel, then arguably his connection with the fate of his people reached its high point in the cross. There that solidarity extended to bearing in his own body the judgement he foresaw as coming upon Israel, sacrificing himself as the Maccabean martyrs had done before him, on behalf of the people.

G. B. Caird and N. T. Wright are less clear that the motif

of judgement took the reduced role in Jesus's ministry that Meyer suggests. They are both inclined to see a greater continuity here between John the Baptist and Jesus. Caird (1965) refers in particular to Jesus's criticism of 'this generation' and of 'Jerusalem' (Mark 8.11–13; Luke 11.49–51). It is important to note that on this view as well as on Meyer's, judgement has specific historical and political dimensions to which religious questions are related but are if anything subsidiary.

In this there can be no avoiding the fact that the Gospel narratives do implicate some Jewish people at least in the events that led to Jesus's death. In many contemporary discussions of this issue (as Prusak 1991 has noted), while few – if any – dare blame all Jewish people for the death of Jesus, there nevertheless remains the subtle implication that there were very few people wanting to be on his side when he died. Much more plausible historically is the notion that, as even the Gospel of John relates, Jesus's popularity with the people remained but they were those who lacked access to the political and military power to intervene on his behalf. Gerard O'Collins (1983, 75) may be close to the mark when he says, 'by the time of Jesus' arrest no major religious group of his society was willing to intervene to save him. . . . Enough powerful leaders were ready to see him executed.' In short, *Jesus may have been abandoned by the powerful but not by the people.*

On what basis, then, was his proclamation of judgement made, and to what did it refer? Wright summarizes 'Jewish restoration eschatology' as follows: 'the "apocalyptic" hope of Israel was not an expectation that God would soon end the entire space-time order, but was the hope that he would soon, within the continuing course of history, act to vindicate his own name by delivering his people from their current political and social predicaments' (Wright 1985, 79; cf. Sanders 1985, Part I). Jesus was able to discern the inevitable destructive consequences of Israel's pursuing a path to vindication that depended on nationalist ambition, but for Wright this is only part of the story. Equally important is Jesus's understanding of Rome as the means by which the wrath of God was executed, as the prophets before him had understood Babylon. It is in this context that

Jesus's ministry operates to supply a fresh paradigm of national renewal and hope focused on the nation but eschewing a crude nationalism. So Brandon and others were correct to stress the political context of Jesus's ministry, and indeed Jesus was to die the characteristic death of the zealot, but his zeal had a different quality.

Sayings about 'taking up the cross' have a particular plausibility in the context of life under Roman occupation; the impact of the practice of crucifixion, particularly of political insurgents, was profound on Jewish culture of the first century (see Young 1990). Indeed, Genesis Rabbah, the oldest Jewish commentary on Genesis, relates Isaac's carrying of the wood for the sacrifice in Genesis 22 in terms that liken it to a condemned man taking his cross upon his shoulders. It is plausible that Jesus's saying has deep roots in the sufferings of his people during the time of the second temple. For Jesus and the midrash the cross became a metaphor for the suffering of the innocent in obedience to the commandment of God and on behalf of the struggles of the people as a whole. (For further discussion of the relations between the offering of Isaac and Christian understandings of the cross, see Vermes 1973, 193–227).

The turmoil in Israel under Roman occupation was formed by a powerful amalgam of religious factors, and therefore in that context also political factors, and grievances still left over and festering from the Maccabean crisis. It was a potent mix of religious allegiance, national desire for freedom, and Roman oppression in which the shape of Israel's destiny was essentially contested.

Wright, however, while retaining the emphasis in Jesus's preaching on the coming judgement on Israel, interprets the course of Jesus's ministry as one in which Jesus comes to see that the realization of Israel's future deliverance from judgement will be focused on him. In this sense the principal actor in the passion narratives becomes Jesus himself.

Jesus, as Israel's representative, took upon himself the judgment which he pronounced upon the nation. . . . Jesus saw Israel as courting political and historical disaster by that national ambition which would lead Rome to crush her, as so many other peoples had been crushed: and . . . he identified himself as a matter of vocation with Israel. . . . He was to suffer the characteristic fate of those who rebelled against Rome. He was in fact, to die Israel's death (Wright 1985, 86).

This view depends again on reading messiahship not as a quasi-divine title but as a description of one who stands as a representative of and for the people, one whose fate is bound up with the people as a whole and vice versa (see also Caird 1982; 1983). An interpretative gloss on Wright's position could be to say that the repressive consequences of the authorities' misinterpretation of Jesus's increasing popularity as revolutionary fervour were borne by Jesus in order that they might not be borne by Israel. Jesus takes Rome's wrath upon himself, and thereby into the life of fellowship between him and his heavenly Father, in order that Israel may be free not to experience that wrath.

In this the martyr traditions of the Maccabean period of course form a further basis for seeing the death of Jesus as a sacrificial self-giving on behalf of the people, a religiously inspired suffering that would have redemptive consequences for Israel as a whole (cf. Dunn 1991a). Before Jesus's time there were already indications in Jewish literature from previous political/religious struggles that the death of martyrs could atone for Israel (see 2 Macc 7.37-8). This theology was to come to fuller expression in the literature written after Jesus's time (see 4 Macc 17.21-2; also the literature cited in Lyden 1992, 48). In this there is a resonance with ideas found in other cultures of the ancient world, where the death of the one on behalf of his city, people, and so on, had religious as well as political overtones. In an interesting parallel to John 11, Hengel notes the advice of Rabbi Yehoshua b. Levi regarding handing a person over to the Roman authorities: 'It is better that this man should be killed than that the community be punished for his sake' (Genesis Rabbah 94.9; see Hengel 1986, 203).

Jesus's identification with his people extends to sharing the fate of the zealot whose aspirations he has radically transformed.

Yet as Messiah, as representative of Israel, he takes Israel's fate upon himself and dies in Israel's place.

> On the cross it becomes clear that Israel's real problem is not external (the Roman occupation) merely, but internal also: he shares in the ultimate form of her political and social predicament and hence reveals in his last symbolic act, that the nationalist rebellion whose bloody logical outcome he now shared was something for which Israel was being judged by God, and from which she needed to be saved. . . . He dies Israel's death in order that Israel may not die it (Wright 1985, 89–90).

If such a view, or even a modified version of it, were ultimately sustainable, it would have the consequence of clarifying two crucial points. First, Jesus's challenge to Israel and his message of judgement to his people had their referents prior to the cross in the social and political realities of that time. Any attempt to use them later to justify hostility to Jewish people based on Jesus's death is fundamentally to misunderstand Jesus and his message. Second, Jesus intended in his death to take upon himself the judgement that was due to Israel. The 'sting' of God's wrath is drawn, borne not by the people but by Jesus on their behalf, as their representative and in their place. The political realities may have remained and come to expression in the destruction of the temple and its aftermath, but these events can no longer be easily seen as the expression of God's wrath or of judgement, as Jesus has carried these in his death.

Systematic Resonances

The preceding discussion may well appear to be some distance away from the traditional dogmatic questions surrounding the cross, which tend to centre on questions of the universality of sin and on the cross as a means of dealing both with sin and with the restoration of humanity's relationship with its Creator. However, the themes of the one and the many, of one doing for others what they could not do for themselves, are clearly close to traditional atonement concerns. Israel itself had some sort of representative role in relation to the rest of humanity even if that role was a burden too heavy to bear. It is a short step from here to Paul's representative view of Christ in his Adam Christology and thereby to the heart of his theology (see again Dunn 1991a; also the classic treatments in Hooker 1990). The benefit of seeing Jesus's solidarity with Israel as at the heart of the meaning of the cross is that it is not obviously driven by traditional atonement concerns although it resonates with them at key points, giving them back the flesh and blood of which, as abstract ideas, they are all too often bereft (Wright 1985, 93).

The understanding of the cross presented here, using solidarity as a prime motif, also has some parallels with Moltmann's important version of a critical theology of the cross (see 1981; 1992, 123–43, especially 130–1). Perhaps the most important feature of Moltmann's rehabilitation of the notion of 'Christ as brother' is his grounding of the concept in his understanding of the cross. With the image of the suffering servant in Isaiah 53 in our minds, Moltmann (1992, 130) invites us to consider Christ's death as an expression of his solidarity with us, and especially with the weak, the suffering, and the oppressed.

> The messianic Son of God unreservedly takes on himself the conditions of our vulnerable and mortal existence. . . . He takes the way of non-violent suffering. He carries and endures – suffers and suffers under – injustice and violence, betrayal and denial, forsakenness by God and by human beings, and dies on a Roman cross. . . . He is the divine martyr among the millions of unknown martyrs in the suffering histories of Israel, humanity and nature.

In this Moltmann sees additionally and perhaps primarily Jesus suffering in solidarity with his people. Even if in conflict with religious leaders, Jesus dies as a Jew entering into the fate of God's people. The sufferings of Israel are matched by the sufferings of Israel's God who makes Israel's sufferings his own. Punishment is replaced by the fellow-suffering of the covenant God and his covenant people.

If Jesus died a Jew's death, then the sufferings of Christ are open for solidarity with 'the sufferings of Israel' – the Israel of that time and the Israel of today. . . . If the sufferings of Christ and the sufferings of Israel are linked, and belong within the framework of God's sufferings over the world and with the world, then it is not merely possible to see Golgotha and Auschwitz in a single perspective; it is actually necessary (Moltmann 1990, 168).

The passion of Christ is the driving force of the passion story, which has at its heart the Christology of solidarity seen in the Christ who is our brother. Golgotha happened in order for God to be with us in our suffering and our pain so that at the points of our deepest need or oppression we might not be abandoned without hope. Yet there is for Moltmann not only solidarity but substitution at the cross, even if not understood in penal terms. If only the suffering God can help us in our need, then only the God of forgiveness can bear our guilt away and liberate us from it. 'God is himself the atoning God. . . . God transforms human sin into his suffering by "carrying" human sin. . . . Christ is not only the Brother of the victims but also the expiation for the culprits' (1993, 26).

Needless to say, Moltmann goes on beyond substitution to orthopraxis in his description of the followers of Christ as those called to take up their cross and follow in his way, the way of compassionate solidarity, protest and liberation. Christology and christopraxis must meet in a life of discipleship patterned on the messianic example of Jesus (cf. McFadyen 1990, 42–66).

Conclusion

The present study is no more than a sketch of one way of dealing with the fundamental problem of aligning responsible Christian action and belief in relation to the cross in the context of Jewish-Christian relations. If it holds true on its terms then perhaps the most important test of its future usefulness will be in assisting Christian theologians to address the pressing contemporary questions surrounding the land and state of Israel, which is for many Jewish people the physical first-fruits of genuine redemption. An understanding of Jesus's solidarity with Israel exemplified at the cross as the basis of what Jesus *did* must still be fashioned into fresh understandings of who Jesus *was*, and of the *meaning of his suffering death*, if even the most basic questions raised by the holocaust are to be addressed. Indeed, serious theological reflection will be required if such a reading is not simply to provide fresh grounds for Israel's replacement by the church, as Wright's work might. The future agenda will need to include the impact on Israel of the traditions of the resurrection, not least because the New Testament holds crucifixion and resurrection together dialectically.

This dialectical unity is only matched by its equal insistence that prayer and righteous action go together. To call on the name of the Lord is also to be called by him to a life lived in imitation of him, including his unshakeable yet not uncritical solidarity with his people Israel.

11

Atonement and Mercy:
Islam between Athanasius and Anselm

GEORGE BEBAWI

A PAINTER ONCE came to undertake some work in our flat in Cairo. On the wall he saw an icon of Christ on the cross, and I heard him muttering at it. When I asked him what he was saying, he told me that he was urging Jesus not to humiliate himself. To a Muslim, such self-lowering was quite unacceptable for one who was supposed to be the Son of God. On another occasion, I was strap-hanging on a bus in Cairo when a man offered me his seat. I asked him why he had done so, thinking he might be someone from our parish. 'It's that cross tattooed on your wrist', he explained. 'I don't want to sit under the cross.' The cross stands between Islam and Christianity. Dialogue cannot remove its scandal, and in due course a Muslim who might come to believe in Jesus has to face it. But are there ways of facilitating dialogue at some points?

The prophet Muhammad lived midway between two great influential figures in the history of Christianity in the East and in the West, Athanasius and Anselm, and consideration of these figures may open the way to a consideration of this question. Prior to Anselm there was no doctrine of the atonement, in the sense that Christian understanding had not been formulated in such a way as to explain the significance of the death of Christ. This does not mean that Christians did not believe in salvation or in the death of Christ to save us. But prior to Anselm there is no atonement theory which deals only with the death of Jesus. In ancient Christian theology, soteriology was an integral part of the doctrine of the Trinity and of Christology. It revolved around consideration of the incarnation, baptism, death, resurrection, and glorification of Jesus, and not merely the cross, and also involved consideration of the work of the Holy Spirit in creation and salvation. Anselm created a major change of emphasis here. The emphasis on the divine reprieve or amnesty as a result of Christ's death was initiated by the Scholastics and developed by the Reformers.

Athanasius: Creation According to the Divine Image and its Implications for Redemption

How does Athanasius differ from Islam, and from the Qur'an in particular? First, in the thinking of Athanasius a central place is occupied by the creation of humanity according to the divine image. In contrast, the divine image in humanity is not essential for orthodox Islamic anthropology. It does come in the writings of the Muslim sufis but it has no clear place in the writings of Sunni Muslims. The Eastern Christian tradition, and Athanasius in particular, emphasizes that humanity has been created to enjoy its existence and to live like God. The human race was given a double share in the divine grace: the grace of life or existence, and the grace of the image. This double grace means that from the beginning grace is part of the creation of humanity; it belongs to our creation and not only to our salvation. Even to transcend our life and bring the divine image into a state of being is in itself the expression of grace. Therefore sin is indeed 'missing the mark', but the mark is not an ethical or moral goal, but the conformity of human existence to the image of God. Sin is a loss of life and a loss of being according to the image of God, and conformity instead to the image of nothingness, the self-image discovered by humanity as a result of turning away from the source of life, God.

Second, since death is the natural end of life, Athanasius and the Fathers see death as a wound which has been inflicted on humanity by humanity itself. God is not directly involved. As Gregory of Palamas (1296–1359) later put it, God did not say to Adam, 'If you eat I shall kill you', but 'If you eat you shall die' (1865, 1157–60). God is not involved in the human dilemma of death as judge or as direct cause of death, but is the 'philanthropic God' (a common title for God in the East). The opposite is true for Augustine and later Western theologians, who may even be prepared to speak of God killing Adam. God has judged humanity and put it to death. Here Islam, which accepts that God is the Creator of both life and death, is nearer to the West than to the East, except that death has no relationship to the sin of Adam.

In *The Incarnation* Athanasius uses a number of metaphors to highlight the victory of the Son of God over death. The dwelling of a king in one house in a city brings honour and glory to house and city (ch. 10). A picture (an image) is renewed by copying the features of the original (ch. 14). A powerful wrestler meets his enemy on his terms (ch. 28). Other metaphors or illustrations are used (chs. 8, 15, 28, 41, 44), all to express the power, goodness, and love of the Word.

When speaking of sacrifice, offering, and redemption, Athanasius uses the Old and New Testament vocabulary in a way that suggests several different concepts of sacrifice. It is a sacrifice without blemish (ch. 9), a sacrifice of his body (ch. 10), a sacrifice for all (ch. 15), a sacrifice of life (ch. 21), and – in a very important exchange of the words 'sacrifice' and 'temple' – a sacrifice of his temple. Evidently Athanasius is not confined to the Old and New Testament concept of sacrifice, because there the temple is not sacrificed.

The writings of Athanasius have been used as a hunting-ground by all who have wanted to prove this or that theory of the atonement. The fact remains that his language and concepts are alien to all atonement theories.

First, when he speaks of the Word incarnate offering his body to death and to God the Father, this must not be confused with later concepts. Jesus offered his body to death; the significance of the verb 'offered' is that it suggests this was a voluntary act. The Word incarnate accepted death in his flesh which was 'capable of death' in order to abolish what we human beings have inflicted on ourselves. He offered his body to the Father in order to 'undo', to 'abolish', the law of death, and also to show the divine love and goodness and the fact that God remains 'truthful' and 'honest', because the 'Father of all truth' does not lie to save humanity from death.

Second, an understanding of Athanasius's approach to the atonement requires an appreciation of his key phrase 'the Word who is above all'. The phrase is used emphatically in the context of both sacrificing his flesh and meeting 'death' in his flesh. The idea of substitution which modern writers have discerned in the writings of Athanasius needs to be understood in its own terms. In what sense is the Word incarnate 'mediator', 'ambassador', 'redeemer', and 'substitute'?

He is the Word-Creator, who created us according to his own image, for he alone is the true image of the Father. The Word is responsible for our creation and sustenance. Creation could not have survived if the Word-Creator had decided to abandon it or even to separate himself from it. All the way along, the relationship between the Word and creation was maintained by the Word after Adam's sin and in preparation for the restoration and re-creation. The Word was a mediator and an ambassador from the beginning, not just from the incarnation or the cross, because he is the one who supplies creation with life and supplies humanity with life and knowledge. This teaching was abandoned in the West.

The Word stands between the Father, the Holy Spirit and creation before Adam's sin and after it. What is new is his incarnation, which in goodness and love changes the human nature in himself, in the desire that his human body become the first of a kind and the beginning of the new creation, through cross and resurrection. Athanasius speaks of the Word 'redeeming his own body' (*Against the Arians* 2.61) and granting this to all those who are 'knit' to him.

Third, the Word who is above all thus has the source of life, the power to change and the will to re-create in himself what has fallen into corruption and evil, because human beings cannot do it for themselves. This 'substitution' effected by means of his death and resurrection must be seen in the context of the goodness and sustaining power of the Word over against the sinful, weak, enslavement of humanity to death, the devil and corruption.

188

Fourth, Jesus is certainly the 'mediator', as the one who from the beginning was the Word-Creator. Terms such as 'debt' and 'ransom' must also be treated in the context of the work of Athanasius himself. 'Since the Word is above all, consequently by offering his temple and the instrument of his body as *antipsuchon* [substitute] for all men, he fulfilled the debt by his death' (*The Incarnation* 9.9). The debt is the human 'loss' of the 'image' and the 'law of death' which must be fulfilled. The Word is above all. The words of Athanasius indicate that the Word, the incorruptible Son of God, has been united to all by taking a body similar to theirs. Consequently he endued all men with incorruption by the promise concerning his resurrection. Thus the Word who is life bestowed life and 'the grace of the resurrection' on mortals. The 'Fountain of Life and Knowledge' is the one who can bring about this change because he is above all. The 'substitute' is not to be understood in the context of the later development, because Jesus is the 'second Adam', the 'new head' of the 'new human race', who alone can grant 'stability' to creation. Jesus replaced 'Adam' in a cosmological context and, as far as the human race is concerned, he is the 'substitute' for the old and first 'Adam'.

Fifth, Athanasius uses words that could be translated as 'ransom' and 'substitution', but the context does not support the meaning of 'payment' or the kind of substitution developed in later periods. Jesus surrendered his body to death on 'behalf of all'. Jesus is the only one who can do so. He is the Word incarnate who alone does not die the same death as other human beings. 'The Lord is not weak but is the power of God and the Word of God and life itself.' He does not die as a result of weakness, because if he 'suffered through the weakness of his nature', Jesus would no longer be 'superior over men'. 'But because he was life and the Word of God, and because death had to take place on behalf of all, therefore as he is life and power, he gave strength to the body and as death had to occur, he took the occasion provided not by himself but by others, to complete the sacrifice' (ch. 21). The 'ransom' is not a payment but a voluntary act of the powerful and strong one who did not die because of weakness, but because of power. Thus the Lord ransomed and redeemed humanity. 'How then could the end of death have been demonstrated and victory over it, unless in the sight of all he had summoned it and proved it to be dead and thenceforth rendered void by the incorruptibility of his body?' (ch. 23).

Sixth, Athanasius subsequently deals with the 'curse'. Having quoted the declaration 'cursed is he who is hanged on wood' he says, 'Furthermore if the death of the Lord is a ransom for all and by his death "the wall of partition is broken down"', then the death of Christ has reconciled the Jews and the Gentiles, the death of the cross itself being the manner by which 'he would ransom all men' (ch. 25). These words not only rule out the idea of a payment, but also establish the positive side of the ransom, the end of hostility, reconciliation; the 'way to heaven has been opened'.

Seventh, Athanasius does not separate the death of Jesus from his resurrection. Salvation is not two steps, death and resurrection; rather, accepting death abolishes its power and re-creates a new life, so the cross and the resurrection go hand in hand. The evidence of this can be seen in the stress Athanasius laid on the incorruptibility of the body of Christ even after his death. Jesus died the death of the Creator-Word, not the death of a sinner. Similar statements can be read in the writings of all the Eastern Fathers, among them the two Gregories, Cyril of Jerusalem and John Chrysostom. Sin could not have put Jesus to death. This means that none of the Fathers of the Eastern church had in mind any of the later forms of 'substitution'. Their emphasis is not so much that Jesus died because he had to carry our sins in his flesh on the cross but that his will and power made him accept death and destroy death. Modern books dealing with the history of the atonement have not paid attention to the great influence that John 10.17–18 exercised on all the Fathers of the East. It is enough to quote the words of Cyril of Alexandria (1864, 1053–6) on the passage:

> Moreover, Christ declared that he was loved by the Father, not merely because he lays down his life, but because he lays it down that he may take it again. . . . For if he had only died,

and had not risen again, what would have been the advantage? And how would he appear to have benefitted our nature, if he remained amongst us, dead, under the bonds of death, subjected to consequent corruption in the same way as others? He in this way saved our nature perfectly, bringing to naught the power of death; and he will display us as new creation. . . . Jesus says 'I have power'; he used his power with regard to both his death and his resurrection, in order that the action of power and ability might not appear to be that of another.

Anselm's Teaching on Creation, the Fall and Redemption

In Athanasius the creation of humanity according to the divine image is central. His emphasis with regard to sin (and redemption) is that sin brought about a change in human nature which has resulted in death; thus in his work death is more central than sin. Since Athanasius's day, central importance had come to attach to the idea that sin put humanity in debt to the devil and that on the cross Christ was paying that debt. Anselm in turn is interested in showing that paying a ransom to the devil is an unacceptable idea, and in order to undermine this idea completely, he goes on to define sin as a violation of the divine honour and glory, not an indebtedness to the devil. Anselm does not make use of the idea of humanity's being created in God's image. He is interested in the ideas of justice and debt, and therefore in satisfaction. His legal, even moralistic, feudalistic understanding of sin coheres with his theology as a whole. Every concept of sin presupposes a certain remedy, as much as any particular remedy is designed for a particular disease (as Jenny Sankey and Sally Alsford have noted). These differences also illustrate how we have to deal either with sin in isolation or with sin and death together. To deal with sin as a self-contained theme in Christian theology leads towards a God-ward understanding of atonement. If we deal with sin and death, we are bound to face the human need of the gift of eternal life.

The legal concept of sin is no obstacle to Islam. Humanity has been given the law as a guide. Whoever disobeys (*ya'sa* in

Arabic) will surely be punished or, if he or she repents, will surely be forgiven. So Anselm's concept of sin is not foreign to Islamic thinking in general, and in particular to the Qur'an. Humanity has in Adam disobeyed God. What is foreign to Anselm is that in the Qur'an death is not a punishment for sin; it is a natural phenomenon. God is the Creator of both life and death. The penalty for the sin of Adam and Eve was not their death but their banishment from paradise. Islam and the Eastern Christian tradition agree that death is the natural end of life. Athanasius relates death to the Christian concept of creation from nothing. What came out of nothing does not possess the power or energy to last forever. It will die and revert to nothingness, because it is God alone who by his grace sustains creation. Humanity could have escaped death by remaining in communion with the only source of life, which is God. So death is both natural and avoidable.

The fundamental notion of humanity being created in God's image is absent from Anselm because he did not consider the divine image to be definitive of human life. Still less was human participation in the divine image and life which was given at the beginning any longer an organizing principle in theological systems. Already in Augustine's writings it plays no obvious part, even though it is mentioned. In contrast, in the East the divine image and sin are treated together as the one basic component of Christian anthropology, and there are coherent links between the notions of humanity made in God's image, of grace at work in the world from the beginning, and of the Word himself becoming a human being. In the absence of such anthropology, redemption cannot be coherently treated as the work of grace of a divine redeemer.

Anselm is interested in exploring the 'rational basis' of Christian faith, not in order to approach 'faith by way of reason, but to delight in the comprehension and contemplation of the doctrines'. This particular form of rationalism raised basic questions for Anselm which he himself formulated in this way: For what reason and on the basis of what necessity did God become a human being? And how did God by the death of his Son restore life to the world?

The restoration of humanity appears on almost every page of the first book of *Why Did God Become a Human Being?* Anselm's explanation of restoration is particular to him. His basic interest is the death of our Lord rather than the incarnation or the resurrection. The latter two important parts of the life and work of the Redeemer are not directly related to the questions which Anselm asked about sin, to death as a punishment for sin. Anselm does say that 'the Father did not delight in the Son's torment. However, the Son said that the chalice could not pass from Him except He drink it. This He said not because He was unable to avoid death if He had willed to, but because (as I said) it was impossible for the world to be saved in any other way' (1.10). The centrality of the cross becomes inevitable as a result of a clear teaching which can only contemplate salvation in a particular way.

On what basis does God forgive people their sins? To understand this more clearly, let us first see what sinning and making satisfaction for sin are (1.10–11). To sin is nothing other than not to render to God what is due. It is also defined as not being subordinate to the will of God; this is the debt of sin and everyone who does not pay it does sin. Compensation is required for the painful wrong in 'proportion to the injury'.

This watertight approach does not leave room for goodness and mercy. Anselm becomes aware that Christians are commanded to forgive those who sin against them freely. He puts the words on the lips of Boso that if we forgive sins 'it seems inconsistent that [God] commands us to do what it is unfitting for Him to do'. This objection is not answered completely, 'because God gives us this command so that we should not arrogate to ourselves His prerogative. For to take vengeance belongs to no one except to Him who is Lord of all' (1.12). Further objections about God, the law, and his freedom to exercise kindness are also answered not by denying kindness or freedom but by appealing once more to 'reason' (1.12). Reason prevents Anselm from considering a place for God's humility and kindness. It is here more than anywhere else that the spirit of feudalism is evident. Humans must not think about God in a way that seems to 'oppose His dignity'. Freedom seeks 'what is advantageous or what is fitting'. Kindness must not perform any work that is 'unbefitting to God', because this would no longer be 'kindness' (1.12).

Anselm is eager to explain divine 'freedom' and 'will' and the 'good' and 'just nature of God'. God can will and do what is in harmony with his nature. He is also clear that humans cannot deprive God of his honour; the sinner pays or God 'takes it from him against his will' (1.14). God does not 'allow it to be even slightly violated' and 'nothing can be added to or subtracted from His honor'. The honour of God is kept by creatures in obedience, which is the honour due to God. Thus by staying in their proper place in the universe and preserving the beauty of the universe, humans honour God (1.15). Here, at least, Anselm comes very close to considering the cosmic implication of human sin. It disturbs 'the order and the beauty of the universe'. This is followed immediately by a precise statement that the violation of the order and beauty of the universe does not injure or tarnish 'God's power or dignity' (1.15). Nonetheless, God cannot fail to govern if creatures decide to take a different course contrary to the one designed by the creator. This brings creatures two options: to submit to the divine will or to run beneath the divine punitive will.

Human beings are made in order to replace evil angels and to make up the number of the citizens of the heavenly city. The gift of the divine image to humanity is entirely absent from the presentation of *Why Did God Become a Human Being?* The final destiny of humans is to be good like the good angels and to share in their eternal destiny (1.15). This is striking because in patristic theology, restoration and redemption were never divorced from the concept of humanity's being made in the divine image, which is one of the reasons for the incarnation of the Son who is the image of God.

More important is the treatment of death in the second part of *Why Did God Become a Human Being?* If human beings had never sinned, they would never have died, says Anselm (2.2). What would have been the final human destiny? Anselm says that human beings would 'have been transformed into incorruptibility' of the body (2.3). So there is a natural incorruptibility in humanity, such as we see in Athanasius. Anselm does not say how natural incorruptibility related to death, and he would have felt that death as a punishment could be regarded as part of nature as it was created. When Anselm defends his concept of paying the 'debt' due to God, he does not single out the Father. Although the emphasis lies there, Adam sinned against the Son as well as the Father (2.9). The centrality of the cross is not without basis. It rests on the doctrine of the two natures 'of the Son of God'. In Christ the diversity of natures and the unity of person served the following end. If the human nature was not able to do what was required for restoring humanity, then the divine nature would do it; and if what was required did not befit the divine nature, then the human nature would do it. Not two different 'persons', but one and the same 'person' existing perfectly in two natures, would pay through his human nature what that nature ought to pay and would be able through his divine nature to do what was required (2.17).

The debt of humanity was great. God is the only one who could pay it. How and what did the human nature do? It was necessary for God to assume a human nature into a unity of person, so that the one who with respect to his nature ought to make payment, but was unable to, would be the one who with respect to his person was able to (2.17). This dynamic Christological approach needs further development. Anselm subsequently comes nearer to the late Eastern Orthodox development at the Council held in 1157 in Constantinople. Anselm and the Council state clearly that the sacrifice or the offering on the cross was not to God the Father alone, as was commonly accepted. 'The Son of God . . . offered Himself to Himself . . . for His own honor. That is, [He offered] His humanity to His divinity, which is one and the same divinity common to the three persons' (2.18). It may it be that Anselm was aware that his interpretation was a novelty, for in the same breath he says, 'in order to say more clearly what we mean, while still abiding within this truth, let us say . . . that the Son freely offered Himself to the Father. For in this way we speak most fittingly' (2.18).

This trinitarian aspect needed further development. Indeed,

none of the Fathers of the Eastern church except Cyril of Alexandria provides us with a similar statement of the Son's offering to the Three Persons a sacrifice for our redemption.

The Atonement in Islamic Apologetic Writings

Islamic apologetic writings go back to the encounter between Al-Hashimi and Al-Kindi about 923, and before that to the work of Ali Ibn Rabban Al-Tabari, who died about 885 (and must not be confused with the great thirteenth-century commentator Al-Tabari). He was a convert from Christianity to Islam and wrote a book entitled *Al-Radd ala al-Nasara* (*An Answer to Christians*). This most influential writer opened the way for many Muslims who read his works, copied his arguments, and read the Christian sources which he used.

The crucial subject was and still is the doctrine of God. The Trinity is denied and so consequently is the divinity of Jesus. The cross is also used as an argument against the divinity of Jesus Christ, because God does not suffer and indeed does not die.

Muslims seem to have read one particular atonement theory which has its roots in folk religion. The Son of God deceived the devil by hiding his divinity under an assumed form. Jesus delivered the human race from the power of the devil in two ways, by deceiving the devil on the cross and by descending to hell to save the souls of the human race who were enslaved by the devil. Muslims like Ali Al-Tabari were familiar with Good Friday and Easter services. They quote some of the prayers of the Syrian church which speak of the defeat of the devil and the destruction of sin.

Apart from the letters of Ikhwan Al-Safa (The Brotherhood of Purity), Muslim sources deny the crucifixion of Jesus. It did not happen. The most common story is that Jesus projected his likeness upon one of his apostles. This apostle 'looked like Jesus'. The Jews arrested him and crucified him, while Jesus was taken up to heaven. Muslim writers depend on one Qur'anic text in Al-Nisa' (4.156–8), which seems to deny the crucifixion of Jesus, without giving those details. Eastern Christians prior to Islam all maintained that it is the humanity of God incarnate alone that was put to death, while his divinity did not suffer – or if his divinity suffered, this is not a physical suffering. It is a mystery which is beyond expression. What is emphatically denied is the death of the divine nature. This was part of the heated debate of the fourth and fifth centuries which created a consensus among the entire Eastern Church that the divine nature did not suffer death.

In *Kitab Tamheed Al-Dalael* the eleventh-century Muslim writer Al-Baqlani asked the Christians how they could say that one nature died while the other remained alive. Death means the death of the entire or the whole person. Al-Baqlani does not seem to be aware that Islam does not accept the death of the human soul. At death every soul or spirit remains alive and is taken to its proper place. He questioned the union of the divine and the human during the crucifixion.

> If the union remained, one must ask how anyone can say that he who was crucified, who has two natures, the eternal Son and the human body, has died on the cross. If they [Christians] say that he truly died, that means he is not God; if they say that he is human and that he died as human, then he is not God.

The temptations of Jesus in the wilderness, his eating, fasting, sleeping, etc., are all evidence that Jesus was truly human and thus cannot be God incarnate because all these human actions could not have happened had Jesus been God.

The doctrine of the incarnation was rejected because it went along with an understanding of redemption as a battle between God and the devil. Muslims cannot tolerate such an idea. Al-Aziz (Almighty God), Al-Qawi (the only Powerful One), cannot accept a challenge to his power and might by one of his slave-creatures. God does not engage in a dialogue with any of his creatures nor is there anyone who can stand against his power. The idea of God deceiving the devil by sending his hidden Son could be traced back not just to Origen of Alexandria but also to Ignatius of Antioch. In spite of being a folk-story, it has behind it a certain spirituality which is deeply rooted in the ancient understanding of 'pride' and 'humility'. Muslims do not tolerate any hint at any form of divine humility or condescension. God is Al-Aziz, and this means he has the power, the only power, that can decide.

Written in the context of the flowering of Arabic Christian writing in the thirteenth century, a treatise known by the title *Al-Abd Al-Mamluk* (*The Owned Slave*) opens with the fall of Adam, who was the owned slave of God. Adam became a slave of the devil through his obedience to him. Adam sold his being. Then the treatise engages the divine Trinity in dialogue. The main argument in the dialogue is the discrepancy between 'justice' and 'mercy'. If God punishes Adam, where is the mercy? If God forgives Adam what happened to justice? There is a nineteenth-century English dialogue between Justice and Mercy which is not different in essence from the old Arabic treatise. In *Al-Manar*, a commentary on the Qur'an, the contemporary Islamic writer Rashid Rida has compiled twenty-eight objections to this modern understanding of atonement which can also thus be traced back to the medieval period. Rashid Rida and other modern writers regard such a dialogue as utterly blasphemous. No one can question God's mercy or justice. God who is perfect does not suffer from an inner paradox of mercy and justice. More important, if anyone repents, God will surely forgive them. It is futile to argue about forgiveness with Muslims, because forgiveness is secured by repentance and by repentance alone.

Athanasius, Anselm, and Islam

It is not difficult to see that if the starting-point of our teaching on salvation is sin or the fall, we have hardly anything to say to Muslims who believe in the 'commonsense of the divine mercy'. How important is sin for a Christian teaching on redemption? There is no one answer to this question, for all depends on the school of theology we refer to, how that school defines sin, and therefore how it defines salvation or the atonement. Before we come to a definition of sin, let us remind ourselves that the nature and the eternal destiny of human beings must not be divorced from sin and from redemption. These three subjects must be examined together. Each of them presupposes the other and none can be treated separately. If we presuppose that human beings were created 'according to the divine image', then sin incurs a loss of grace rather than a debt, unless we define the debt as the loss of what belongs to God – that is, human life itself. This also means that salvation or atonement is a 'restoration', a 'healing' of human nature, rather than a paying to God of what belongs to God. Further, restoring humanity to its original state presupposes the involvement of God our Creator, who alone can restore creation.

Athanasius was more aware than Anselm of the link between creation, the grace of the divine image, the sin of Adam, and redemption. Yet the treatments of both Athanasius and Anselm are still unacceptable to Muslims. Death is seen as a natural corruption of the created nature in Athanasius, Anselm, and Islam. If we can say that it is not a punishment from God, but that our sins accelerated the decay and subjected us to an obvious futility (Rom 8.20), we may be able to say more about redemption.

First, redemption is brought about by the free love and mercy of God, who came to rescue us from death, which had become a good ally of sin and futility. Sin brings 'self-injury' which involves not only one individual, but others also. Futility is obvious in the premature death of human beings and in the unexplained deformation of creation which needs healing and restoration by the Creator.

Second, the death and resurrection of Jesus is a message which solves the problem of natural decay, sinful decay, and the futility of death, and brings eternal life through the resurrection. The Qur'an seems to make the virgin birth the 'sign', whereas the New Testament makes the resurrection the 'sign'. Islam does not ignore or deny the resurrection of the body. On the last day all humans will rise from the dead. This is attributed to the divine power of the Creator. This belief provides a good opportunity to speak of the resurrection of Jesus as God's power being manifested to us as a declaration of his faithful love to his creation. If we can go back to the old Easter hymn that

Jesus 'abolished death by his death', the resurrection of Christ can become once more 'the good news' which ties our salvation not to any conditions, but to God's love and power. The resurrection of Jesus provides evidence for the belief which a Muslim wishes to hold but lacks the evidence for.

Third, Anselm and the Council of Constantinople in 1157 make the offering and the sacrifice of Jesus on the cross the corporate and common action of the Trinity. Two important points deserve our attention. One is that the Islamic emphasis on monotheism must not be treated as an obstacle. Here this neglected aspect of the atonement as the work of the 'One God' must surface to help us and to help Muslims see that there are not two gods or more who are separated by their actions of giving and receiving, but one God acting for the salvation of humanity as Father, Son and Holy Spirit. The other point is that the involvement of the One God with us through his own sacrifice must be related to the entire cosmic sacrificial system. The sun, the moon, the stars, water, air, the trees and the rest of creation offer life without conditions in a free and generous way. God is not less than his creatures and the generosity of creation is but a reflection of the divine generosity. This may create a better opportunity for dialogue with Islam on the sacrifice of the cross as the model or embodiment of a cosmic self-giving death-resurrection system which expresses the hidden redeeming love of God.

Fourth, in order to begin conversation with Muslims can we change our approach to the crucifixion of our Lord? Can we gather together some elements from the New Testament and the Old and present the crucified Christ in a way that Islam may be attracted to? In considering the relationship between God and human beings Islam has three essential verbs, to forgive, to purify, and to have mercy. The three verbs identify the activities of God in creation: God is generous, God is compassionate and merciful, and in fact grants forgiveness to those who approach him, without any condition at all except right faith and repentance. So if we compare two thirds of the Qur'an with the Book of Psalms and certain parts of the prophets such as Isaiah and Jeremiah, we will discover that the divine gift of forgiveness is free, we are forgiven on the basis of our repentance, our prayer, and our commitment to amend our life.

If we are to approach Muslims in order to speak to them about the cross, we will thus do well to look at certain parts of the Old Testament, especially the prayers in the Psalms which ask God for mercy and forgiveness. The Psalms provide us with a very powerful sense of trust in the mercy and the kindness of God. Repentance is required but forgiveness comes because God is most merciful. So what is the problem in the conversation? In part it comes from our own Christian tradition. One way in which we speak of redemption is as purification. Muslims will understand that word to denote ritual and inner purification. What do we ourselves mean by purification? It involves leading a different form of life. The blood of Jesus is a means of purification (1 John 1.7; Heb 1.3): Christ died for our sins in order to purify our life from the love of sin. To die to sin means to look at the crucifixion as an end of an old life and the beginning of a new life.

If redemption or atonement is a means of purification, why did Jesus die on the cross to achieve it? Part of the answer is that he died on the cross to reveal to us the very nature of sin. He accepted death when he was innocent. What is the relationship between sin and death? Romans 5.12 says that sin came into the world through one man and death through sin, and so death spread to all. That is as far as the text will go because all sinned 'through their attempts to avoid death' (as the Byzantine lectionaries put it). We sin through death. We are afraid to lose our life. We hang on to our own life, we try to preserve our life at the expense of others, even nature. So Christ came to tell us that the only way to preserve our life is to die, to die with him on the cross. Christ did not merely die for us; he died with us in order to show us the way to true life. And that is to be crucified with Christ and to accept death. We all are afraid of death and that is why Jesus died to purify us from our sins, from the fear of death. The power of death in us is the cause of so many sins in our life. So Christ offered us a new way, a purification from our fear. By his blood we are forgiven, yes indeed, and that means we are purified. We have been redeemed by the blood of Christ indeed, but that means we have been illuminated. We have been given a vision of how to accept the destructive power of death which is in us, in order to accept a resurrected life and to be transformed.

This is not all that needs to be said about the cross in the discussion of Christian doctrine. My concern has been to see what points of contact we have with Muslims. I have therefore omitted consideration of more 'objective' atonement theories, traditional and modern, and ignored Moltmann's stress on God's own suffering with us which is also in such tension with Muslim thinking on God's pride. As often happens through dialogue, I hope to have shown that consideration of the cross from a Muslim angle enables us to see aspects of the significance of the cross more clearly, even while we have had to ignore others.

I began by mentioning an icon which offended a Muslim. On another occasion a school colleague brought me a painting of a burial. A Muslim asked me about it and I explained that it represented the burial of Jesus. 'Go on, tell him, George', one of my Christian colleagues said, 'It's a painting of the burial of God!' The man was scandalized. 'What sort of people are you to believe in the possibility of God dying?' More recently we entertained a British Muslim leader to a meal. I assured him that we had bought halal meat and had observed the requirements of his religion in preparing the meal. We had a fine time of discussion and even hugged each other. Then we moved from the dining room to the lounge, where he saw a cross, and the atmosphere between us froze. I said to him, 'The cross still stands between you and me.'

12

The Atonement and the Post-Modern Deconstruction of the Self

MICHAEL ALSFORD

Simplifying to the extreme, I define *postmodern* as incredulity towards metanarratives.

(Jean-Francois Lyotard 1984, xiv)

CHRISTIAN THEOLOGICAL ANTHROPOLOGY is inevitably dependent upon a notion of normativity: it understands there to be a normative form of human being. It is to the doctrine of creation that theology has tended to look for its understanding of human being as a creature of God, whose very existence is derived from God and whose nature and mode of being issues from the divine intention to create a being of a certain kind. The twin doctrines of fall and atonement speak of deviation from and restoration to this normative mode of human being.

It is to this very notion of normativity that post-modernism is opposed in its suspicion of what it regards as a single, inflexible and absolute view of reality – what has come to be referred as a metanarrative or grand narrative. The status and nature of the human being or self has come under particular scrutiny by a variety of thinkers loosely federated under the post-modern banner, and a degree of consensus has emerged that, crudely put, the 'self' has to go. The question we will be addressing in this chapter is precisely what notion of the self is being deconstructed by post-modernism, and to what extent this ought to affect the contemporary Christian theological enterprise.

According to Charles Jencks (1984), the post-modern era commenced on 15 July 1972 at 3.32 in the afternoon. This was the moment at which a prizewinning modernist housing development in St Louis was demolished on the grounds of its being an uninhabitable environment. While Jencks is making a symbolic point with this remark, it does capture something quite significant from the often elusive nature of that configuration of socio-cultural elements commonly referred to as postmodern.

Post-modernism might be said to begin with the demolition of the Enlightenment capital in which Western culture has invested so heavily. However, while post-modernism's character as opposition to Enlightenment-resourced modernism is something of an uncontentious truism, the inability of both modernists and post-modernists to provide a precise definition of their respective movements does nothing to aid us in our inquiry into this crisis point for Western thought in general and for Christian theology in particular.

What I propose to do here is to identify something of the flavour of post-modernism by sketching out some of the central themes of the modernism against which post-modernism sets its various faces and then by putting names to some of these faces. While post-modernist theoretical writings tend to be both demanding and idiosyncratic, I hope to convey something of the constructive as well as deconstructive contributions made by various key thinkers to the post-modern movement.

Before embarking on this course I would like to return briefly to the opening quotation from Lyotard. The post-modern movement, in all its disparateness, is indebted to Lyotard for one of its most characteristic rallying themes, the end of the grand or metanarratives. Lyotard argues that the era of the all-encompassing account of reality is at an end; he has particularly in mind the great totalizing systems of Kant, Hegel and ultimately Marx, which seek to provide a single hermeneutical key with which to unlock ultimate meaning. For the post-modern there is no one truth but a plurality of truths, no one privileged and exclusive basis for knowledge but a multiplicity of modes of apprehension or ways of seeing. In short, there can be no normative perspective on reality, no one story about the world, no single or grand narrative.

It is in its opposition to any form of metanarrative that post-modernism comes most obviously into conflict with the Christian tradition. This, one might argue, is one of the grandest of all narratives – as Hollywood would have it, *The Greatest Story Ever Told*.

Post-modernism presents a challenge to all those (such as Marxists) who have committed themselves substantially to the Enlightenment. Christianity, on the other hand, has its roots sunk elsewhere. Assuming post-modernism is understood in the first instance as a threat, when exploring the post-modern affect upon the Christian tradition we must keep in mind the question to what extent theologians are protecting from legitimate critique baggage carried out of the eighteenth and nineteenth centuries by Christianity. Is there scope within the Christian tradition for a post-modern transformation? Is it possible that such a transformation might in fact catalyse a return to a more authentic mode of Christian religious awareness?

Many leading figures among the post-modern intelligentsia are by no means uninterested in theology. Some level of affinity indeed exists between the post-modern enterprise and the Judeo-Christian tradition: consider Derrida's struggle with negative theology, Levinas's concern with otherness and his deep immersion in the Talmud, Irigaray's use of religious language (e.g. 1991), and Kristeva's interest in Christian mysticism, the Virgin Mary, and *agapē* (e.g. 1986). Exactly where we might find this patch of common ground and whether it is large enough to build upon remains to be seen.

The Prioritizing of the Self

It could be argued that the major intellectual shift characterizing the Enlightenment was from issues of being and existence to issues of knowing. This philosophical focus upon how and what 'I' know had its formal origins in the work of René Descartes. The Cartesian epistemic programme was to change the face of intellectual life in the West and to exercise a dramatic influence upon culture in general.

Descartes's primary concern was (if I may be anachronistic) to undermine both the scepticism which was to receive its most developed treatment in the work of David Hume and also the attack subsequently launched upon transcendental absolutes by Nietzsche. To this end Descartes deployed three epistemic strategies: methodological doubt, the notion of clear and certain ideas, and most significantly the principle expressed in the phrase 'I think, therefore I am'. The combination of the method of doubt with the epistemic criteria of clarity and certainty debarred as knowledge anything which could not be absolutely verified. The only epistemic certainty to be salvaged from this manifold of uncertainty was the thinking self, which alone (according to Descartes) could be self-evidently guaranteed.

Of course Descartes, as a good Christian, wished to preserve a place for God within his epistemology. It is only the self-evident existence of a perfect God that guarantees human sense experience, argues Descartes, insofar as an infinitely perfect God would not be a party to duplicity and so would not permit our senses to mislead us. Thus we move from certainty of self, to certainty of God, and finally to certainty of external reality.

With John Locke's denial of the existence of innate ideas the Enlightenment took its leave of God and sought to move directly from certainty of self to certainty of reality mediated via sense experience.

The first formal misgivings over the direction in which Western thought was proceeding came from David Hume, whose scepticism concerning human ability to apprehend the world as an ordered unity threatened to undermine the burgeoning confidence in the new scientific world-view. It was in response to Hume's scepticism that Immanuel Kant sought to map out the relationship between the knower and the thing known (the 'subject-object dichotomy').

For Kant, knowledge does not issue out of a conformity of the mind to external objects but is the result of the mind's providing conceptual structuring to the manifold of experience provided by the material world. Knowledge thus involves the conformity of external objects to the *a priori* categories of the human mind, categories such as substance and causality. It is solely through these categories that we apprehend reality as anything other than a chaotic mass of uncoordinated sense-impressions (Kant 1982, B xvi). Here we come to the heart of

Kant's understanding of the priority of the subject, a necessary development of the Cartesian turn to the subject minus the transcendentality of God.

As the inheritors of the Enlightenment legacy we are presented with a complex formation of ontological and epistemological notions which are intended to function as transcendentally normative subsequent to the death of God. Human being, defined in terms of the autonomous Cartesian self, stands as the guarantor of true knowledge, the final arbiter of what is clear and certain, the one who brings the creative ordering of the categories of thought to the chaotic manifold of sense experience. Truth is that which the constituting subject may assimilate and structure. That which cannot be so treated is denied the status of knowledge. In a very real sense what we have here is the establishing of the modernist creation myth where the god of human reason brings order out of chaos. Taking the Baconian maxim that knowledge is power and tracing a line through the idealist tradition of Kant, Fichte, and Hegel, we see that in the modernist programme the relation of subject to object is one of dominance. The object, the other, is constituted by the subject; the whole of so-called objective reality, the not-I, is derived from the transcendental self (cf. Fichte 1982, 71). It is the active subject that is prior to all things; the 'other' is concomitantly subordinate to it. The value of the external world, if it has any value, lies in its contribution to the development of the transcendental ego or self.

It is against this prioritizing of the autonomous self with its attendant notion of a unitary and indubitable knowledge base that post-modernism contends.

The Death of Man

It has been suggested that the post-modern crisis represents, in Nietzschean terms, a second death of God. This time, however, it is the Promethean god of the Enlightenment whose passing is either being mourned by the disenchanted devotees of modernism or vigorously denied by its apologists. This second death of a transcendental has often been referred to as the 'death of man'.

Since Descartes's initiation of the modernist quest for clarity and certainty, all subsequent epistemological initiatives have presupposed a subject-centred rationalism. The high point of the modernist epistemology is clearly seen in the constitutive powers allocated to the autonomous subject by Kant (see 1982, A 125).

It is precisely with this notion and centrality of the transcendental subject that post-modernism takes issue. Indeed, if we were looking for a rather less jocular definition of the beginnings of post-modernism than that given by Jencks, we might well focus on the work of Nietzsche, which arguably represents the first sustained critique of modernism and the transcendental subject (cf. Habermas 1987, 85–6). For Nietzsche modernity represents a twilight existence and those who inhabit it are little more than a herd, slavishly following one way of knowing, one way of behaving. This is an existence conditioned by two millennia's adherence to a single metaphysical norm, that of Christianity, a norm that has been replaced in the modernist schema by the transcendental self.

In his reaction against metanarrative, Nietzsche is as post-modern as Lyotard. The Enlightenment trinity of reason, naturalism, and progress are understood by him to be revered out of fear, fear of the chaos and nihilism attendant on the dissolution of Christian Europe.

> In the anxiety created by doubts about divine authority, and in the chaos created by so many irreconcilable attempts at a secular basis of moral order, we have, in a kind of panic, taken refuge in each other, in safety, or the lowest common denominator (Pippin 1991, 92).

This 'lowest common denominator', a bulwark against a failing metaphysic, manifests itself in the Enlightenment deification of reason and its preoccupation with law, universal principles, objectivity, and clear and certain truth.

Of course Nietzsche's view of Christianity as an enfeebling tradition that fosters egalitarianism out of fear of originality, creativity, and power provides much of the impetus for his criticisms of modernism as a mere redoubt in which the post-Christian West lies huddled seeking refuge from the ruins of its religious absolutes. His message, and indeed that of post-moderns in general, is the abandonment of modernism's ersatz deity (the transcendental self enthroned by Descartes) and its replacement by an historically situated subject – in other words, the death of the modernist God.

It was Michel Foucault who took up and developed Nietzsche's initial attempts at a deconstruction of the subject. However, we need to approach Foucault and his contemporaries by way of Martin Heidegger (1977), who identified most incisively modernism's dependence upon the Cartesian subject. Modernism, argues Heidegger, regards the autonomous subject as self-constituting and as the focus for truth and meaning. Clear and certain truth is at the disposal of the subject by virtue of its ability to abstract, to occupy a so-called Archimedian point in its apprehension/possession of the objective world. Heidegger rejects this prioritizing of the subject, arguing that human existence is characterized by its historical situatedness. The subject does not occupy a transcendental epistemological high ground.

Heidegger's attack upon Cartesian-backed modernism is both ontological and epistemological. A historical notion of human being is at the very heart of his notion of *Dasein* ('being-present-here'), our unnegotiated presence in a world into which we have been thrown and which defines us through an already existing past and context. This notion of *Dasein*, of being-in-the-world, represents the radical departure of Heideggerian thought from the Cartesian transcendental subject which exists, in effect, outside of the world. While the modernist project sought to provide us with an epistemological microscope through which we might examine the world as if on a microscope slide, Heidegger draws attention to our own presence not behind the lens but on the slide itself. It is our determination by a past, our involvement in a present, and our orientation towards a future which are constitutive of human being.

Michel Foucault deploys a similar (but not identical) argument when he seeks to identify the problems inherent in modernism's notion of the subject. In identifying the concept of

man, the human sciences are locked into the irresolvable problematic of man as both the subject and object of the inquiry.
Man as an essential subject is nothing more than a construct
of modernist epistemology, and one which, ironically, fails to
provide the very epistemological key it has always pretended
to. A new epistemology is required, one which unmakes man
as a transcendental subject and reconstructs the subject (with a
small 's') as particular historico-cultural beings. This eviction
of man from his position of epistemological transcendentality
provides a new kind of freedom, one which it is almost impossible for us to grasp from our present position:

> It is no longer possible to think in our day other than in the
> void left by man's disappearance. For this void does not create
> a deficiency; it does not constitute a lacuna that must be filled.
> It is nothing more, and nothing less, than the unfolding of space
> in which it is once more possible to think. . . . To all those who
> still wish to talk about man, about his reign or his liberation,
> to all those who wish to take him as their starting-point in their
> attempts to reach the truth, to all those who, on the other hand,
> refer all knowledge back to the truths of man himself, to all
> those who refuse to formalize without anthropologizing, who
> refuse to mythologize without demystifying, who refuse to think
> without immediately thinking that it is man who is thinking, to
> all these warped and twisted forms of reflection we can answer
> only with a philosophical laugh – which means, to a certain
> extent, a silent one (1989, 342–3).

In this way Foucault has established himself as the arch anti-
humanist, earning the enmity of existentialists, Marxists and
structuralists alike.

Foucault is ultimately concerned with the dissolution of a
particular understanding of the subject rather than the dis-
appearance of the subject in itself. The same is true of Jacques
Derrida. While Derrida most assuredly places himself within
the Heideggerian 'death of man' tradition – arguing in fact that
Heidegger does not go far enough – he equally clearly wishes
to preserve a situated as opposed to a transcendental subject

and to undermine the modernist dualism which prioritizes the subject over the object or other. Indeed much of Derrida's work may be understood as an identification of such enforced hierarchies within modernist thought ('binary oppositions') which may only be disrupted by the privileging of the subordinate other. Derrida calls this process of destabilizing hierarchies 'deconstruction', which (he argues) always involves the overturning or inversion of the order of things – in this case, of the aforementioned hierarchies.

> In a classical philosophical opposition, we do not find a peaceful coexistence between the two sides, but a violent hierarchy. One of the two terms dominates the other (axiologically, logically, etc.), occupies the higher place. To deconstruct the oppositions one must first of all, at a given moment, reverse the hierarchy (1981, 56–7).

Once again the target of post-modern critiques of modernism is thus the privileging of the subject – not the subject indiscriminately understood. Indeed Derrida goes as far as to admit that the subject is 'absolutely indispensable'(1970, 271).

There is a great deal to be said for Derrida's deconstruction and destabilization of the transcendental subject, but there are also a number of potentially devastating critical attacks that can be deployed in opposition to it. The most sophisticated and nuanced of these attacks comes from feminist theorists such as Luce Irigaray (see Whitford 1991). While undeniably indebted to Derrida for his deconstruction of male-female hierarchy, Irigaray is all too aware of the double-edged nature of the Derridian sword when used as a feminist weapon. She argues that the process of deconstructing the notion of the human self (regarded within modernism as essentially male) inevitably deconstructs the feminine also, deconstructs the very ground required for feminist political action. Women who have been denied the privilege of autonomous self-identity by Enlightenment-resourced modernism are thus equally denied a place of enunciation by the post-modern programme. Indeed, Irigaray suggests that deconstruction is in itself both privileged and gendered male. In his deconstruction of the male-female binary opposition Derrida maintains that he may speak 'like a woman'. Irigaray regards this as an all-too-familiar attempt by patriarchy simply to absorb female perspectives rather than allowing them autonomy.

The last thinker that I wish to introduce here is Emmanuel Levinas. The work of Levinas holds a certain fascination for the Christian theologian due to its deep engagement with the Hebraic tradition, which he regards as offering an ethical relationship to the world as opposed to an ontological one. Levinas's treatment of the subject is at the very heart of his philosophy, and like other post-modern theorists he is concerned to decentre rather than to destroy the subject. He seeks to develop an ethical subversion of the subject, by a radical prioritizing of the other. Levinas's discussion of the priority of the other is complex and highly nuanced. The flavour of his thinking in this area emerges in a conversation with Richard Kearney. Kearney has inquired of Levinas whether he wishes to preserve subjectivity in some form or another, in the light of his concerns over the ethical 'I':

> It is not that I wish to preserve, over and against the structuralist critique, the idea of a subject who would be a substantial or mastering centre of meaning, an idealist self-sufficient cogito. . . . Ethical subjectivity dispenses with the idealizing subjectivity of ontology which reduces everything to itself. The ethical 'I' is subjectivity precisely in so far as it kneels before the other, sacrificing its own liberty to the more primordial call of the other. For me, the freedom of the subject is not the highest of primary values. The heteronomy of our response to the human other, or to God as the absolutely Other, precedes the autonomy of our subjective freedom (Kearney 1984, 63).

Levinas (1979) regards the priority given to the self in Western thought as the root cause of those essentially violent totalizing structures in which the 'I' seeks to subsume the other. The 'other' loses its distinct otherness and becomes the 'same'.

It has been observed in this connection that an adequate

account of the reality of other 'minds' is highly elusive within the Cartesian schema. John Macmurray (1957, 73) argues that post-Cartesian thought 'fails to do justice to, and even to allow for the possibility of our knowledge of one another; and this failure arises because its formal conception of knowledge excludes this possibility by postulating the "I think" as the primary presupposition of all experience.'

By the time we arrived at the Kantian development of 'I think, therefore I am', the self (as we noted above) became the constituting self, the self which creates its world of objects but also of other selves. Along with all other objects, other selves must submit to the synthesizing structure of the mind, in order to become recognizable as knowledge, for the subject. This would appear to be the only way in which the reality of the other self might impinge upon the subject – that is, at least in part, as constituted and modified by that subject. The possibility of engaging with the other-in-itself is simply beyond the constitutive capacity of the categories of human thought. It is this dominance of the autonomous self over the other, as the self construes the other, that Levinas condemns as ultimately totalitarian and unethical.

Modernism, then, privileged the autonomous self; post-modernism attacks this. While there is much to be suspicious of within the post-modern movement (not least as identified in feminist critiques) there is also much of value. It would be a great pity if the terms post-modern, post-structuralist, and deconstructionist joined other pejorative labels such as liberal, fundamentalist, and relativist, which function as shorthand for 'anything I disagree with'. Post-modernism does involve a move away from absolutes and a strong inclination towards epistemic relativity, and this is problematic for religion. But there is more to post-modernism than that.

The Atonement and the Deconstruction of the Self

If post-modernism teaches us anything, it is to be wary of inflexible and totalizing normative structures. In seeking to establish the existence of a normative mode of human being, the Christian tradition has often found itself marginalizing those who do not readily conform to such norms. The experience of women in this regard is an obvious case in point. Nevertheless it seems inevitable that the Christian religion engage in the articulation of some normative definition of human being. In part this is because the triptych of the Christian story – creation, fall, and redemption – demands the use of normative language. In part it is because some such definition has an essential place in the empowering of any Christian ethical or political activity.

What is essential in any deployment of the language of normativity is a degree of provisionality. To return to the language of Heidegger and Derrida, every norm must be placed 'under erasure': at the very moment of suggesting a norm we must be aware of its failure, its inadequacy to the task of presenting human being to human beings. This is the essence of Foucault's critique of the human sciences, and it is a critique of equal relevance to Christian theology. Levinas observes that 'the best thing about philosophy is that it fails'; although it is forced to make use of ontological language, the language of norms and limitations, its strength lies in its ability 'to deconstruct what it has constructed and unsay what it has said' (see Kearney 1984, 58). This must equally be true of theology, and the theologian must be aware of this throughout the attempt at normatizing the two mysterious foci of the theological enterprise, God and human being.

Where the Christian tradition speaks of a normative mode of human existence it is fundamentally a relational one. The term I favour in this regard is 'coadunate' (see M. Alsford 1990). Coadunacy speaks of a radical unity of one with the other such that true selfhood is a function of alterity, that is of a mutual interchange and self-giving. The notion of coadunacy involves an understanding of human being which privileges the other over the self and understands human fallenness in terms of the breakdown of human relationality and the prioritizing of the self over the other. In this regard coadunacy, which I argue to be a thoroughly Judeo-Christian theological notion, may be seen as in accord with one of the central themes of the post-modern programme, the de-centring of the self and the prioritizing of the other. Clearly any understanding of reconciliation and atonement must have at its centre some such notion of human restoration to oneness with God and with others.

In saying that coadunacy is in some sense normative for human being, we are reiterating the biblical observation that it is not good that we be alone and that the ideal mode of redeemed existence is to be all one in Christ. The theological foci of normative human coadunacy have to do with human creatureliness and the twin doctrines of the image of God and the Trinity.

The claim that human beings are first and foremost creatures is already to establish them as in relation. Human being is always one pole of the creator/creature relationality which, within the Christian tradition, is characterized as an interpersonal relationship of familial intimacy. Human sociality is of fundamental significance in that it has to do in the first instance with humanity's relationship with its Creator. The very fact of our creatureliness establishes us as fundamentally relational (cf. Bonhoeffer 1963, 40–1; Greenberg 1971, 33, 35). It is precisely because the statement 'It is not good that we be alone' derives its force from the logic of the creator/creature dynamic that we may maintain the primal significance of human relationality. In arguing for the constitutive significance of human relationality or human coadunacy, the logic of the Christian tradition permits us to make sense of the clearly observable brokenness of human mutuality and the dysfunction experienced with regard to self/other engagement.

The image of God has always been central to any theological explication of the essential nature of human being, and consequently the Christian doctrines of God and humanity are inextricably linked. The idea of the image of God is by no means an unproblematic one, and questions concerning its constitution and its status, particularly in the light of human sin, make it a difficult doctrine to build upon. Yet two things may be said. First, the image of God has constitutive significance, as is indicated by the references to the image in biblical passages concerned with creation (Gen 1.26; 9.3–6; Col 1.15–17; 2 Cor 4.4). Second, while the image has been understood in a variety of ways throughout Christian history (notably as rationality in

Augustine, Aquinas, and Calvin), the tendency in modern theology has been to understand it as fundamentally relational. Indeed, it appears thus in Luther, implying a life orientated towards God rather than having to do with any precise human power, 'living just as God lives' (Luther 1958, 62–3). This understanding is taken up and developed by Karl Barth (1958; cf. 1960, 222, 250). To be created in the divine image is to be created after the image of the triune God who is always in relation. Indeed for Barth it is Christ's perfect relationship with the Father which identifies him as truly the image of God (cf. also Pannenberg 1985, 53; cf. 1968, 194–5).

The doctrine of the image of God becomes particularly significant for the issue of human relationality within the context of a trinitarian understanding of God. The Christian confession of God as Trinity is derived uniquely from his act of communing with humanity in their historical situatedness. In the person of Jesus Christ we are permitted to gaze upon the mutuality of God in the Son's addressing the Father as a discrete person. We are led further into the divine mutuality with the coming of the Spirit, sent by Christ and described by him as the mediator of his continued presence and activity to and for the church.

At this point we may begin to see some parallels between the Christian theological enterprise and the post-modern themes adumbrated above. In its attempt to avoid both modalism and tritheism the doctrine of the Trinity seeks to express the mystery of the divine unity in particularity. Avoiding the subsumption of the other by the subject as in modernist thinking since Descartes, the doctrine of the Trinity refuses to subsume particularity into a single totalizing subject. The trinitarian understanding of God as the unity of three persons speaks of radical reciprocity, not of absorption. Thus Pannenberg insists that trinitarian formulations ought to begin with Jesus's relationship with the Father, as opposed to beginning with metaphysical debates concerning divine ontology; the point parallels aspects of post-modern methodology. Clearly the Gospel accounts of Jesus's relationship with the Father illustrate both particularity and intimate self-constituting communion (cf. Schillebeeckx 1973, 61).

It is from this mode of existence, as beings in the image of the God who is always in relation, that humanity has fallen, and it is thus to this mode of existence that we are to hope for restoration. This it seems to me is at the very heart of the doctrine of the atonement – the restoring of the lost or damaged image of God. To characterize Jesus's message and mission as one of redemption, reconciliation, or salvation, is to prompt the question – redemption from what?

Christian theology has always recognized human fallenness as characterized by the breakdown of humanity's relationship with its Creator, and concomitantly of relationships among human beings, with death as the outcome of deadliness in relationships (Jüngel 1974, 109; cf. Barth 1981, 212; Pannenberg 1977, 26). But sin cannot be understood as a mere disjunction between the self and the other, be that other God or human being. It involves violence toward the other. Sin is the prioritizing of the autonomous self over the other, the ego's attempt at creating the world in its own image, the domination of 'I' over 'You', what Levinas calls the totalism of the self and Foucault sees as the laughable pretension of the reign of the transcendental self. It is what Pannenberg calls egocentricity and what Heidegger understands as the human tendency towards abstraction and privileged epistemological isolation. The Judeo-Christian tradition has from its earliest times understood sin as human beings' wish to become as God: post-modernism informs us that the modernist programme was in fact a coup to this end.

The consequence of dislocation from God and from others is that we no longer consider ourselves to be our brother's or sister's keeper. Our current experience of relational brokenness prompts us always to encounter the other first and foremost as stranger. Indeed, even God is now considered to be a stranger by human beings (cf. John 1).

Our experience of the other as stranger is born, in part, out of fear. It is fear of, or at least anxiety over, the sin of Cain, fear of the potential for violence and animosity inherent in the mysterious stranger. It is this which represents the tragedy and paradox of relational brokenness, for while it is the mysteriousness and dangerousness of the stranger which fuels our fear, it is our fear which helps to fuel our continued estrangement from the other.

The reality of human sinfulness, experienced in terms of relational brokenness and the prioritizing of the self, takes the form, in part, of a tragic condition which unaided humanity is incapable of resolving. It is for this reason that the Christian tradition speaks of the need for grace and for divine empowering to a restored humanity, for the restoration of the divine image.

This having been said, it is also necessary to maintain a perspective on human culpability and responsibility. The Christological restoration of human coadunacy – the atoning work of Christ – must be understood as operating in two modes. We may speak of Jesus Christ as an exemplar, the true human being whom we must imitate, and also as the one who in the face of the tragedy of human brokenness empowers us to the restored image of God. The empowering Christ speaks to our inability to transcend our own situatedness, while Jesus the exemplar speaks to our particularity, our freedom and responsibility. It is in these two modes that we encounter the atoning work of Christ.

To maintain that human being is communal being, simply by virtue of its creatureliness and its imaging of a God who is understood as essentially relational, is to fall short of the true radicality of the Christian anthropology. This radicality is to be found precisely in the imitation of Christ. While Jesus's teaching is clearly concerned with relational themes – forgiveness, love, service of others – it is his life which concerns us most here. As Pannenberg points out, it is Jesus's relationship with the Father that is the paradigmatic form of interpersonal relationality, and it is self-giving to the Father and to others which is at the heart of Jesus's being as human. The mode of relationality most characteristic of Jesus's engagement with others is one of self-abandonment. Jesus is the one who gave himself completely to others, without condition or reserve even to the point of death. His relationship with others is never conditioned by fear or animosity, even in the face of hostility. He is the one who is always available to the other, with all the risks that such unconditional availability involves.

He is the image of God, and is therefore true human being. It is through his person and work that human being is re-created and restored. This image of God is restored by Christ by virtue of the reconciliation he establishes between human being and its Creator, and within humanity itself. It is this Christological empowering to reconciliation and restored coadunacy which breaks into our existential experience of fear and estrangement.

In Christ as the agent of creation, human being has restored to it, by grace, the conditions necessary for coadunacy: reconciliation with God, restoration of the image of God, freedom from fear and, as Pannenberg argues, hope for a communal destiny with God and other human beings. The presence of Christ among those who acknowledge him as Lord always results in an empowering to community. In this respect the church represents a witness to the potential for restored human coadunacy and also points forward to a destiny where humanity may be one in Christ.

In Jesus Christ we see the perfect example of coadunate humanity. He is the true image of God, the one who abandons himself to humanity in the face of estrangement and violence. Both in his person and in his teaching, Jesus exemplifies the denial of estrangement which is proper to those who are in the image of the triune God. Alongside human empowering to coadunacy in Christ, where God is actively engaged in an act of re-creation, there must also be a human response, which takes the form of a strategy for the imitation of Christ in his abandonment to the other (cf. Phil 2.1–8).

The overcoming of estrangement and the denial of the other as stranger calls for a movement towards the other that imitates the radicalness of Jesus's relationship with the Father and with others. The dynamic of coadunacy entails nothing less than self-abandonment as the primal mode of human relationality and indeed of human being. This principal message of the Christian religion is resonant within the post-modern deconstruction of the autonomous transcendental self, and the privileging, particularly in Levinas, of the other.

The notion of self-abandonment to the other as a self-constituting act could easily be misused to legitimate gender and racial oppression. If women and marginalized groups are denied autonomous self-possession, they cannot be expected in the name of coadunacy to abandon themselves to the other. Coadunacy depends on self-possession, as Irigaray hints. That having been said, the attempt to establish discrete stages in the process of coadunate existence is not very helpful. Some notion of perichoretic reciprocity may be more usefully deployed. We may also need to reconsider the value of the model of Christ himself as victim (see the chapters by Sally Alsford and Christina Baxter above).

Further, self-abandonment must not be taken to imply self-negation. As Foucault argues, it is only through the abandoning of the mythical transcendental subject that we may become truly human beings inhabiting a real world. True personhood is not achieved by absenting ourselves from our historical situatedness, by removing ourselves from the world, by existing as one pole of a duality where the 'I' confronts and attempts to dominate all that is 'not-I', the other. Through self-abandonment we follow the example of Christ who abandons himself to the will of the Father, to the abuse of humanity and ultimately to death, without ever turning that abandonment to the other into self-negation. In Christ we see total availability to and for the other without reduction of self. In self-abandonment we are not dealing with a weak-willed acquiescence to the domination of others, as Nietzsche suggests, but rather with a will to self-availability to the other, empowered by the reconciling and atoning work of Christ.

It is this self-abandonment in the presence of the power to be purely for self – that is, in the presence of the power to deny the other – which constitutes the basis for the dynamic of coadunacy. It is to this reality that the church is called; we are called to love one another as Christ loves us and gave himself for us. This community of self-abandonment is what Stanley Hauerwas (1981) means when he talks of the church as 'a community of character, a 'contrast model' to a world constituted by strangers and dominated by fear. Yet true coadunate existence is, as we have intimated, the birthright of human being *qua* human being. The church is but the custodian of the dynamic empowering to overcome the self's estrangement from others and from God. Thus the encountering of the other primarily as friend cannot be confined to the community of faith alone. As Christ taught, the loving of those who love us must be coupled with the loving of those who do not.

Christian theology has much to learn from post-modernism's analysis of the dominance of the self in modern Western thought, while the attempt by post-modern theorists such as Levinas to redefine the self in terms of a radical orientation towards the other is indeed fully in accord with the central anthropological concerns of the Christian tradition. Whether post-modern theory can truly go beyond this analysis and present us with a non-transcendental strategy for an effective de-centring of the subject is doubtful. As we are quite rightly informed by post-moderns, human being is situated being. We are incapable of abstracting ourselves from our situation. It is Christianity's appeal to transcendental empowering through the atonement which ultimately forces it to part company with the post-modern programme.

While the dethroning of the ego as the transcendental guarantor of truth is a necessary step in the deconstruction of the Enlightenment's usurpation of religion, Christianity clearly represents a narrative of the grandest kind. At this point religion must conflict with post-modernism. Insofar as post-moderns such as Derrida, however, wish to emphasize the creative act of reception – a multiplicity of ways of reading and perceiving and a variety of ways of knowing – then this can function as a timely reminder of the ultimately mysterious nature of reality and its Author. If post-modernism can help to remind Christianity that mystery rather than Cartesian certainty and clarity lies at its heart, then it will have done us a great service.

13

Is the Message of the Cross Good News for the Twentieth Century?

COLIN GREENE

HOW ARE WE to communicate the meaning of the cross to our contemporaries? It is this task which faces all those who believe that the reality of Christ's atoning love is still at the heart of the good news which it is both our responsibility and our joy to share with others. David Lowes Watson (1983) has suggested that the best model to use in connection with communicating the gospel is that of journalism. The journalist always seeks to address a particular context mindful of the social and cultural presuppositions that will determine whether or not he or she gains a hearing.

In a recent article examining the relationship between cultural assumptions and the missionary task of remaining faithful to the essentials of the gospel, Robert Priest (1993, 100) has issued a bleak warning to all those of an evangelical persuasion who might attempt this particular task.

> Evangelicals respond to a secular culture with apologetics, philosophy, and a defense of the historicity of the faith, while that culture with its discourses quietly chips away at biblical foundational assumptions of who we are as humans – giving new categories to think with and grounding its assumptions in sophisticated empirical studies. The result is that we defend, philosophically and historically, a faith that ceases to make sense of our condition, a faith that in terms of our subjective perceptions ceases to have face validity or subjective plausibility. With the demise of sin, hell becomes indefensible, grace loses its appeal, mission faces a crisis of legitimacy, and the cross of Christ has no meaning.

Such a statement might lead us to despair of any attempt to make the word of the cross either relevant or intelligible to contemporary culture. The problem as Priest sees it is that most attempts at contextualization tend to stray into two related errors: cultural insensitivity or cultural accommodation. In an article in the *Church of England Newspaper* of 29 January 1993, Bishop Paul Richardson, who has worked in New Guinea, provided an interesting example of the former.

> Central to the world view of the Chimbu people is the concept of reciprocity. Relationships are initiated, deepened and sustained by the exchange of gifts. No expression for 'thank you' exists in their language; favours must always be returned in kind. When the first Lutheran missionaries arrived in the 1950s, they put the cross and justification at the centre of their preaching. They emphasised how much God had done for the Chimbu people by dying to take away their sins, and that Jesus' death sealed their salvation once for all.

At first the missionaries appeared to be very successful. Converts were plentiful and much land was donated for church building and the like. Behind all this apparent generosity, however, was the cultural assumption that the Chimbu people must reciprocate and pay Christ back what they owed him. In due course their enthusiasm for the Christian faith waned when they considered they had done enough to repay their debt.

In the context of Western secular culture the problem is more likely to be that of cultural accommodation. An example was the widespread rejection of traditional substitutionary-sacrificial atonement theology by nineteenth- and twentieth-century liberal theology. Liberalism identified the human predicament as ignorance rather than sin and guilt and so construed the meaning of the cross in largely exemplarist terms. In distinctly Abelardian fashion the death of Christ was viewed as the supreme example of God's love for the world. As such it solved the problem of humanity's substantial ignorance of God's unconditional and unrestrained love and mercy, rather than objectively providing expiation for the burden and constraint of sin and human wrongdoing. It is unfortunately the case that much contemporary preaching is still wedded to some form of the moral influence theory and is consequently unable to develop a theology of atonement that addresses the cultural assumptions and values of our contemporaries. Luther resolved to make the cross the criterion that judges all things, but Jürgen Moltmann has commented that Luther's dictum has proved difficult to maintain in the history of the church because the tradition of the theology of the cross 'was never much loved' (1974, 3). The antecedents of this tradition are found in Paul's resolve to remind the Corinthians that 'we proclaim Christ crucified, a stumbling block to Jews and foolishness to Gentiles' (1 Cor 1.23).

The situation Paul faced at Corinth is similar to our own. He, too, had to advance the cause of his theology of the cross by avoiding the twin errors of cultural accommodation and cultural insensitivity. At first glance it might appear that the former was his main concern. In a context of extensive religious pluralism, where dangerous liaisons of religious and philosophical ideas were rife, Paul resolved not to deviate from what P. T. Forsyth (1909) later called the cruciality of the cross. He was very well aware that for the Jew the phrase 'crucified Messiah' was a contradiction in terms. 'Messiah' was synonomous with power, splendour, triumph, and glory, while 'crucifixion' could only be defined in terms of the exact opposite – weakness, humiliation, defeat, the curse of God. The two words simply did not cohere. In a Greek culture dominated by ever more esoteric varieties of philosophy and 'worldly wisdom', the word of the cross was viewed as an affront to human reason and intelligibility. In both contexts the word of the cross constituted an alienating foolishness. Nevertheless the affront of the cross could not be removed. It also made its demand on the Christians at Corinth whose preference for charismatic gifts and rarified spiritual experience threatened to bypass the apparent foolishness of the cross and other fundamental principles of personal morality and practical discipleship.

On the other hand, Paul did not fall into the trap of cultural insensitivity. He maintained an apologetic concern to relate the word of the cross to the cultural values and expectations of his hearers. He was concerned to demonstrate that the word of the cross, which in one sense cannot be limited by the criteria of reason, nevertheless possessed its own inherent rationality and wisdom (see 1 Cor 1.17–18). To those enamoured with an undifferentiated worldly wisdom, Paul offers Christ crucified, the quintessential expression of God's power and wisdom. While this wisdom and power are found in what are most certainly paradoxical circumstances, it is nevertheless true wisdom, and in due course Paul was to speak of Christ as the very personification of that wisdom, the revelation of God's eternal saving purposes (see the Christological hymns of Phil 2.6–11; Col 1.15–20; also 1 Cor 1.20, 27; 2.5, 13; 3.18–20).

The cultural context in which the church exists in Western Europe is variously described as the end of the Constantinian era or the demise of Christendom. This has hastened a return to a religious pluralism such as was faced by the first apostles. It is doubtful if the church has fully come to terms with what is effectively the disestablishment of the Christian faith by secular, political, and religious alternatives to the vision that inspired Christendom. That vision was based on the belief that the unity of religion was essential for the unity of society. It was for this reason that Theodosius outlawed all non-Christian religions so that the confession of one holy, catholic and apostolic church would also guarantee political authority and stability.

This vision which upheld old Christendom, and made the Christian faith the natural inheritance of every citizen of the empire, was effectively destroyed by the confessional wars of the sixteenth and seventeenth centuries, which took place as a consequence of the Reformation. This in turn produced two further consequences. It led to the emergence of the nation state which replaced religion as the guarantor of political sovereignty and stability, with the consequent marginalization of the Christian faith from the public realm of political and social concern. And it led to the unleashing of a new intellectual impulse which sought to reformulate the basic concepts of law, morality, economics, science, and religion on the basis of that which is common to human nature.

In the intellectual maelstrom that ensued, science supplanted religion as the only secure path to truth, and reason replaced authority, whether that of the church or the Bible, as the arbiter of truth. Two hundred years later the vision that governs the public sphere of contemporary society is avowedly secular. For many of our contemporaries the very word God has become as enigmatic as a blank face (Rahner 1978, 46). The secular state tolerates and condones religious diversity as long as no one religion puts forward an exclusive or authoritarian claim for truth. If secularism seeks to liberate societies from religious control and domination, then the rise of modern atheism has sought to debunk the religious thesis altogether. Many of our contemporaries are imbued with the spirit of Feuerbach, Marx and Nietzsche. Religion is regarded as at best an escape from reality, the so-called opiate of the peoples, or at worse a form of alienated self-consciousness which inevitably leads to political and social oppression and militarism of one form or another.

If it is the case that we are presently being engulfed by 'the crisis of modernity', or have indeed moved into a form of post-modernism, then that is because we are witnessing the demise of the secular alternative to the vision that maintained Christendom. The myth of technological control and expansion has ceased to be a credible alternative to theism. The nuclear and ecological crisis has produced a situation where such unbounded optimism in the transcendence of human reason is now being confronted with numerous 'frontier situations' which could lead to catastrophe and the early demise of the human experiment altogether.

It is just such a complex situation which any renewal of atonement theology should seek to address, avoiding the twin errors of cultural accommodation and insensitivity. The refusal to contextualize the word of the cross as Paul sought to do in Corinth leads to theological discourse which is jejune and irrelevant. In this chapter we can only begin to scratch the surface of this positive endeavour. We will do so, however, by addressing three areas of atonement theology which appear to have become increasingly problematic in the light of the cultural context we have sought to describe.

The Word of the Cross and the Task of Evangelism

We are now in the context of a new commitment to the cause of evangelization. Where the word of the cross has been understood as central to the task of evangelism it has often been associated with what is referred to as the moral or juridical theory of atonement. The death of Christ is understood as in some way making reparation or compensating for the moral failure of human sinfulness. The origins of this view are associated with the medieval theologian Anselm. His answer to the question *'Cur Deus homo?'*, 'Why did God become a human being?', presupposed a framework of universal moral law (cf. Gunton 1988, 87–93). God is the just ruler of the universe and sin violates the moral fabric of his universe. There are two courses of action open to him. Either he destroys the cause of the offence or a satisfactory bargain is struck which compensates for God's violated honour and justice. The bargain or transaction takes place through Christ's death on the cross, through which mercy once again prevails over the concerns of justice.

In Anselm's thought, unlike that of the New Testament, God is no longer the subject of reconciliation but instead the object to whom a reconciling compensation is made. The Son faces the Father with his back to us and the infinite worth of his sinless life is sufficient to make reparation for the accumulated burden of sin. The benefits or merits of Christ's death were mediated to the sinner through the medieval penitential system. Now evangelicalism traces its roots back to the Reformation, and despite Luther's unease with many aspects of meritorious satisfaction, neither he nor Calvin broke fundamentally with the juridical or moral framework of discourse which controlled Anselm's theology of atonement (cf. Althaus 1966, 218–23, against Aulén 1931). Instead, violated honour is replaced by violated righteousness, which unleashes God's wrath and anger upon the sinner. For Luther, the cross is that 'happy exchange' whereby God's wrath is placated. For Calvin, Christ accepts the punishment of sin in our place and God's anger is propitiated. Luther thus replaced the incertitudes of the medieval penitential system with the doctrine of justification by faith. Through baptism, sinners can participate in the life and righteousness of Christ and live outside ourselves. God imputes to us the benefits of that 'alien righteousness' which Christ's justifying death achieves.

A number of factors make the juristic metaphor of the atonement inherently problematic in the context of contemporary culture.

The major difficulty in the context of secular Western culture is the almost complete dissolution of the framework of universal moral law. This constitutes part of the 'crisis of modernity' (cf. Newbigin 1989). Anselm's atonement theology was formulated in the context of old Christendom where the universal moral law was commensurate with feudal concepts of justice and obligation. There is now no universally acceptable religious or anthropological basis to morality. Instead, moral values, like questions of religious belief, are understood to be issues of personal preference or choice (MacIntyre 1981). Not surprisingly, this change has been accompanied by a serious weakening of the idea of sin as moral failure which makes us both culpably responsible for our actions and answerable to the righteous provision of God's moral law. In such a context the message of Christ's saving death as the means of forgiveness for sin and moral failure easily fails to connect with contemporary self-awareness.

Faced with this fact, the preacher or evangelist can resort to using the word of the cross as a way of trying to inculcate a sense of guilt and shame which appears to be absent in the recipients of the message – particularly if the theology of atonement presupposed is one of penal substitution. The proclamation of the saving death of Christ, instead of being the occasion where we meet God's forgiveness and grace, becomes a dubious meditation upon the baleful reality of human guilt and sinfulness.

It is not often recognized how vulnerable such an approach is to the devastating critique of the cultivation of guilt-consciousness which was first directed towards the Christian religion by Friedrich Nietzsche (1887, Essay II). Nietzsche recoiled from what he regarded as the arid moralism and self-hatred of his pietistic upbringing. He consequently viewed a bad conscience as a mental disease (cf. Pannenberg 1985, 151; 1991, 65). In his view, Christianity fostered a masochistic obsession with guilt and sinfulness which hindered the recovery of genuine self-identity. Similar views were later put forward by Sigmund Freud (1918). He concluded that religion was an expression of mass neurosis stemming from guilt-consciousness. For both writers, the reality of a sense of guilt was an expression of self-alienation or self-aggression. The influence of both thinkers in some aspects of post-modernism and the dissemination of their ideas in contemporary consciousness should not be underestimated.

The Christian is under no obligation to accept the naive optimism that underlies this view of human nature. It cannot simply be presupposed that unbridled self-expression is synonymous with psychological health and well-being, while the repression of certain basic drives and instincts is not. On the other hand, like Paul we must attend carefully to the indigenous cultural values and aspirations that form our particular missionary context. The word of the cross will always relativize such 'worldly wisdom', but if the cross is indeed to be the criterion that judges all things, then this will also apply to our own apologetic presuppositions.

It is a further shortcoming that the juridical model restricts the meaning of sin to the notion of moral failure or transgression of the law. This is only one among a family of biblical ideas and motifs which together outline the nature of sin (cf. Chapter 3 above). Sin can equally well be understood in terms of infidelity and disloyalty to the God who loves us with an exclusivity that demands a similar response. Or in a manner that appears more applicable to our own culture it can be seen as the failure to adhere to our God-given destiny and vocation.

In the doctrinal tradition the classical exposition of the nature of sin was undertaken by Augustine in terms of concupiscence and pride. In both respects this describes humanity as turned in on itself and so unable to relate properly to the world around. In Chapter 9 Sally Alsford has noted how such a view has come under fire from feminist writers who argue that this is a particularly male concept of sin which does little to illuminate female experiences of estrangement. The same criticism could be levelled at the juristic metaphor, where the idea of sin as transgression of universal law refers to a form of self-assertion and titanism remote from 'feminine' sins of compliance and passivity. All this links with that plurality of religious experience and belief to which we have already alluded. In such a situation it seems unwise to rely on a metaphor fashioned in a wholly different context, though we need to uphold the basic insight of the juridical model, that moral anarchy requires divine atonement rather than human adjustment.

The Word of the Cross and Substitutionary Atonement

A similar situation obtains when we probe more deeply into what we mean by the representative function of Christ's death. His death can only be understood as vicarious if it is undertaken on our behalf. The recurrent phrase *huper hēmon*, recognized as belonging to the oldest of the New Testament traditions, conveys this sense of representation. Christ dies on our behalf, the just for the unjust, the righteous for the unrighteous; 'while we still were sinners Christ died for us' (Rom 5.8). The notion of representation is not restricted to the end of Jesus's earthly life; it is there also at the beginning. The one who becomes incarnate and assumes flesh does so on our behalf in order that he might redeem and liberate. Gregory Nazianzen's dictum which Christina Baxter has discussed in Chapter 8, that which Christ did not assume he did not redeem, presupposes the principle of representation. But it is in the word of the cross that the idea of representation is most sharply accentuated.

Christ's dying 'on our behalf' could mean his dying instead of us: he stands in for us as our replacement. His death is then understood in terms of substitution. In Anselm's thought the concept of substitution is understood in terms of moral reparation or compensation. The value of Christ's sinless life is sufficient to compensate for the accumulated weight of human sin and moral failure. With the Reformers, however, particularly

Calvin and Grotius, substitution is put within the context of criminal law. Christ bears the wrath and anger of God in our place and so is punished as our substitute. Calvin did not think of this punishment in a mechanical and impersonal sense, but he did believe that Scripture, particularly Isaiah 53, attests that the Son took upon himself the full severity of the Father's wrath. The punishment for sin that was our just deserve was transferred to the one without sin. This is the meaning of his being wounded for our transgressions. Penal substitution has remained one of the distinguishing markers of the evangelical tradition, even though it is often asserted that such a punitive notion of substitution is both morally repugnant and incomprehensible to our contemporaries. Critique of it has already been offered in these pages.

Stephen Travis has noted that the idea of retributive punishment is not at all central to the Pauline theology of atonement. While Paul does acknowledge that we are habitual lawbreakers and that our very nature is caught in sin, he does not understand the solution for our predicament in terms of the placating or propitiating of an injured Father by the sacrifice of the Son. 'To conceive Jesus as primarily the victim of divine punitive justice is to commit three sins: to treat one metaphor of atonement, the legal, in isolation from the others; to read that metaphor literally and merely personalistically; and to create a dualism between the action of God and that of Jesus' (Gunton 1988, 165).

Tom Smail has indicated how penal substitution is based on the notion of forensic imputation whereby sins and their consequences are transferred from us to Christ. It is precisely this notion of transference that takes us outside the realm of personal relationships to that of legal transaction. Is it not the case that sins are so identified with their perpetrators that they cannot simply be transferred from one person to another as if by legal fiat?

It would appear that the concept of substitution, while it belongs within a legal framework, is not best understood in a punitive sense. Rather it is the transformative grace of God that is here at work (see Gunton 1988, 166). Punishment is not inflicted on the Son by an injured Father. Rather, as a consequence of obedience the Son takes upon himself the results of our captivity to sin and evil. It is also the case that when substitution is understood in a punitive and exclusive sense, the act of atonement is so objectivized that it appears to be an event or transaction whereby we are simply removed from the scene. Christ becomes the sacrificial victim who is punished instead of us, the whipping-boy who appeases the wrath of God, or the exchange mechanism that balances the heavenly ledger. How are we involved in any of these so-called divine transactions?

Mindful of the difficulties that surround the concept of substitution, there are those who have sought to abandon it altogether in favour of the notion of representation. Dorothee Sölle (1967) asserts a concept of representation which implies both personality and temporality. In time and history, one person is capable of representing another. The historicity of Jesus points to his unique representative role. It is this particular life and death that is chosen to represent all previous and subsequent living and dying. This also implies universalization. Jesus the Messiah could not be confined to Judaism, as the first Christian martyr proclaimed to his cost; he could not be confined to a previous covenant, but creates a new one comprising people from every race, tribe and nation. To all this must be added the voluntary personal identification and association of the representative with those whom he represents. A second Adam to the fight and to the rescue came. As such he is able to represent us before God and God to us.

The question remains, are we to understand Christ the representative in the exclusive or inclusive sense? Albrecht Ritschl (1900) first developed this distinction, arguing that representation in the New Testament must be understood inclusively. Does the Saviour represent us in a way that includes us, holding our place open for us before the Father, or does his action on our behalf effectively displace us altogether? As Sölle points out, Karl Barth was a convinced exponent of the exclusivist position. He equates the terms substitution and representation through his use of the German term *Stellvertretung*, 'place-taking'. In order to act effectively on our behalf, Christ must effectively take our place. Barth employs this imagery in order to uphold the essential truth that we are not capable of acting on our own behalf, but in so doing we become displaced persons. Our place has been 'occupied' by another, who has 'relegated' us and moved us to another sphere.

According to Sölle, there is a philosophical distinction which can prise apart the concepts of representation and substitution.

> Representation regards man from the standpoint of time. It gains time for the man who is for the moment incapacitated. Substitution, on the contrary, is a spatial concept. In space, one thing can be replaced by another thing; in time, it is possible for one person to be represented by another person (1967, 91).

Whether or not Sölle's distinction can be maintained, in her case it serves a dubious theological purpose. Her final thesis is to argue that representation understood in the personal and temporal sense also entails provisionality. Jesus does not replace us because his representative function is only a temporary one. He may be the forerunner who goes ahead of us, but when we catch up with him through the acceptance of our own responsibility and discipleship in the world, he is no longer required. Then it is the church that becomes the new temporary representative.

It is theologically more appropriate to maintain that representation and substitution are interchangeable concepts, provided that both are understood in the inclusive or participationist sense. Christ is our substitute because he accomplishes what we cannot do by or for ourselves. In that atoning action, however, he does not replace us. Rather he brings us with him, because as God incarnate he is also our representative. He goes where we cannot go (because it would be our destruction) and the judgement that he endures is both instead of us and for us, so that we might be transformed into his likeness. It is clear that Paul was able to think of Christ both as our representative and our substitute (cf. 2 Cor 5.14–15, 21).

> Jesus is both our representative and, if it is desired to retain the word, our substitute in the sense that He stands as the living

233

symbol of the God who empties Himself in love even to the point of crucifixion, and who takes to Himself and embodies in the person of His Son the creation for which He is responsible and which He wills to restore to unity in His own image and likeness (Moses 1992, 119–20).

Moses's hesitation over the concept of substitution alerts us once again to the issue of cultural insensitivity. If substitution suggests that persons can be displaced, replaced, or simply pushed aside for the sake of some divine transaction, then it easily makes connections with similar depersonalizing elements that form part of people's experience of Western technocratic culture.

In a world where 33 million people are refugees, displacement is a prevalent phenomenon. Countless suffer displacement through inadequate social, financial, and material provision, while others become 'displaced persons' through political and social expediency and injustice. Personal vocation and achievement are replaced by new technology, which together with complicated bureaucratic procedures, tend to depersonalize, alienate, and turn persons into expendable commodities. The search for self-identity often leads to nihilism and atheistic acceptance of the belief that we are alone in the 'unfeeling immensity of the universe' (Monod 1972, 167). In such a situation we must beware a theology of atonement which reduces the event of the cross to another bureaucratic procedure, creating a further sense of displacement and insignificance.

How does the cross delineate the issue of our sinfulness? Does it reveal persons who are incapacitated before God, weak, enfeebled, and in need of rescue, or does it point to persons so corrupt and despoiled that they must simply be pushed aside? In just such a context we must surely maintain the conviction that Jesus's death is in fact inclusive of all people. He holds our place open for us, enabling us to make our own personal response to his self-giving on our behalf. He takes us with him down into death so that we may be raised to new life with him.

The Word of the Cross and the Wrath of God

The difficulties we have encountered in regard to the intelligibility of the concept of substitution would appear to pale into insignificance when we turn our attention to another closely related topic. What sense can we make of the notion that the death of Christ propitiates or appeases the wrath of God? This also forms part of our Reformation inheritance. The Reformers interpreted the Pauline references to the wrath of God as the manner in which God's judgement is directed against the affront of sin and evil. Luther, utilizing patristic imagery, viewed the cross as a kind of extraordinary battle, the place where a dramatic conflict takes place between the executants of God's wrath, the law, death, and Satan, and the Son who experiences the full fury of their combined assault. In the end love triumphs over the agents of wrath. As we have noted already, for Calvin penal substitution is the way in which the wrath of God is propitiated or turned away from the sinner. New Testament scholarship from C. H. Dodd to J. D. G. Dunn has protested that Paul did not conceive of the divine wrath in a retributive sense. Rather it is a matter of God allowing us to experience the consequences of our captivity to sin and alienation from him. God did not punish but 'gave them over' to experience the consequences of degradation, disunity and distrust. When God cannot woo us with 'the wine of divine love' he leaves us to 'the vinegar of his wrath' (Robinson 1979, 19). The wrath of God is not his personal response to sin and evil but the way in which individuals and nations reap the harvest of their own wrongdoing.

In more recent systematic theology the notion of the wrath of God has all but disappeared, to be replaced by the supposedly more morally acceptable view that the death of Jesus expresses the suffering identification of God with the oppressed and the God-forsaken. In a century which more than any other has experienced the continual trauma of mass death, the theology of the pathos of God developed by writers such as Abraham Heschel, Kazoh Kitamori and Jürgen Moltmann is to be welcomed. Where such concerns for theodicy effectively replace the traditional concerns of atonement theology, however, then we are witnessing another example of cultural accommodation.

The wrath of God speaks to us not just of a handing over to the bitter consequences of our actions, but of divinely imposed limits to human autonomy and domination. The judgement of God is felt most keenly wherever human beings overstep these limits and bring catastrophe upon themselves. It is precisely the nuclear and ecological crisis of the present era that directs us to the limits of technological control and expansion. We were asked to be stewards of God's good creation and have become instead technocratic abusers, endangering the very stability and future of our natural habitat.

Once we have removed the retributive framework in which the notion of the wrath of God has been housed, the atoning death of Christ does not need to be understood as an appeasement of God's anger and hostility toward sin. However, the wrath of God does have to do with the maintaining of justice amongst the orders of creation. We require systems of justice which protect the rights of peoples and nations and of other species from those who seek to dominate, oppress, and control. Inevitably that directs our attention to limits that are there to guarantee the future of creation and preserve the sanctity of life itself. If the death of Christ was indeed the objective, actual, reconciliation of the whole created order to God, then the Son suffered the effects of violated justice. As Paul reminds us, the whole creation was thrown into confusion and estrangement through the misuse of human freedom, the consequences of which Christ endured so that the restoration of unity and harmony would express the redemption he has secured for the children of God (cf. Rom 8.18–25).

Atonement and Eschatology

We have investigated three integrally related areas of atonement theology which require careful explication in the light of our contemporary cultural context. We have also noted how any attempt to contextualize the word of the cross runs the risk of cultural insensitivity or accommodation. All the metaphors of atonement were framed and deployed in particular historical contexts and some do not translate easily from one culture to another. That does not necessarily mean that they become redundant, but it does demonstrate the need for versatility and the ability to find a framework of discourse which combines metaphors in such a way that we gain new insight into the meaning of atonement. The substitutionary-sacrificial framework of reference has been well tried and tested, but insufficient attention has been paid to the eschatological dimensions that form the backdrop to the New Testament theology of atonement.

Theologies of atonement often break apart the eschatological unity of cross and resurrection. Paul understands the cross and resurrection of Christ to be the anticipation of eschatological judgement, reconciliation, and fulfilment. Here a number of metaphors are combined to delineate cross and resurrection as the division between the old creation and the new. For the benefit of the Corinthians he claims that the word of the cross is a message of foolishness to those caught up in the vicissitudes of a world which is perishing, but to those who know already the reality of the age to come, it is the power and wisdom of God. The best framework for understanding the cross might then be not universal moral law or retributive justice, but eschatological crisis, judgement and transformation. Paul argues in Romans and Galatians that the law is superseded by the gospel of God's righteousness which is both judgement and justifying grace. The cross of Christ shows us why we live in a world which is perishing, which cannot endure and is caught in the futility of sin, evil, death, suffering and decay. It is a world upon which God has passed judgement, a world in the process of being brought to an end. The cross is the means by which simultaneously judgement is passed and salvation offered to all people regardless of ethnic affiliation and nationality (John 12.30–1). Similarly, the adversarial role of the Holy Spirit is to convince the world that judgement has already taken place (John 16.8–11). It is because of this that Christian existence is defined in terms of imminent expectation. 'The end of all things is near' (1 Pet 4.7); 'the present form of this world is passing away' (1 Cor 7.31). Moltmann has contextualized this eschatological horizon in terms of our modern experience of reality:

Today, the expectation of the impending end is realistic, compared with this modern time myth. Hiroshima 1945 fundamentally changed the quality of human history. Our time has become time with a time limit. . . . Humanity is now engaged in the struggle for survival between the end-time and the end of time (1990, 159).

In such a situation, it is also clear that the significance of Jesus's death must be conceived in broader terms than the juridical metaphor often allows. Judgement is passed on the collective expressions of socio-political injustice, oppression and sinfulness. We have to accept responsibility for the world we create, a world that opposes the saving purposes of God and is therefore always in a state of perishing or passing away. But into just such a world has come the reality of cross and resurrection, the source of redemptive power and recreation. To be in Christ is to be already participating in the reality of that which is to come. Consequently it is Christ's atoning death and resurrection which provides the impulse for missionary proclamation and service. It is precisely this wider context of corporate sin and injustice which many of our contemporaries do understand and so they need to hear that into our world have come new impulses for the shaping of public, social and political life (cf. Moltmann 1967, 324).

The task of evangelism is to proclaim judgement, reconciliation, and transformation. It is to explain why the world is perishing and why we consequently suffer from the accumulated effects of corporate sin and guilt. It is also to proclaim the forgiveness of sins, the reality of the new birth, and the hope of re-creation.

The retrieval of this eschatological context also unites the metaphors of representation and substitution. 'God was pleased' to have all his fullness dwell 'in him . . . and through him . . . to reconcile to himself all things, whether on earth or in heaven, by making peace through the blood of his cross' (Col 1.19–20). Christ is the new Adam, the eschatological fulfilment of human life and personal identity. His death for us and on behalf of us was not a past metaphysical transaction nor a divine legal fiat but an eschatological accomplishment. Jesus's death anticipates the universal death of a perishing creation and so Jesus is able to keep our place open for us. Our own personal existence and worth are not nullified but maintained. He does not brush us aside and replace us, but becomes instead our representative who continues to intercede for us at the Father's right hand. The word of the cross that comes to us in the power of the Spirit invites us to participate in his death and resurrection. 'It is the function of God the Spirit, the Lord and giver of life, to particularize the universal redemption in anticipation of the eschatological redemption' (Gunton 1988, 170).

Finally, the eschatological consummation of the created orders forms another context in which the wrath of God can be understood. Frances Young argues that the phrase refers to 'the eschatological woes, the great cataclysm of agony, destruction and disaster which had begun to afflict the creation' (1982, 70). In that sense it describes for us the birth-pangs of the new creation which Jesus's death and resurrection has ushered in. The crucified and resurrected Saviour is the one through whom the whole created order will be restored to unity of purpose and in whom the destiny of creation is secure. In the interim period, however, 'there is a purgatory of judgement through which the creation must pass before the final destiny of participation in God's glory can be realised' (Moses 1992, 164).

It would seem as if this eschatological framework of meaning, which declares final judgement and transformation, is better able to negotiate the difficulties in atonement theology which we have considered. It is also able to communicate the meaning of the cross to our contemporaries in a way that avoids the twin errors of cultural insensitivity or accommodation. The gift of salvation is both contained within and conveyed by the procla-mation of the gospel. It is the forgiveness of sins, the overcoming and neutralising of the powers of sin and evil, the offer of fellow-ship with God and one another, and the promise of the final redemption of human existence in the glory of the coming king-dom of God.

14

Illusions of Guilt and Innocence

GORDON OLIVER

THERE IS A vast literature on psychotherapy and counselling;
a good reader surveying both the general and the Christian
material is Michael Jacobs's *Fear to Faith*. Much of the secular
literature has something of an evangelistic feel to it. We find
there more than a suggestion of discoveries about the means of
salvation from our troubles. The most popular works are the
least theoretical and the most concerned with offering methods
of understanding the relationship between therapist and client.
Although many of them address the issue of guilt, it is very
often with the assumption that guilt is a pathological notion
which is to be resolved by 'insight'. Conflicts of values are part
of the everyday reality of the therapeutic relationship. The aim
is to enable the client to become free in relation to the values
they live out in their daily experience – in other words, to allow
the client's implicit values to become explicit and to be owned by
becoming freely chosen values instead of inherited, supposed,
or imposed values. This 'taking of adult responsibility' is the
successful outcome of the growth out of immaturity or other
restrictive inhibitions.

Transcendence as a concept in therapy (rare under this name)
would be seen as the client gathering strength as their self-
identity is renewed in order to be free to transcend formerly
restrictive boundaries of being, living, and acting. The radical
discontinuity that Christians call sin tends to be absent or to be
used as a focus for exploring restrictive illusions.

The Christian-based literature on counselling, if we exclude
that produced in circles such as the Crusade for World Revival
which has closer affinities to some forms of spiritual direction
than to counselling in the generally accepted sense, is little

different from the secular literature upon which it draws heavily and often uncritically. The SPCK 'New Library of Pastoral Care' provides some of the better examples, sensitive to issues of faith and values, but not offering an exposition or critique at the level of presuppositions; for instance, the client-centred therapy approach is frequently simply taken as a 'given'. Within the popular Christian literature on counselling, Gary R. Collins's *Christian Counselling* is an exception; it gives a clear account of its confessional basis (1985, 13–56). Otherwise in Christian and secular works the notions of personal freedom, responsibility, and transcendence are broadly similar. The nature and effects of sin (except the effects of being a victim of the sin of others) are rarely addressed.

There is also evidence in the field of spirituality and spiritual direction that, while the tangible experience of guilt is widespread and often deep, the notion of sin is found to be confusing, and the part which confession of sin plays in the lives of individual Christians is distorted in the direction of virtual absence or (less commonly) virtual obsession. (The relationship between therapy, confession, and spiritual direction is very helpfully discussed by Kenneth Leech in *Soul Friend*, ch. 3.)

If these generalizations bear some approximation to some realities, it is hardly surprising that there also appears to be a sense of confusion about the significance of the cross of Jesus. In Chapter 5 above, Tom Smail has commented that the cross is seen in terms of God's identification with the suffering of people, but that its relationship to sin and to the consciousness of guilt is harder to conceive. After all, if the key human problem is suffering and alienation, then the models of atonement that are lived out in a church fellowship and interpreted in its preaching are likely to be dominantly relational rather than forensic or structural-analytical. And there is surely something right about that.

In seeking for a model to reflect on the notions of guilt and innocence in relation to the atonement, I have chosen the experience of illusion.

Invitations to Live with Illusions

Genesis begins with the manifesto statement that God's call is to live with reality that is relational rather than with the illusion of isolation (Gen 1—3). If the origin or editing of the creation narratives is located within an exilic or post-exilic context, it serves as a clarion call to face up to the reality of the political, ecological, and human world as the sphere of God's freedom and of God's call to freedom for God's people. Over against this call, the invitation of the serpent in Genesis 3 is first the invitation to humanity to live instead with the illusions of parity with God (verse 5). When that fails, the invitation is to live in longing for but independence of God with all its consequences. Reality is relational when it is sustained and energized by relationship with the Ultimate Reality, but apart from that sustaining, it degenerates into life lived within illusion.

The Bible contains a whole series of dominant models of this kind of illusion. Examples of such illusions are:

- that covenant without loyalty is a viable proposition (cf. Jer 7.4–10; Hos 6.1–7)
- that law without love can truly be characterized as Torah (cf. Matt 23.23–38, with the comments in Ricoeur 1967, 118–39, on the vocation of the Pharisees in relation to Torah)
- that faith without works constitutes authentic discipleship (cf. Jas 2.14–17)
- that discipleship without mission reflects the vocation of God's people (cf. Isa 42.5–9)
- that (in a sort of backward-looking eschatology) God's time and God's action are confined to the past (cf. John 8.39–42, 56–9)
- that you can be a sinner without being affected by the power of sin (cf. Rom 6.1–4, 11–14).

All these illusions may be reflected on as ways of dealing with guilt and innocence – or (in other words) as ways of trying to come to terms with issues of identity and relationship; I shall return to this theme. The common ground of the various scriptural genres (wisdom, prophecy, torah, apocalypse, epistle, gospel) is that they all represent the call to live a life set free from the Adamic illusion, to see things as they are, to live lives of reality that are rooted in relationship with the Ultimate Reality.

Stated in the stark terms I have used, the illusory nature of those illusions is obvious – insofar as we manage to persuade ourselves that illusions are other people's wrong thinking, whilst ourselves being under the illusion that we have no such illusions. Even if we cannot describe in rational detail what an illusion is – after all, illusions are somewhat illusory – we need to get at least this clear: an illusion is not first a wrong idea arising from incorrect reflection. An illusion is an alternative kind of reality. An illusion is not first something that we think ('thought' comes later). An illusion is something that we live within. As one might say, it is something that thinks us. For as we live within an illusion we begin to take on its life. We live our life under the permission of its conditions of existence. We live within its life context, its life purpose, its life structures – in fact within its very citizenship. Describing an illusion as an alternative reality if anything understates the case. To live within an illusion is to take on the citizenship of its country with all the conflicts and hopes that are part of its landscape and with the difficulties it has with foreign relations, particularly those over the border with the country of Ultimate Reality, who insists on continually calling out in love.

In everyday life children and adults use illusion as a form of playing. Peek a boo! Bang! You're dead! I'll get up now – it's time to play something else. The writers on play and clowning tell us that these are oblique means of reflecting behaviourally upon the relationship between actual experience, fantasized experience, and hoped-for experience (see the creative early treatment of this theme in Saward 1961). Healthy people move freely between the different kinds of experience. The establishing of this emotional facility is crucial to healthy development in persons and in communities (in relation to paths of personal development and its effects on the possibility and the nature of personal faith, see Fowler 1981; in relation to the importance of play in the development of the life of communities, in this case explored as 'ritual', see Turner 1974). Being adults involves becoming persuaded that we can move freely between the instinctive and the elective modes of the 'play' of illusion and the rest of life. For many practical purposes this is true.

But that very freedom of movement also enables us to develop a kind of blindness in relation to the major theological illusions I listed earlier, within which God's people have sought and still seek to live. In particular, the blindness is toward the structure and purpose of the illusions. The very viability of the illusion as a context for living depends on its remaining unrecognized and unexplored. It has to remain illusory.

In pastoral practice the failure to recognize the structure and purpose of the illusions (we might call them hobby-horses, hang-ups, defences or whatever) which sustain people's lives and very character, at the same time as sustaining their problems, can lead to the extremely dangerous perspective that sees Christian ministry as all about the breaking of false images, the shattering of illusions.

If, as I have tried to suggest, an illusion is something to live within, then it is in some literal sense a life-sustaining structure. It is capable of containing – at least up to a point – hope, fear, conflict, love, and of course personal and group identity. If this is so, then to set out to break or shatter that illusion without providing a route via exodus through desert to a new land, is to commit a most terrible crime. To take away the illusion by force leaves the group or person homeless, hopeless, incapable equally of engaging in conflict or in creativity, deprived of the very structures that give vitality and purpose to identity. To take away the illusions that sustain a group or person is to break into pieces the symbols that connect them to their imagined, internalized, perhaps inarticulated past. Such symbols are among the most basic components which enable orientation in the present on the basis of a negotiation with the past, and which offer at least some sense of future, however limited. To take them away is literally to condemn people to utter aloneness, to death in the sense of annihilation of any possibility of relationship with God. All that remains is what F. J. Hoffman (1959,

151) called 'the naked fact of an isolated self', but without the possibility that as they hide their nakedness in the bushes, someone will come seeking and asking 'Where are you?' It is to condemn them to hell.

In this hell there is recognition. Some things become clear:

- Covenant without loyalty is revealed as romantic historical fiction
- Torah without love is revealed as yesterday's bread incapable of giving liberating energy today
- Faith without works is revealed as empty piety whistling in the dark
- Discipleship without mission is revealed as institutionalized religious selfishness
- Time is revealed as a sealed train leading to a dead end
- Being a sinner without being affected by sin is revealed as the phony self-righteousness it is, the only kind of righteousness we can finally have in a world of illusion.

Two diagrams may serve to illustrate the hopefulness and hopelessness of illusions of guilt, innocence, and identity.

Isolation from Ultimate Reality as the Actuality of Illusion

Diagrams A and B are rather simple, even simplistic diagrams, but they describe effectively the paradox of life within the illusion as bipolarly hopeful and hellish (I suspect that illusions are inherently dualistic). It needs to be recognized, however, that whilst the poles mark extremes, the majority experience will be somewhere between them.

We need to ask where the idea of guilt fits into this picture. Guilt is a very slippery and elusive term to define, but we can say some things about it. First, guilt is about being accused of doing or not doing something or of being or not being something.

People can be guilty without feeling guilty.
People can feel guilty without being guilty.

DIAGRAM A

Hope as the Fulfilment of Illusion

When conditions of worth function 'well' they are life- and status-sustaining, albeit what they sustain is an illusion which is soon to come under judgement (Gen 11.1–9).

Conditions of worth become the means of perceiving the world and God. They also become the conditions under which relationship with others and with God is willed, chosen, and enacted.

Conditions of worth have a tendency to become absolutized. Then they take on the character and oppressive functions of principalities and powers.

People can be treated as guilty without being personally guilty (for instance, when treated in a racist way).
People can experience ontological guilt, guilt for being alive as who they are.

Second, the reality and experience of imputed or owned guilt causes people to be pushed to the edge or beyond the edge of something:

DIAGRAM B
Isolation from Ultimate Reality as the Actuality of Illusion

Removal by force of conditions of worth is life-threatening

Conditions of worth are the boundaries of perceptions and identity that protect the isolated self with power from invasion.

The unconditional love of God comes into contact with conditions of worth at the cross and invites but does not coerce the responses that lead out of illusion toward Reality.

---

to the edge or out of a social group,
to the edge or outside of a dominant culture,
to the edge or out of one's mind,
to the edge or out of one's life,
to the edge or out of participation in society (in it but not of it),
to the edge or out of any sense of righteousness, or
to the edge or out of fellowship with God.

It is vitally important to notice that guilt can have very positive and enabling effects as well as negative or disabling ones. Just as some pastoral carers have the knee-jerk reaction to another's pain that it must be taken away without proper attention being paid to its cause, many of us in counselling have the knee-jerk response that guilt must be inappropriate and should be disposed of as soon as possible. Positively, however, the experience of guilt can be very creative, especially if it is used as a basis for reflecting on the relationship between illusory reality and Ultimate Reality. For the presence of guilt may be a clear and pressing sign that the world of illusion is under strain, and that the possibility of serious engagement with Ultimate Reality is very near, whether by repentance, confession, or some other means. Crucial to this idea is the conviction that confession is primarily about identity (the primary Christian confession is 'Jesus is Lord') and only secondarily about wrong actions. As the experience of guilt pushes us to the edge of illusion, it may bring us near to the embrace of recognition, belonging, and vocation toward God's future.

But this does not come about without someone somewhere undertaking a huge engagement in pain and cost.

Atonement, Acceptance and Guilt

In *Atonement and Psychotherapy* the American pastoral theologian Don Browning gives a useful analysis of the relationship between these two, and engages in sustained reflection on the way the psychotherapeutic relationship may be used analogically to explore affective aspects of the atonement. His aim is to evaluate which of the traditional great models of the atonement may come closest to sharing the dynamics and aims of the psychotherapeutic relationship. To do this he evaluates a number of therapies and selects as representative the Rogerian client-centred therapy, probably the most most influential in Christian circles, whether liberal or evangelical.

In this model the psychotherapeutic relationship depends for its success as a health-promoting environment on the client's conditions of worth coming face to face with the therapist's unconditional empathic acceptance. The therapist's unconditional empathic acceptance is seen as an analogy of God's totally unconditioned empathic acceptance. I will outline here some of Browning's main reflections on therapy and atonement.

The therapist must be willing to be the 'further end' of the client's negative feelings, as well as all other feelings. This means that the therapist must allow his own feeling processes to be qualified by the client's hostility, just as he would receive all the client's other feelings.

> The eminent instance of unconditioned empathic acceptance is precisely that structure which is *unqualified* (absolute) in its capacity to be qualified (relative) by the feelings of another – even [especially] the other's most negative and hostile ones. Since empathy is perfect and absolute in God, he truly feels, in the depths of his own being, all hostile and negative feelings expressed toward his acceptance. . . . It is because his acceptance endures unqualified *even though* he fully understands (fully feels) our hostility that we are 'persuaded' to come to trust him – that he may be trusted with my conditions of worth because in him there are no conditions of worth (1964, 203, 204).

For Browning the symbols of the cross and resurrection take on special meaning within the structure of God's characteristic of unconditioned empathic acceptance. He intends his use of the word 'symbols' to be understood as implying that cross and resurrection refer to something essential to the nature of God. Browning seeks to interpret the cross in the light of God's empathic acceptance of our most negative feelings. The ultimate objective of sin's hostility is to sustain the illusion by negating empathic acceptance as a threat to (sin's) conditions of worth. Browning sees the idolatries that arise from the absolutizing of human conditions of worth as equivalent to the Bible's 'principalities and powers' (Eph 6.12) in their nature and oppressive ways of functioning (1964, 182–5).

The logical and inevitable end of the confrontation between one offering empathic acceptance and sin's conditions of worth – its idolatries – is the death of the one offering the relationship. Because the illusion is life-sustaining it will fight to the death to sustain its 'reality'. The cross of Jesus Christ, then, expresses God's capacity and unassailable will to feel fully the depths of sin's hostility – to feel fully within himself its intention to negate him; and the resurrection is the declaration in Jesus Christ of God's capacity not to be qualified or conditioned (contained) by the onslaught of sin's feelings. 'The resurrection points to the *absoluteness* of God's relativity, i.e. of God's empathic feeling. The cross points to the *relativity* of God's absoluteness. . . . [This] is the very structure of love. . . . It is in this never-ending relationship that God lives *justification* into the world' (Browning 1964, 205).

> It is God's cross-resurrection activity that overcomes the supra-individual structures of bondage (principalities and powers) which intersect, support, and form a continuity with the self's conditions of worth. . . . God helps the self to come to learn that there are no conditions prerequisite to God's justifying love. . . . God makes [the self's] hostile defense useless by *accepting* it. . . . As [the principalities and powers] begin to lose their grip, the energy that supports man's conditions of worth is 'released' and made available once again to the more fundamental fulfillment of man's basic nature

in life outside of the illusion.

> What appeared as God's *creative* caring and fellowship with the world before the fall now appears as God's *graceful* [*sic* – and life-sustaining] caring and fellowship. . . . Grace is in no way a *contingent* element in the nature of God. Grace is God's creative feeling of our feeling *enduring* as absolute and unconditioned even after the fall. This also gives us our ultimate clue about the nature of forgiveness (Browning 1964, 205–7).

Browning sees forgiveness as the continuation of God's uncon-ditioned empathic acceptance in spite of man's rejection of it. 'Forgiveness is the nature of grace. It is continuous with God's creative fellowship. Yet it is this same forgiveness and grace that constitutes God's *judgment* in its primary sense.' Since God's love is unconditional empathic acceptance, the very absence of conditions contradicts and judges sin's conditions of worth. 'It is this same forgiveness and grace that constitutes the primary sense in which the world is measured and found wanting' (1964, 207). If this process is characteristic of God's relationship to the world, why should there be a need for a special event of God in Jesus Christ? Browning argues that the psychotherapeutic analogy generates a principle that points to the necessity of God's special act in Jesus, and he finds the linkage by meditating on the incarnation of Jesus Christ as reflecting God's eternal and essential character. The primordial character of God, the incarnation of Jesus, and the death and resurrection of Jesus, are all essentially manifestations of one nature as fellowship in community and in mission. Conditions of worth are taken over from within a social environment. To be unlearned, they need to be unlearned with reference to someone within our social environment. The sinner 'cannot be freed from his conditions of worth until someone emerges *in the world*, emerges at the place where he is looking, who places no conditions on his acceptance' (and total commitment to his liberation) (Browning 1964, 209).

Models and Metaphors

Although Browning reflects on other models of the atonement, and shows considerable respect for a particular version of the moral influence model (Bushnell 1866), his preference for the *Christus Victor* model (Aulén 1931) becomes clear, without becoming dogmatized. It seems to me that part of the genius of the New Testament is that it offers us symbols of the atonement without offering us a detailed and definitive exposition of them. This opens up the possibilities for well-grounded thoroughly contemporary reflection; indeed they are not only open to us but incumbent upon us. As Tom Smail said in introducing the lecture which appears as Chapter 5 above, 'We cannot understand the atonement, but we owe it our minds.'

The great historical models that have emerged within the context of the struggles for coherent soteriology, Christology, community, and mission, all have the status of primary symbols. That is to say that they all invite serious engagement with the reality of the human situation in relation to God, calling forth decisive allegiance, whilst simultaneously refusing the tyrannous demand of the choice of one (often misrepresented) model against others. It is of the character of symbols that they hold together openness and hiddenness – like 'Yahweh', the name of God. Symbols can and often must be interpreted, but we cannot and must not pretend finally to interpret symbols of God. To do so would be to deify the symbol and thus reduce it to a mere sign by restricting it to participation in the world of illusion – to impute conditions of worth to the Unconditioned One.

Indeed, perhaps the only possible choice is to choose them all, and then to move reverently but hard-headedly among them with the conviction that in the historical, incarnate, crucified and risen Jesus Christ the great realities of the atonement are indeed wrought. Here the unconditioned love of God and the conditions of worth (the idolatries of illusion) are confronted as here – in the place of God's own suffering – 'righteousness and peace embrace each other'.

The atonement constitutes the event, the possibility and the call to live outside of the idolatrous illusions of the world and toward the ultimate reality of God in the world and for the world. Discerning by the grace of the Holy Spirit the difference between illusion and God's reality is one of the key issues in Christian discipleship, as we look for and long for the moment when 'we will know fully, even as we have been fully known' (cf. I Cor 13.12).

15

What Difference Does the Cross Make to Life?

DAVID ATKINSON

WHEN THE NEW TESTAMENT refers to the difference the cross makes to our life and our living, the cross is (almost always, I think) bracketed with the resurrection. I believe we need to think of the way the cross impinges on life as part of the way our human stories engage with, or are caught up into, the whole of the broader story of Jesus's birth, life, suffering, death, burial, resurrection, ascension and parousia (see Calvin, *Institutes* II.16.19). What difference does the story of Jesus, especially his death and resurrection, make to our human stories – to my human story?

I Judgement and Death as Part of our Story

When the New Testament indicates that the new humanity is seen in Jesus, it presents this as the fulfilment of God's promise of blessing to Abraham, and therefore as God's ultimate reply to the curses and judgements of Genesis I — II. In Christ, there is a renewed creation (cf. 2 Cor 5.17). The kingdom of God is 'creation healed'. The Genesis story displays the ambiguity of this world. Some strands proclaim 'this is good'. Others speak of God's curses and judgements in response to the world's disorders. Particularly in Genesis 3, these disorders are depicted in terms of the desire for self-advancement and a lack of trust in God's word, instead of the desire for growth in the knowledge of God on the basis of obedience. The result, in the stories of Adam, Cain, Lamech, Babel, is a context of mistrust in place of trust; of shame in place of openness in relationships; of guilt in place of responsibility; of conflict in place of communion.

All relationships – between people and God, people and each other, people and their environment, people within themselves – become estranged. Complementarity of the sexes becomes subordination; work becomes toil; mutuality and fellowship become banishment and alienation (cf. Atkinson 1990). This is the anatomy of disorder, which can most broadly be described as the 'rule of death'. Instead of growth, delight, creativity, freedom, and fellowship, human life is marked also by the anxiety of mistrust, the frustration of shame, the bondage of guilt, the loneliness and bitterness of conflict.

It is fascinating how Erik Erikson's psychosocial approach to human development picks up many of these themes. In his chapter on 'Eight ages of man' (1977) he suggests that the processes of human development usually include critical phases in which the growing person has to deal with various tensions in their personal and interpersonal lives. The most basic question for the baby is whether the external world is ultimately trustworthy or not. As the baby grows, will its life be marked by autonomy or shame, by initiative or guilt, by industry or inferiority? Will the adolescent's life be noted for a sense of identity or one of confusion – will a person be able to offer intimacy in relationships, or be isolated in loneliness? Will adult life be one of creativity and integrity, or of stagnation and despair?

Whereas Erikson is seeking to describe a process of psychosocial maturation, the struggle with ambiguity at each point involves mistrust, shame, guilt, inferiority, confusion, isolation, stagnation and despair. Here is a developmental psychologist describing the dark side of our nature, the 'rule of death'.

Ernest Becker (1973) sees the rule of death in other ways, notably in our persistent human denial of it. He argues that our 'innate and all-encompassing fear of death' drives us to 'attempt to transcend death' through various cultural symbols and practices. 'A "no!" to death is profoundly rooted in the very being of man' (Berger 1971, 81). That No! is surely also the motivation for Dylan Thomas's angry poem in the face of the death of his father:

> Do not go gentle into that good night . . .
> Rage, rage against the dying of the light.

The sense of disorder is also powerfully explored in *King Lear* (I.2):

> These late eclipses of the sun and moon portend no good to us: though the wisdom of nature can reason it thus and thus, yet nature finds itself scourg'd by the sequent effects: love cools, friendship falls off, brothers divide: in cities, mutinies; in countries, discord; in palaces, treason; and the bond crack'd 'twixt son and father. . . . We have seen the best of our time: machinations, hollowness, treachery, and all ruinous disorders, follow us disquietly to our graves.

Psychologist, sociologist, and poet are all profoundly disturbed by the negative, disordered, destructive dimensions of the 'rule of death' in life, and yet hold out a hope that life must be more than this.

It is at this point that Leon Morris's book *The Cross of Jesus* rings true. He argues that the atonement is vaster and deeper than many of the traditional theories suggest, and that some of the aspects of the cross to which the New Testament points have not received the attention they deserve. The cross is God's response to the human experience of futility, ignorance, loneliness, sickness, selfishness and death. This provides a language of atonement for today. Whereas some patristic authors understood the cross mostly in terms of slavery and ransom, whereas Anselm opens us to the feudal categories in which sin is understood as dishonour, and Calvin uses his legal mind to focus mostly on guilt and acquittal, and whereas Aulén's *Christus Victor* could catch the headlines in 1930s Europe with its return to the military categories of conquest, today we need to hear more about sin in the terms we drew from the Genesis prologue. Mistrust, alienation, shame, guilt, conflict, and disorder are some of the primary effects of sin depicted in Genesis 1—11. 'Alienation', in particular, speaks of a deep force which seems to pull us all away from our centre in God. This is part, I think, of what Simone Weil (1952) means by 'gravity' (and cf. Dillistone 1968; Fiddes 1989).

2 Jesus Becomes Subject to the Rule of Death, and Overpowers It

One of the key features of Jesus's life is his identification with the poor, the outcast, those who are under threat. His application to himself of the Isaianic prophecy concerning good news for the poor, release for the captives, recovery of sight to the blind, and the setting at liberty of those who are oppressed (Luke 4), is paralleled by his being known to be on the side of outcasts and sinners, and eating with them (Luke 15.2). The healing ministry of Jesus, particularly when seen in the light of the Old Testament laws concerning uncleanness, is also an expression of his bringing life into the rule of death. Wenham (1982, 115–16) understands the uncleanness laws in terms of a fundamental antithesis between life and death. Certain impure conditions, such as diseases like leprosy, certain bodily discharges, and touching a dead body, are polluting because they symbolize the impurity of the whole people of God. Jesus, by touching the leper, by healing the woman with a discharge of blood, by holding the hand of the dead, is declaring that the antithesis of life and death is bridged. God is a God of life, normality and health. Jesus's healings demonstrate God's infusion of life into the rule of death.

This process is seen at its fullest in Jesus's own taking on himself the rule of death, and yet being raised to life again. In the Gospel narrative of the passion, trial, and crucifixion of Jesus, we see a man betrayed – his whole environment was untrustworthy. Even his closest friends forsook him and fled. We see a man naked and exposed to mockery and shame. We see a man dying alone. We see the agony of uncertainty in the Garden, and the agony of separation from the fellowship of his Father in the cry of dereliction: 'My God, why have you forsaken me?' Such a death is the death of one who is cursed by God (Gal 3.13; Deut 21.23). Paul sums up the whole experience for us in the remarkable phrase 'God made him to be sin, who knew no sin' (2 Cor 5.21). Jesus experienced in his passion, trial, suffering and crucifixion all the effects of the rule of death in human life: mistrust, alienation and frustration, shame, guilt, conflict, confusion, loneliness, and despair. His death is the summation of the rule of death. 'A sight most pitiful in the meanest wretch, past speaking of in a king!' (*King Lear* IV.6).

And then in his resurrection we see what we might call the death of the rule of death. Jesus 'let himself be swallowed by death, as it were, not to be engulfed in its abyss, but rather to engulf it' (Calvin, *Institutes* II.16.7).

Jesus's death and resurrection are the means by which the rule of death in this world is broken. He takes on death, dies its death, and yet is raised to new life. He partook of our nature 'that through death he might destroy him who has the power of death, that is the devil, and deliver all those who through fear of death were subject to lifelong bondage' (Heb 2.14 RSV). God's deliverance is made possible through the combined power of Jesus's death and resurrection. Without the resurrection, any talk of the power of Jesus's death is incomplete. The purpose of the Lord's dying, and of all dying in him was 'that He might turn again to incorruption men who had turned back to corruption, and make them alive through death by the appropriation of His body and by the grace of His resurrection' (Athanasius, *The Incarnation* 8).

Since only weakness appears in the cross, death, and burial of Christ, faith must leap over all these things to attain its full strength. We have in his death the complete fulfillment of salvation, for through it we are reconciled to God, his righteous judgment is satisfied, the curse is removed, and the penalty paid in full. Nevertheless we are said to 'have been born anew to a living hope' not through his death but 'through his resurrection' [1 Peter 1:3p.]. . . . 'He was put to death for our sins, and raised for our justification' [Rom. 4:25]. . . . Sin was taken away by his death; righteousness was revived and restored by his resurrection (Calvin, *Institutes* II.16.13).

257

The ambiguity, suffering and struggle of which psychologists and poets speak can also be understood as the labour pains of God – to bring forth a new people, restoration, new life, new hope (cf. Rom 8.22–3). Frances Young links this to teaching about hope in the New Testament, with its two aspects. 'The first is its acceptance that the present state of the world is far from satisfactory. The second is confidence that nevertheless it is all under God, and God's purposes will be worked out. Atonement is to do with making that hope credible' (1982, 54).

The Bible emphasizes that the motivation behind the death of Jesus is the self-giving love of God, the God of life, whose infusion of life into the rule of death opens up the possibility that true human life can yet be lived. It is from the creative heart of the Father that his saving love extends to his disordered and perishing world (John 3.16). Within the life of the love of God, the obedience of Jesus to his Father's will is the means by which the Father's saving love comes into the world. The death and resurrection of Jesus are to do with God, in love, taking responsibility on his own shoulders for the disorders of the world, integrating everything back into line with his creative purposes, sharing in the sufferings of his suffering world and yet not being crushed by them. A human being has 'engulfed' the power of the rule of death and so brought life and immortality to light once again (2 Tim 1.10). In our disordered and alienated world one of us has broken through the power of this world's disorders, and – like God in the opening of the creation saga – has brought order again where there was chaos.

It is through the work of the Holy Spirit, uniting us to the life and death of Jesus Christ, that the Father's love seen in Jesus is shed abroad in our hearts, bringing life where death rules. It is by reference to the work of the Holy Spirit within the love of the Holy Trinity, that we can approach the question: what difference does the story of Jesus make to my human story? What difference does the cross make to life?

3 We Are United with Christ in His Death and in His Resurrection

In the incarnation of Jesus, the Son of God assumes our out-of-line humanity under the judgement of God. God and humanity are inextricably and indivisibly united in the person of Jesus Christ. It is as representative and authentic true human being that Jesus dies and is raised to life again. If we are to be affected by the life and death and resurrection of Christ, we must be united with him, incorporated into him, actually share his life. And this is what the New Testament means by the power of the Holy Spirit incorporating us as living members into Christ's body, the church.

> The objective union which we have with Christ through his incarnational assumption of our humanity into himself is subjectively actualised in us through his indwelling spirit, we in Christ and Christ in us thus complementing and interpenetrating each other. In other words, there takes place a relation of mutual indwelling between Christ and the church which derives from and is grounded in the mutual indwelling of the Father, the Son and the Holy Spirit in the Holy Trinity (Torrance 1983, 77).

The cross and resurrection of Christ do not affect us merely by some moral influence, offering a powerful example which we then imitate (as some have interpreted Abelard, and Rashdall). The cross and resurrection do not affect us at all through some legal fiction of imputed guilt and imputed righteousness (as some have interpreted the penal substitution theory). They affect us because we are really and actually united with the Christ who died and was raised, in our very beings. As he engulfs the power of the rule of death and is raised to life again, we, united with him, are also set free and made new creatures in him (2 Cor 5.17), by the gift of the Spirit.

> By His own blood then the Lord redeemed us, and gave His life for our life, His flesh for our flesh; and He poured out the Spirit of the Father to bring about the union and communion

of God and man, bringing down God to men through the Spirit while raising man to God through His incarnation and His advent, surely and truly giving us incorruption through the communion which we have with God (Ireneaus, *Against the Heresies* V.1.2).

'If we have been united with him in a death like his, we will certainly be united with him in a resurrection like his' (Rom 6.5). As we, as individual believers, are incorporated into the body of Christ when we receive grace and are baptized, we are incorporated into the Christ whose death overcame the rule of death and whose resurrection is in truth 'the power at work within us' (Eph 3.20; cf. 1.19–20).

For those baptized into Christ, the story of Jesus now includes our own. Our life stories are changed by being incorporated into his. This change is both gift and task (see Rom 6). There is a change in our status: 'We know that our old self was crucified with him. . . . If we have died with Christ, we believe that we will also live with him.' There is also a summons to live a new life: 'You also must consider yourselves dead to sin and alive to God in Christ Jesus. . . . No longer present your members to sin . . . but present yourselves to God.'

4 Life in the Body of Christ

What does that mean in the actual experience of living? The traditional categories of atonement theology are sin and forgiveness. I have tried to broaden the concept of sin to include not only the moral guilt of ungodly behaviour, which separates us from fellowship with God, but the wider themes of mistrust, shame, guilt, and conflict. By mistrust, I mean anxiety and frustration in the face of an uncertain world, in which powers greater than our own threaten us. By shame, I mean our own sense of personal failure, and the inability to hold up our heads with confidence and gratitude that we are who we are. By guilt, I mean the state in which we put ourselves through violation of God's moral character. By conflict, I mean the confusion, alienation, and isolation in our relationships with one another and with our environment.

Forgiveness, likewise, can have a narrower or a broader focus. It is essentially a relational word. Forgiveness is appropriate in a situation where things are wrong. It does not pretend that there is no wrong. It does not offer peace at any price. Forgiveness is a dynamic process of change. It breaks down the idealizations that pretend that the world is all angel or all devil. It recognizes ambiguity: that there is real evil, wrong, and injustice, but that there is also hope of change. Forgiveness attempts to respond to wrong in a way that is open to new possibilities, seeking to reshape the future in the light of what is wrong, in the most creative way possible. It moves beyond the determinisms of fatalistic anxiety, despair of change, the law of retaliation, and the bitterness of resentful conflict. Forgiveness is costly, and hard work, but essentially filled with hope – the offer of re-creation.

In other words, forgiveness is the process by which the life of resurrection, through the power of the Holy Spirit, engulfs, transforms, and replaces in us the rule of sin and death. Forgiveness and the presentation of ourselves to God is a process, a journey, something dynamic and changing, not static and fixed, a pilgrimage – even an adventure. Forgiveness is a relationship word, and relationships happen over time. As the Skin Horse said to the Velveteen Rabbit, 'It doesn't happen all at once. . . . You *become*. It takes a long time.'

Let us see what forgiveness means in response to four of the features of what we earlier called 'the rule of death', drawing on Pruyser (1991) and Oates (1973).

(i) MISTRUST

What difference do the cross and resurrection of Jesus make to someone who is given up to anxiety? For some people, anxiety is terrifying. The world is filled with terrifying powers over which I have no control. I may be stuck in what I once heard called a 'required relationship' – a pattern of life and attitude from which I dare not move, because if I were to move there would be some terrible catastrophe, a hole would open in the universe and I would fall down it. Some of us hold on to depression, because what underlies the depression is too awful to face. For others, the feelings may not be so debilitating, but are none the less their basic attitude to the world. The world is not safe.

So I build idols to worship, to take my mind off life's uncertainties. Humankind, as Eliot said, cannot bear very much reality. I put my faith in horoscopes, tarot cards, the stars, materialism, noise, other people who will come and rescue me; perhaps parents deify their children. Oates quotes Tillich: 'Idolatry is the elevation of a preliminary concern to ultimacy.' When our devotion is given to something partial, conditioned, finite, we are resting our faith on something very fragile, and transient. 'Gordon Allport identified one characteristic of the mature religious sentiment as being comprehensiveness. To fix one's life commitment on a restricted, finite, and temporary object of devotion is to have a noncomprehensive sentiment in one's faith' (Oates 1973, 204). But it is sometimes easier, at least temporarily, to believe in the images which press upon me from the culture around, unreal as they often are, and then despair that I cannot live up to these unreal expectations. I am living in untruth, not in faith, trust, and obedience.

By contrast, forgiveness opens up the possibilities of hope again. In his cross and resurrection Jesus Christ has gone the way of anxiety and despair before me. He is the pioneer who for the joy that was set before him endured the cross, despising the shame. He has gone the way of uncertainty, ahead of me, and broken the powers that so frighten me. The ineffectiveness of these other gods is now shown up.

> Repentance of the sin of idolatry means to change one's god from a constricted, narrowed and dying god to a universal, comprehensive and eternal God. This calls for a change of mind, a transformation of loyalty, and a release of one's clutch on family, nation, denomination, race, sex, school, teacher, or ideological bias (Oates 1973, 205).

And if God did not spare his own Son, will he not with him also freely give us all things? Nothing in the whole of creation can now separate me from his love (Rom 8). My hope now lies in the fact that he promises to hold on to me in my uncertainties. Through the valley of every shadow he is with me. I can therefore, really and truly, cast my care on to him, for by his death and resurrection he has brought me, really and truly, into the place where I know that he cares for me, and that all things will one day be brought to their fulfilment in him (Eph 1.7–10).

If sin is about mistrust, idolatry, and lack of faith, forgiveness through the death and resurrection of Christ is about God's providence, the 'enlargement of life' (Oates), the journey of pilgrimage, living in hope. The evil powers have been conquered (Aulén). 'We know that the Son of God has come. . . . Little children, keep yourselves from idols' (1 John 5.20–1).

(ii) SHAME

What difference does the cross and resurrection of Jesus make to someone who is shrivelled through shame? Shame only comes into existence in a world of division (cf. Bonhoeffer 1959, 78–81). This began with the division between man and woman. In the Garden they were naked and not ashamed, but the division between them means that neither can now lift up their heads with confidence before the other. Shame also expresses the division within myself – between my hopes, desires, aspirations, and my failure, falling short, and disappointment. Shame makes it hard for me to sing 'Thank you, Father, for making me me.' Through my own wrongdoing as well as through my failure to achieve, I believe myself to be of little worth. I do not like myself. And I am wading, head turned down, in a murky pool of stagnant water – the water of my disappointed hopes, lost opportunities, and inability to reach the standards I and others had set. If my personal worth depends on my achievements, I am worth little.

Forgiveness opens up to me the resources of grace. Forgiveness is rooted in the gift of God's grace to us in Christ. Through his death and resurrection, God loves us. We are given the gift of belonging to Christ, of knowing that he has held his head in shame, crowned with thorns, but now holds it high, crowned with glory. If we are incorporated into Christ in the whole story of his suffering and humiliation, as well as the power of his new life, our lives are set in a new place. The old equation 'worth equals works' can now be replaced by 'worth is a gracious gift'. This, I think, is the existential meaning of justification by grace through faith. Jesus Christ is the Justified One, and I am justified because I am incorporated into him.

> When one comes to terms with, confesses, and rethinks his behaviour and makes a decision to change, a reward of forgiveness resides in the decision: He has now thrown off the sense of weakness and begun to feel real strength. The result of feeling genuinely forgiven is freedom from impotence and helplessness. The resolve itself is a source of strength (Oates 1973, 208).

And so forgiveness breaks down idealizations. I no longer have to think of myself in the either/or terms of either wonderful and achieving, or failing and worthless. If I forgive myself, I realize that this side of heaven I will always to some extent get it wrong, I will fail, I will hurt people and they will hurt me. But I can also realize that my identity is not now defined by such things; my identity is centred – indeed given – elsewhere. I am now united with one who has identified with this world's failures and was not crushed by them, one who therefore is (in the words of Heb 4.15) 'not untouched with the feeling of our infirmities' (AV), who can 'sympathize with our weaknesses' (NRSV), and who promises 'grace to help in time of need'.

If sin is about shame, forgiveness (especially of myself) is about the development of a realistic self-concept. It is about knowing myself as united with the crucified and risen Lord, with my identity now given, not through my own divisions and failure, but in grace.

Joanna and Alister McGrath (1992) have developed an account of self-esteem which draws on the attachment theory of John Bowlby in *Attachment and Loss*, linking his ideas concerning the implications of parental attachment and separation to the theological concept of being 'bonded to Christ'. A

Christian, once separated by God through her or his sin, can find their true self-worth and acceptance grounded in an attachment to God through Christ. As Abelard says, the cross manifests God's accepting love. Now I must 'put on love'.

'So if you have been raised with Christ, seek the things that are above. . . . For you have died, and your life is hid with Christ in God. . . . Put to death, therefore, whatever in you is earthly. . . . Clothe yourselves with love' (Col 3).

(iii) GUILT

Implicit in the notion of sin is my moral accountability before God, as a person capable of choice. Whatever may be true of the limits within which my freedom is exercised, genetic or environmental, I still have the freedom to choose how much to collude with, confront, accept or deny the attitudes and patterns of behaviour with which I have grown up. I can understand my moral accountability in terms of a development from a prudential morality (in which I do certain things to avoid punishment or pain), through an authoritarian morality (in which I do certain things in response to external authority), to a personal morality (in which I take responsibility – within appropriate limits – for my choices and behaviour) (adapted from Kohlberg 1976).

To acknowledge my sin includes acknowledging that some at least of my choices and behaviour patterns are out of line with the purposes and character of God. Sin includes transgression, and its result is guilt. Guilt has both an objective dimension as the state of a moral person who has violated or transgressed a moral law, and a subjective dimension, in which guilt is 'a feeling of having done something wrong, and cannot be analysed away into anything else' (McKeating 1970, 16). This is that aspect of my personality commonly referred to as my conscience. (There is also what Buber calls 'civic guilt', the sort of legal guilt which arises through the infringement of certain social conventions – which may or may not include objective moral guilt; this does not concern us here.) I may be objectively guilty and not feel guilty (because my conscience has been worn down); I may subjectively feel guilty when I am not objectively guilty (because my conscience is over-scrupulous).

If I am to speak of sin in relation to guilt, I am referring primarily to the objective moral state of having violated God's purposes, law and character. It is a refusal, as Barth says, to let God be God. This may or may not include some subjective feelings associated with this. But true moral guilt is a trap, a bondage, from which I need to be set free. Behind wrong behaviour usually also lies a false belief. Behaviours are the expression of faith, which is why Paul says 'Whatever does not proceed from faith is sin' (Rom 14.23). The cognitive therapists, who work with the destructiveness of irrational beliefs and their consequent behavioural responses, remind us of the trap of guilt which follows wrong faith and wrong doing.

By contrast, forgiveness liberates me from condemnation, and enables me to live in freedom. It can speak of the truth which sets free. How does this happen?

The Object Relations approach of Melanie Klein (e.g. 1960) is the nearest I think psychoanalytic theory gets to providing a model of the inner changes which forgiveness brings. Klein illustrates the emotions of our adult world by reference to what she calls their 'roots in infancy'. In Klein's understanding, the maturing process in the child goes through various stages. For a child who has related to mother in contradictory ways (the nourishing mother whom I love; the depriving mother who leaves me to cry, whom I hate), the development to seeing the mother as a whole person – sometimes nourishing, sometimes depriving – includes a realization of true guilt, that I have screamed at the one who is my provider and who loves me. There is a deep sense that wrong must be punished and a penalty paid. How is the child to move from incapacitating guilt to the capacity to give and receive love creatively towards mother and others? Klein says this comes through making reparation. Motherhood needs to provide the facilitating context in which emotional reparation can be made, and the demands of moral order satisfied. Then life can become creative.

Whatever we think of this as a model of child development (and the inner workings of a baby's mind are, of course, untestable), it provides a model for understanding the changes which forgiveness can bring in our adult world. For guilt to be handled, there must be reparation. The demands of right and wrong must be satisfied. Only then can life go on creatively.

In connection with Jesus's cross and resurrection, those strands of the New Testament which speak of the cross in terms of God's curse, of an expression of divine wrath, and of the punishment for sin, are speaking of a divinely provided means by which reparation can be made. Anselm is right that God's honour needs to be satisfied, even if his model of satisfaction is inappropriate in a post-feudal world. Anselm is right that sin must be taken seriously enough. He is also right that only God can provide the means for making reparation. We must beware here of dividing up the Holy Trinity, as though the Son was appeasing the Father. One way of expressing this is to say that the interpersonal self-giving love within the Persons of the God-head flows out into the suffering and guilty world of persons who are trapped in their guilt. In costly grace it unites with them in their guilt, and then in them and on their behalf makes the reparation needed to satisfy the honour of the God at whom we have screamed, despite his being our provider and the one who loves us. In Christ, God makes the costly reparation; in Christ, we are liberated to live creatively again.

This is close to the language of Romans, which pictures the consequences of sin in terms of four barriers between us and God: wrath, the condemnation of law, the power of sin, and the rule of death. Paul's gospel is that through divinely provided and costly grace we are free from wrath (5.9), free from sin (6.7), free from condemnation (8.1), and free from the law of sin and death (8.2). It is close, also, to the language of Galatians, which urges us to *live as* freed people.

(iv) CONFLICT

Part of the meaning of sin is conflict: this may be alienation between people and God, or people and each other. It may be the destructive jealousy of Cain towards Abel, or the deep-seated vengeance of Lamech. It may be the disintegration of society as a whole through its abandonment of a centre in God (as at Babel). It may show itself in the way we take our stand on the law of retaliation: you owe, so you must pay – a law which Jesus repudiates in the parable of the unjust steward. It is perhaps most evident in the third of what Stephen Neill (1959, 190–213) calls the 'three great enemies of the human race: fear, frustration and resentment.' Resentment is a bitterness which cripples, decays, destroys.

Many other aspects of sin are included in this destructive kaleidoscope of conflict. As Oates puts it (1973, 211):

Sin as alienation from God and man is the composite and end result meaning of sin. Idolatry alienates one from God and those persons and/or things that are put in God's place. Shrinking back from participating with God and man in the demands of growth in personal and corporate life alienates and estranges a person. Destructive habits preoccupy and hinder one's relationships to self, others and God. Dividing walls of hostility estrange the self-elevated and ambition-ridden person. The foolish person seems to be asking to be cast out, estranged and isolated.

The result is enmity not only between us and God, but between people, cultures, and races, and between ourselves and our environment. We stand on our rights, we demand our dues, we insist on fairness, and we trample on one another to get it.

Forgiveness, by contrast, is a refusal to be trapped by the law of retaliation. Forgiveness is a willingness to move beyond the requirements of mere fairness into the justice which reflects the *redemptive* justice of God. Forgiveness does not demand an eye or a tooth, but is willing – in costly sacrifice and without minimizing wrong – to seek to make good the wrong as far as possible, and to move from stultifying bitterness and resentment into the fresh air of grace.

In the cross and resurrection God does not demand his dues from us. In costly self-giving he vindicates his justice and righteousness from within his own heart. But he moves beyond requirement into gift, beyond death into life. Forgiveness is about life continuing despite the rule of death.

There is a personal, social and political dimension to forgiveness in this sense.

Personal forgiveness may be seen in conflict resolution

between marriage partners, in the recognition of and repentance from blameshifting, domination, and manipulation of one person by another, in the healing of memories in a person who has been hurt or abused, and in the letting go of a justified sense of bitterness in one who has been unjustly treated by another, all this in imitation of Christ (see 1 Peter 2.21–3).

Social forgiveness would provide a creative contrast to the ingrained habits of our culture which seem to insist and require that people's sins accumulate against them. A politician who falls into sin may come to repentance, may start a new life, and may give himself to the service of others. Before God his conscience may now be clean, and the past be put behind him. Not so with the tabloids who keep his story alive, the film-makers who set the story in celluloid, those who will always associate his name with his faults, and will not let him be free.

Can there be a *politics* of forgiveness? Haddon Willmer (1979) has sought to outline what such a political stance might involve (cf. Hinchliff 1982; Atkinson 1985). His thesis is that the biblical concept of justice points towards certain political responses to evil in the world which are very close to what in personal terms we would call forgiveness. It refuses to be trapped in a fatalistic determinism. It refuses peace at any price and seeks to vindicate justice in the face of wrong. It seeks to approach the wrongdoer not in terms of bare retaliation and retributive justice alone, but in a way that is creative of new possibilities. Forgiveness underlines the reality of human frailty and sin, and the limited capacity of human resources to deal with them, but for the sake of the common good it seeks to explore ways of handling wrong and guilt creatively and not destructively. Forgiveness involves a gracious initiative from the party who is wronged. Without forgiveness in the political arena, the options open seem to be either to reject the notion that politics is about conciliation and making the best of faulty people, limited resources, and a distorting heritage, or to abandon all quest for justice in human affairs and to acquiesce in injustice. Willmer's thesis has relevance to the making of political systems and the creating of political structures. Can a state's response to evil be both just and redemptive?

The most poignant biblical example of the difficulties and possibilities of conflict resolution at personal, social and political level is the relationship in the early church between Jew and Gentile. That there was discord is evident from Galatians and from Acts. Attitudes of mutual condemnation in Gentile and Jew are clear in the early chapters of Romans. But Ephesians also speaks of those who were far off being brought near in the blood of Christ. 'For he is our peace; in his flesh he has made both groups into one, and has broken down the dividing wall, that is the hostility . . . [that he] might reconcile both groups to God in one body through the cross, thus putting to death that hostility. . . . Through him both of us have access in one Spirit to the Father' (Eph 2.14–18). In other words, through the death of Christ and the gift of the Spirit of the risen Christ, there is now one living body of Christ in this world. Through our actual unity together in Christ, the walls of hostility are breached. Indeed, because Christ has died, we, in him, have died to the law (Gal 2) – the understanding and application of which has acted as a barrier between Jew and Gentile. Therefore, whether I like it or not I am one with my neighbour. All of us are brothers and sisters 'for whom Christ died' (Rom 15).

(v) CONCLUSION

In summary: forgiveness is part of the love which casts out fear and part of the truth which sets free. Forgiveness extends beyond our 'sins' in the narrow sense of our wrong actions, to 'all other benefits of his passion' (BCP, Holy Communion), within which I would want to include all that makes for healing, wholeness, *shalom*. Forgiveness is the secret of the atonement, namely that there can be life through death.

> When thou dost ask me blessing, I'll kneel down and ask of thee forgiveness: so we'll live, and pray, and sing, and tell old tales, and laugh at gilded butterflies (*King Lear* V.3).

Forgiveness is the *relational* part of the mystery of God's will which he set forth in Christ as a plan for the fullness of time, to unite all things in him (Eph 1.9–10). Forgiveness is the response of the gospel to people under the rule of death, given up to mistrust, shame, guilt, and conflict. It is to them a gift of grace, an infusion of life into the rule of death. It is also a task: thereafter within the body of Christ they are to put to death the old nature and put on the new. This is a journey, a process of change, as our stories are caught up into the ongoing story of Christ in the purposes of God for his world. Beginning with Abraham, and through the story of Israel, focusing all God's judgement and mercy in Jesus Christ, especially his death and resurrection, catching us all up into him in the power of his Spirit, God is creating an authentically new humanity, the Israel of God, of which we are beginning to be part.

Simone Weil (1952, 84) describes the grace which is God's response to the gravity of sin, in terms of 'the cross as a balance, as a lever. A going down, the condition of a rising up. Heaven coming down to earth raises earth to heaven.' The end of the story is the restoration of a renewed Israel, a renewed people of God, who are the true humanity of God's creative purposes, the nations gathered round the throne of heaven in trust, openness, freedom, and love. And the centre of their worship is a Lamb.

Bibliography

The bibliography contains works referred to in the text by author's name and the date of the work. In case of ambiguity, the reference will be to the British edition of a work. Initial dates in brackets indicate when a work was first written or published. ET denotes English translation.

Abelard, P. *Exposition of the Epistle to the Romans* (about 1135). ET of excerpts in *A Scholastic Miscellany* (ed. E. R. Fairweather) 276–87. Library of Christian Classics 10. London: SCM/Philadelphia: Westminster, 1956.

Ackermann, D. 'Critical theory, communicative actions and liberating praxis'. *Journal of Theology For Southern Africa* 82 (1993) 21–36.

Allison, D. C. *The End of the Ages Has Come.* Philadelphia: Fortress, 1985/Edinburgh: Clark, 1987.

Alsford, M. *The Notion of Coaduncy and the Problem of the Self/Other Relationality in Theology With Special Reference to Kant, Fichte, Hegel, Barth and Pannenberg.* Diss. Durham, 1990.

Alsford, S. *Sin As A Problem of Twentieth Century Systematic Theology.* Diss. Durham, 1987.

Althaus, P. *The Theology of Martin Luther* (1962). ET Philadelphia: Fortress, 1966.

Anderson, R. S. *On Being Human.* Grand Rapids: Eerdmans, 1982.

Anselm of Canterbury. *Why Did God Become A Human Being?* (1098). ET in *Anselm of Canterbury* (ed. J. Hopkins and H. Richardson) 3:39–137.

— *A Meditation on Human Redemption* (about 1100). ET in *Anselm of Canterbury* (ed. J. Hopkins and H. Richardson) 1:137–44. London: SCM/New York: Mellen, 1974.

Arendt, H. *The Human Condition.* Chicago: University of Chicago, 1958.

Ashby, G. *Sacrifice.* London: SCM, 1988.

Athanasius of Alexandria. *The Incarnation* (about 318). ET [London] Centenary, 1944/[New York] Macmillan, 1946.

— *Four Discourses Against the Arians* (about 358). ET in *Nicene and Post-Nicene Fathers of the Christian Church* II (ed. P. Schaff and H. Wace) 4:303–447. Reprinted Edinburgh: Clark/Grand Rapids: Eerdmans, 1991.

Atkinson, D. J. *Peace in Our Time?* Leicester: IVP, 1985.

— *The Message of Genesis 1–11*. Leicester/Downers Grove, IL: IVP, 1990.

Augustine of Hippo. *Confessions* (about 400). ET in *Nicene and Post-Nicene Fathers of the Christian Church* I (ed. P. Schaff) 1:27–207. Reprinted Edinburgh: Clark/Grand Rapids: Eerdmans, 1988.

— *Lectures on the Gospel According to St John* (416). In *Patrologia . . . latina* (ed. J.-P. Migne) 35 (1902) 1379–1976. ET in *Nicene and Post-Nicene Fathers of the Christian Church* I (ed. P. Schaff) 7:1–452. Reprinted Edinburgh: Clark/Grand Rapids: Eerdmans, 1986.

Aulén, G. *Christus Victor* (1930). ET London: SPCK/New York: Macmillan, 1931; reprinted 1970.

Bal, M. *Death and Dissymmetry: The Politics of Coherence in the Book of Judges*. Chicago/London: University of Chicago, 1988.

Barnett, V. *For the Soul of the People: Protestant Protest Against Hitler*. New York: OUP, 1992.

Barrett, C. K. *Romans*. London: Black, 1957/New York: Harper, 1958.

— *2 Corinthians*. London: Black, 1973/New York: Harper, 1974.

Barth, K. *Church Dogmatics* III/1 (1946). ET Edinburgh: Clark, 1958.

— *Church Dogmatics* III/2 (1948). ET Edinburgh: Clark, 1960.

— *Church Dogmatics* IV/1 (1953). ET Edinburgh: Clark, 1956.

— *The Christian Life* (1969). ET Edinburgh: Clark, 1981.

Bauckham, R. and Williams, R. 'Jesus—God with us'. In *Stepping Stones* (ed. C. A. Baxter) 21–41. London: Hodder, 1987.

Beattie, J. H. M. 'On understanding sacrifice'. In Bourdillon and Fortes 1980, 29–44.

Becker, E. *The Denial of Death*. New York: Free Press/London: Collier Macmillan, 1973.

Berger, P. *A Rumo[u]r of Angels*. Garden City, NY: Doubleday, 1969/London: Allen Lane, 1970/Harmondsworth: Penguin, 1971.

Berkouwer, G. C. *Sin*. Grand Rapids: Eerdmans, 1971.

Berry, W. W. 'Images of sin and salvation in feminist theology'. *Anglican Theological Review* 60 (1978) 25–54.

Betty, C. C. 'Piet Schoonenberg's theory of original sin'. *Thought* 45 (1970) 83–101.

Blumenthal, D. R. 'Jewish Studies and Religious Studies'. In *Religious Education* 81/1 (1986) 29–36.

Bonhoeffer, D. *Sanctorum Communio* (1927). ET London: Collins, 1963.

— *Creation and Fall* (1937). ET London: SCM/New York: Macmillan, 1959.

Borg, M. 'An orthodoxy reconsidered'. In Hurst and Wright 1987, 207–17.

Bourdillon, M. F. C. and Fortes, M. (eds.). *Sacrifice*. London/New York: Academic, 1980.

Bowker, J. *The Meanings of Death*. Cambridge/New York: CUP, 1991.

Bowlby, J. *Attachment and Loss*. 3 vols. London: Hogarth/Institute of Pyscho-Analysis/New York: Basic, 1969; 1973; 1980.

Brandenburger, E. 'Text und Vorlagen von Hebr. 5:7–10'. *Novum Testamentum* 11 (1969) 190–224.

Brandon, S. G. F. *Jesus and the Zealots*. Manchester: Manchester UP, 1967.

Browning, D. S. *Atonement and Psychotherapy*. Philadelphia: Westminster, 1964.

Brueggemann, W. *Praying the Psalms*. Winona, MN: St Mary's Press, 1982.

Brümmer, V. 'Atonement and reconciliation'. *Religious Studies* 28 (1992) 435–52.

Brunner, E. *The Mediator* (1927). ET London: Lutterworth/New York: Macmillan, 1934.

van Buren, P. *Christ in Our Place*. Edinburgh: Oliver and Boyd/Grand Rapids: Eerdmans, 1957.

Bushnell, H. *The Vicarious Sacrifice*. New York: Scribner's/London: Strahan, 1866.

— *Women's Suffrage: The Reform Against Nature*. New York: Scribner's, 1869.

Caird, G. B. *Jesus and the Jewish Nation*. London: Athlone, 1965.

— *The Language and Imagery of the Bible*. London: Duckworth/Philadelphia: Westminster, 1980.

— 'Jesus and Israel: The starting point for New Testament Christology'. In *Christological Perspectives* (H. K. McArthur Festschrift, ed. R. F. Berkey and S. Edwards) 56–68. New York: Pilgrim, 1982.

— 'The one and the many in Mark and John'. In *Studies of the Church in History* (R. S. Paul Festschrift, ed. H. Davies) 39–54. Allison Park, PA: Pickwick, 1983.

Calvin, J. *Institutes of the Christian Religion* (1534; rev. ed., 1559). ET (ed. J. T. McNeill) London: SCM/Philadelphia: Westminster, 1961.

— *The Epistles of Paul the Apostle to the Galatians, Ephesians, Philippians and Colossians* (1548). ET Edinburgh: Oliver and Boyd/Grand Rapids: Eerdmans, 1965.

— *The Epistle of Paul the Apostle to the Hebrews and The First and Second Epistles of St Peter* (1549, 1551). ET Edinburgh: Oliver and Boyd/Grand Rapids: Eerdmans, 1963.

Campbell, A. Y. *The Gospel of Anger*. London: SPCK, 1986.

Campbell, J. M. *The Nature of the Atonement*. London/New York: Macmillan, 6th ed., 1886.

Carey, G. L. *The Gate of Glory*. London: Hodder, 1986. 2nd ed. London: Hodder, 1992/Grand Rapids: Eerdmans, 1993.

Cargas, H. J. *Shadows of Auschwitz* (1981). New York: Crossroad, rev. ed., 1990.

Chesterton, G. K. 'The Honour of Israel Gow'. In *Father Brown: Selected Stories* 95–113. Ware: Wordsworth Editions, 1992.

Chodorow, N. *The Reproduction of Mothering*. Berkeley: University of California, 1978.

Coakley, S. 'Creaturehood Before God'. In *Theology* 93 (1990) 343–54.

Coates, J. R. (ed.). *Bible Key Words: Sin*. London: Black, 1951.

Cocksworth, C. J. *Evangelical Eucharistic Thought in the Church of England*. Cambridge/ New York: CUP, 1993.

Cohn-Sherbok, D. *The Crucified Jew*. London: HarperCollins, 1991.

Collins, G. R. *Christian Counselling*. Waco, TX: Word, 1980/Milton Keynes: Word, 1985.

Cranfield, C. E. B. *The Epistle to the Romans*. Vol. 1. Edinburgh: Clark, 1975.

Cyril of Alexandria, *Commentary on the Gospel According to John* (about 429). *Patrologia . . . graeca* 73 (1864).

— *Epistles*. In *Patrologia . . . graeca* 77 (1864) 9–390. ET *Letters 1—50*. Washington: Catholic University of America, 1987.

Dalferth, I. U. 'Christ died for us'. In Sykes 1991, 299–325.

Daly, R. J. *The Origins of the Christian Doctrine of Sacrifice*. Philadelphia: Fortress, 1978.

Davies, A. T. *Anti-Semitism and the Christian Mind*. New York: Herder, 1969.

Davies, D. J. 'An interpretation of sacrifice in Leviticus'. *Zeitschrift für die alttestamentliche Wissenschaft* 89 (1977) 387–99. = *Anthropological Approaches to the Old Testament* (ed. B. Lang) 151–62. London: SPCK/ Philadelphia: Fortress, 1985.

Deddo, G. W. *Karl Barth's Special Ethics of Parents and Children in the Light of his Trinitarian Theological Anthropology*. Diss. Aberdeen, 1990.

Derrida, J. 'Structure, sign and play in the discourse of the human sciences'. In *The Languages of Criticism and the Sciences of Man: The Structuralist Controversy* (ed. R. Macksey and E. Donato) 247–72. Baltimore/ London: Johns Hopkins UP, 1970.

— *Positions* (1973). ET London: Athlone, 1981/Chicago: University of Chicago, 1982.

Dillistone, F. W. *The Christian Understanding of Atonement*. London: Nisbet/Philadelphia: Westminster, 1968.

Dodd, C. H. *The Epistle of Paul to the Romans*. London: Hodder/New York: Harper, 1932.

Dods, M. and others. *The Atonement in Modern Religious Thought*. London: Clarke, 1900/New York: Whittaker, 1901.

Dowell, S. and Hurcombe, L. *Dispossessed Daughters of Eve*. London: SCM, 1981.

Dunn, J. D. G. *Romans 1—8*. Dallas: Word, 1988/Milton Keynes: Word, 1991.

— 'Paul's understanding of the death of Jesus as a sacrifice'. In Sykes 1991, 35–56. [= 1991a]

— *The Parting of the Ways*. London: SCM, 1991. [= 1991b]

Earley, G. D. 'The radical hermeneutical shift in post-holocaust Christian thought'. *Journal of Ecumenical Studies* 18 (1981) 16–32.

Eckardt, A. L. and A. R. *Long Night's Journey Into Day*. Rev. ed., Detroit: Wayne State UP/Oxford: Pergamon, 1988.

Erikson, E. *Childhood and Society*. New York: Norton, 1950; rev. ed., 1963/London: Image, 1951; rev. ed., London: Hogarth, 1963; reprinted London: Collins, 1977.

Evans, G. R. *Augustine on Evil*. Cambridge/New York: CUP, 1982.

Fackenheim, E. *The Jewish Bible After the Holocaust*. Manchester UP, 1990.

Fichte, J. G. *The Science of Knowledge*. Cambridge/New York: CUP, 1982.

Fiddes, P. *Past Event and Present Salvation*. London: DLT/Philadelphia: Westminster, 1989.

Finney, J. *Finding Faith Today*. Swindon: Bible Society, 1992.

Flannery, E. *The Anguish of the Jews*. New York: Paulist, rev. ed., 1985.

Forsyth, P. T. and others. *The Atonement in Modern Religious Thought*. London: Clarke, 1900/New York: Whittaker, 1901.

— *The Cruciality of the Cross*. London: Hodder, 1909.

— *The Work of Christ*. London/New York: Hodder, 1910.

Foucault, M. *The Order of Things* (1966). ET London: Tavistock, 1970/ New York: Random, 1973. Reprinted London: Routledge, 1989.

Fowler, J. W. *Stages of Faith*. San Francisco: Harper, 1981.

Fox, M. *Original Blessing*. Santa Fe: Bear, 1983.

Franks, R. S. *A History of the Doctrine of the Work of Christ*. 2 vols. London/ New York: Hodder, 1918. Reprinted as *The Work of Christ*. London/ New York: Nelson, 1962.

Freedman, D. N. and others (eds.). *The Anchor Bible Dictionary*. Garden City, NY: Doubleday, 1992.

Freud, S. *Totem and Taboo* (1912–13). ET New York: Moffat, 1918/ London: Routledge, 1919.

Furnish, V. P. *2 Corinthians*. Garden City, NY: Doubleday, 1984.

Gager, J. G. *The Origins of Anti-Semitism*. New York: OUP, 1983.

Genesis Rabbah (about 400). 3 vols. Atlanta: Scholars, 1985.

van Gennep, A. *The Rites of Passage* (1909). ET London: Routledge/ Chicago: University of Chicago, 1960.

Gilligan, C. *In A Different Voice*. Cambridge, MA/London: Harvard UP, 1982.

Girard, R. *Violence and the Sacred* (1972). ET Baltimore/London: Johns Hopkins UP, 1977.

Glasser, W. *Reality Therapy*. New York: Harper, 1965.

Gorringe, T. J. *Redeeming Time: Atonement Through Education*. London: DLT, 1986.

Gray, G. B. *Sacrifice in the Old Testament*. Oxford/New York: OUP, 1925.

Greenberg, M. 'Mankind, Israel and the nations in Hebraic Heritage'. In

No Man Is Alien (W. A. Visser 't Hooft Festschrift, ed. J. R. Nelson) 15–40. Leiden: Brill, 1971.

Gregory of Nyssa. *The Making of Humanity* (about 380). ET in *Nicene and Post-Nicene Christian Fathers* II (ed. P. Schaff and H. Wace) 5:387–427. Reprinted Edinburgh: Clark/Grand Rapids: Eerdmans, 1988.

Gregory of Palamas. *The One Hundred and Fifty Chapters* (about 1350). In *Patrologia . . . graeca* 150 (1865) 1121–1224.

Grey, M. *Redeeming the Dream*. London: SPCK, 1989. = *Feminism, Redemption, and the Christian Tradition*. Mystic, CT: Twenty-Third, 1990.

Gunton, C. E. *The Actuality of Atonement*. Edinburgh: T & T Clark, 1988/ Grand Rapids: Eerdmans, 1989.

— *The Promise of Trinitarian Theology*. Edinburgh: T & T Clark, 1991.

Habermas, J. *The Philosophical Discourse of Modernity*. Cambridge, MA: MIT/Cambridge: Polity, 1987.

Hall, D. J. 'Barmen: Lesson in theology'. *Toronto Journal of Theology* 1 (1985) 180–99.

Halteman Finger, R. 'How can Jesus save women?' In *Daughters of Sarah* 14 (1988) 14–18.

Hampson, M. D. 'On power and gender'. *Modern Theology* 4 (1988) 234–50.

— 'Theological integrity and human relationships'. Unpublished paper, 1991.

Hardy, D. and Ford, D. *Jubilate: Theology in Praise*. London: DLT, 1984. = *Praising and Knowing God*. Philadelphia: Westminster, 1985.

Hart, T. 'Humankind in Christ and Christ in humankind'. *Scottish Journal of Theology* 42 (1989) 67–84.

Hauerwas, S. *A Community of Character*. Notre Dame: University of Notre Dame, 1981.

Hebblethwaite, B. 'The Jewishness of Jesus from the perspective of Christian doctrine'. *Scottish Journal of Theology* 42 (1989) 27–44.

Heidegger, M. *Being and Time* (1927). ET London: Blackwell, 1962.

— *The Question Concerning Technology, and other essays*. ET New York: Harper, 1977.

Hengel, M. *The Cross of the Son of God*. ET London: SCM, 1986.

Heschel, A. J. *The Prophets*. New York: Harper, 1962.

Hill, D. *Greek Words and Hebrew Meanings*. Cambridge/New York: CUP, 1967.

Hinchliff, P. *Holiness and Politics*. London: DLT, 1982.

Hodgson, L. *The Doctrine of the Atonement*. London: Nisbet/New York: Scribner's, 1951.

Hodgson, P. C. and King, R. H. (eds.). *Christian Theology*. Philadelphia: Fortress, 1982.

Hoffman, F. J. 'Mortality and modern literature'. In *The Meaning of Death* (ed. H. Feifel) 133–56. New York: McGraw Hill, 1959.

Hooker, M. D. *From Adam to Christ*. Cambridge/New York: CUP, 1990.

Hooker, R. *Of the Laws of Ecclesiastical Polity*. 3 vols. Cambridge, MA/ London: Harvard UP, 1977, 1980.

Hubert, H. and Mauss, M. *Sacrifice: Its Nature and Function* (1898). ET Chicago: University of Chicago/London: Cohen and West, 1964.

Hughes, P. E. *2 Corinthians*. London: Marshall/Grand Rapids: Eerdmans, 1962.

Hurst, L. D. and Wright, N. T. (eds.). *The Glory of Christ in the New Testament* (G. B. Caird Festschrift). Oxford/New York: OUP, 1987.

Irenaeus of Lyons. *Against the Heresies* (about 185). ET in *The Ante-Nicene Fathers* (ed. A. Roberts and J. Donaldson) 1:309–567. Reprinted Grand Rapids: Eerdmans/Edinburgh: Clark, 1989.

[Irigaray, L.] *The Irigaray Reader*, ed. M. Whitford. Oxford/Cambridge, MA: Blackwell, 1991.

Isaac, J. *The Teaching of Contempt* (1956). ET New York: Holt, Rinehart and Winston, 1964.

— *The Christian Roots of Antisemitism* (1959). ET Southampton: CCJ/ Parkes Library, 1965.

— *Jesus and Israel* (1959). ET New York: Holt, Rinehart and Winston, 1971.

Isaacs, M. E. *The Concept of Spirit*. London: Heythrop, 1976.

Jacobs, M. *Fear to Faith*. London: DLT, 1988.

Jencks, C. *The Language of Post-Modern Architecture*. London: Academy, 4th ed., 1984/New York: Rizzoll, 5th ed., 1988.

Jensen, P. P. *Graded Holiness*. Sheffield: SAP, 1992.

Jeremias, J. *The Central Message of the New Testament* (1955). ET New York: Scribner's, 1965/London: SCM, 1966.

Johnson, L. T. 'The New Testament's anti-Jewish slander and the conventions of ancient polemic'. *Journal of Biblical Literature* 108 (1989) 419–41.

Jüngel, E. *Death: The Riddle and the Mystery*. Philadelphia: Westminster, 1974/Edinburgh: St Andrew's, 1976.

Käsemann, E. *Perspectives on Paul* (1969). ET London: SCM/Philadelphia: Fortress, 1971.

— *Commentary on Romans* (4th ed., 1980). ET London: SCM/Grand Rapids: Eerdmans, 1980.

Kant, I. *Critique of Pure Reason*. ET New York: St Martin, 1969/London: Macmillan, 1982.

Katz, J. T. *From Prejudice to Destruction: Anti-Semitism 1700–1933*. Cambridge, MA; Harvard UP, 1980.

Kearney, R. *Dialogues With Contemporary Continental Thinkers*. Manchester: Manchester UP, 1984.

Kelsey, D. 'Human being'. In Hodgson and King 1982, 141–67.

Kidner, F. D. *Sacrifice*. London: Tyndale, 1952.

Kirk, A. 'Theology from a feminist perspective'. In *Men Women and God* (ed. K. Keay) 24–45. Basingstoke: Marshall, 1987.

Kitamori, K. *Theology of the Pain of God* (1946; 1958). ET Richmond: Knox, 1965/London: SCM, 1966.

Kittel, R. (ed.)., *Theological Dictionary of the New Testament*. Vol. 1 (1933). ET Grand Rapids: Eerdmans, 1964.

Klein, C. *Anti-Judaism in Christian Theology* (1975). ET Philadelphia: Fortress/London: SPCK, 1978.

Klein, M. *Our Adult World and its Roots in Infancy*. London: Tavistock, 1960.

Kohlberg, L. 'Moral stages and moralization'. In *Moral Development and Behavior* (ed. T. Lickona). New York: Holt, Rinehart, and Winston, 1976.

[Kristeva, J.] *The Kristeva Reader*, ed. T. Moi. Oxford: Blackwell/New York: Columbia UP, 1986.

Lampe, G. W. H. 'The atonement: Law and love'. In *Soundings* (ed. A. R. Vidler) 173–91. Cambridge/New York: CUP, 1962.

— 'The saving work of Christ'. In *Christ For Us Today* (ed. N. Pittenger) 141–53. London: SCM, 1968.

Leach, E. R. 'The logic of sacrifice'. In Leach, *Culture and Communication* 81–93. Cambridge/New York: CUP, 1976. = *Anthropological Approaches to the Old Testament* (ed. B. Lang) 136–50. London: SPCK/Philadelphia: Fortress, 1985.

Leech, K. *Soul Friend*. London: Sheldon, 1977/San Francisco: Harper, 1980.

van Leeuwen, T. M. *The Surplus of Meaning*. Amsterdam: Rodopi, 1981.

Lévi, S. *La doctrine de sacrifice dans les Brahmanas*. Paris: Bibliothèque de l'école des hautes études, 1966.

Levinas, E. *Totality and Infinity* (1971). ET The Hague: Nijhoff, 1979.

Levine, B. A. *In The Presence of the Lord*. Leiden: Brill, 1974.

Lindars, B. *New Testament Apologetic*. London: SCM/Philadelphia: Fortress, 1961.

Littel, F. H. *The Crucifixion of the Jews*. Macon GA: Mercer UP, 1975; rev. ed., 1986.

Loades, A. L. 'Eucharistic sacrifice'. In Sykes 1991, 247–61.

Lodahl, M. E. 'Jews and Christians in a conflict of interpretations'. *Christian Scholars Review* 19 (1989–90) 332–4.

Luther, M. 'Lectures on Genesis Chapters 1—5' (1535). ET in *Luther's Works* Vol. 1. St Louis: Concordia, 1958.

— 'Lectures on Hebrews' (1518). ET in *Luther's Works* Vol. 29. St Louis: Concordia, 1968.

Lyden, J. C. 'Atonement in Judaism and Christianity'. *Journal of Ecumenical Studies* 29 (1992) 47–54.

Lyotard, J.-F. *The Postmodern Condition*. ET Minneapolis: University of Minnesota/Manchester: Manchester UP, 1984.

MacIntyre, A. *After Virtue*. London: Duckworth, 1981. 2nd ed., Notre Dame: University of Notre Dame, 1984.

Macmurray, J. *The Self As Agent*. London: Faber/New York: Harper, 1957.

Marshall, I. H. *Jesus the Saviour*. London: SPCK/Downers Grove, IL: IVP, 1990.

Martin, R. P. *2 Corinthians*. Waco, TX: Word, 1986/Milton Keynes: Word, 1991.

Masterman, M. 'The psychology of levels of will'. *Proceedings of the Aristotelian Society* n.s. 48 (1947–8) 75–110H.

McFadyen, A. I. *The Call to Personhood*. Cambridge/New York: CUP, 1990.

McGarry, M. B. *Christology After Auschwitz*. New York: Paulist, 1977.

McGrath, J. and A. *The Dilemma of Self-Esteem*. Wheaton, IL/Cambridge: Crossway, 1992.

McKeating, H. *Living With Guilt*. London: SCM/Valley Forge, PA: Judson, 1970.

Megill, A. *Prophets of Extremity*. Berkeley: University of California, 1987.

Menninger, K. *Whatever Became of Sin?* New York: Hawthorn, 1973.

Meyer, B. F. *The Aims of Jesus*. London: SCM, 1979.

Milgrom, J. 'Sin-offering or purification-offering'. *Vetus Testamentum* 21 (1971) 237–9. = Milgrom 1983, 67–9.

— 'The priestly doctrine of repentance'. In *Revue Biblique* 82 (1975) 186–205. = Milgrom 1983, 47–66.

— *Studies in Cultic Theology and Terminology*. Leiden: Brill, 1983.

Milne, B. 'The idea of sin in twentieth century theology'. *Tyndale Bulletin* 26 (1975) 3–33.

Moberly, R. C. *Atonement and Personality*. London: Murray/New York: Longmans, 1901.

Moltmann, J. *Theology of Hope* (1965). ET London: SCM/New York: Harper, 1967.

— *The Crucified God* (1973). ET London: SCM/New York: Harper, 1974.

— *The Trinity and the Kingdom of God* (1980). ET London: SCM/New York: Harper, 1981.

— *The Way of Jesus Christ* (1989). ET London: SCM/New York: Harper-Collins, 1990.

— *The Spirit of Life* (1991). ET London: SCM/Minneapolis: Augsburg/Fortress, 1992.

— 'The passion of Christ and the suffering of God'. In *The Asbury Theological Journal* 48 (1993) 19–28.

Moltmann-Wendel, E. *A Land Flowing With Milk and Honey*. London: SCM, 1986/New York: Crossroad, 1988.

Monod, J. *Chance and Necessity* (1970). ET New York: Knopf, 1971/London: Collins, 1972.

Morris, H. 'Shared guilt'. In *Wisdom* (ed. R. Bambrough). Oxford: Blackwell/Totowa, NJ: Rowman, 1974.

Morris, L. *The Cross in the New Testament*. Exeter: Paternoster/Grand Rapids: Eerdmans, 1966.

— *The Cross of Jesus*. Exeter: Paternoster/Grand Rapids: Eerdmans, 1988.

Moses, J. *The Sacrifice of God*. Norwich: Canterbury Press, 1992.

Moule, C. F. D. 'The theology of forgiveness'. In *From Fear To Faith* (ed. N. Autton) 61–72. London: SPCK, 1971.

Mowry LaCugna, C. and McDonnell, K. ' "Returning from the far country" '. *Scottish Journal of Theology* 41 (1988) 191–215.

Neill, S. *A Genuinely Human Existence*. London: Constable/Garden City, NY: Doubleday, 1959.

Newbigin, L. *The Open Secret*. Grand Rapids: Eerdmans, 1978/London: SPCK, 1979.

— *The Gospel in a Pluralistic Society*. London: SPCK, 1989/Grand Rapids: Eerdmans, 1990.

Neibuhr, R. *The Nature and Destiny of Man*. Vol. 1. ET London: Nisbet/London: Scribner's, 1941.

Nietzche, F. *On the Genealogy of Morals* (1887). ET New York: Vintage, 1967.

Noddings, N. *Women and Evil*. Berkeley: University of California, 1989.

Oates, W. *The Psychology of Religion*. Dallas, TX: Word, Inc; © 1973. All rights reserved.

O'Collins, G. *Interpreting Jesus*. London: Chapman/New York: Paulist, 1983.

Oddie, W. *What Will Happen to God?* London: SPCK, 1984/San Francisco: Ignatius, 1988.

Osborn, R. E. 'The Christian blasphemy: A non-Jewish Jesus'. In *Jews and Christians* (ed. J. H. Charlesworth) 211–38. New York: Crossroad, 1990.

O'Shea, K. 'The reality of sin'. *Theological Studies* 29 (1968) 241–59.

Packer, J. I. 'What did the cross achieve?' *Tyndale Bulletin* 25 (1974) 3–45.

Padilla, R. 'The human couple: A biblical perspective'. In *Theological Fraternity Bulletin* 2–3 (1983). = *Evangelical Review of Theology* 8 (1984) 275–88.

Pannenberg, W. *Jesus—God and Man* (1964). ET Philadelphia: Westminster/London: SCM, 1968.

— *Human Nature, Election, and History*. Philadelphia: Westminster, 1977.

— *Anthropology in Theological Perspective* (1983). ET Philadelphia: Westminster/Edinburgh: Clark, 1985.

— *Systematic Theology*. Vol. 1 (1988). ET Grand Rapids: Eerdmans/Edinburgh: Clark, 1991.

Paul, R. S. *The Atonement and the Sacraments*. Nashville: Abingdon, 1960/London: Hodder, 1961.

Peterson, D. *Hebrews and Perfection*. Cambridge/New York: CUP, 1982.

Piper, J. *The Justification of God*. Grand Rapids: Baker, 1983.

Pippin, R. *Modernism as a Philosophical Problem*. Oxford: Blackwell, 1991.

Plaskow, J. *Sex, Sin and Grace*. Lanham, MD/London: UP of America, 1980.

Priest, R. 'Cultural anthropology, sin, and the missionary'. In *God and Culture* (C. F. Henry Festschrift, ed. D. A. Carson and J. D. Woodbridge) 85–105. Grand Rapids: Eerdmans/Carlisle: Paternoster, 1993.

Primavesi, A. *From Apocalypse to Genesis*. Minneapolis: Augsburg Fortress/London: Burns and Oates, 1991.

Prusak, B. P. 'Jews and the death of Jesus in post-Vatican II Christologies'. *Journal of Ecumenical Studies* 28 (1991) 581–625.

Pruyser, P. W. 'Anxiety, guilt and shame in the atonement'. In *Religion in Psychodynamic Perspective* (ed. H. N. Maloney and B. Spilka). Oxford/New York: OUP, 1991.

Rahner, K. *Foundations of Christian Faith* (1976). ET New York: Seabury/London: DLT, 1978.

Rashdall, H. *The Idea of Atonement in Christian Theology*. London: Macmillan, 1919.

Rashid Rida. *Al-Manar*. Cairo, 1954.

Ricoeur, P. *The Symbolism of Evil* (1960). ET New York: Harper, 1967; reprinted Boston: Beacon, 1969.

— *Fallible Man*. ET Chicago: Regnery, 1967.

— 'The hermeneutics of symbols'. In *The Philosophy of Paul Ricoeur* (ed. C. E. Reagan and D. Stewart). Boston: Beacon, 1978.

Riesman, D. *The Lonely Crowd*. Garden City, NY: Doubleday, 1950.

Ritschl, A. *The Christian Doctrine of Justification and Reconciliation* (1870–74). ET Edinburgh: Clark/New York: Scribner's, 1900.

Robinson, J. A. T. *Wrestling With Romans*. London: SCM/Philadelphia: Westminster, 1979.

Rogerson, J. W. 'Sacrifice in the Old Testament'. In Bourdillon and Fortes 1980, 45–59.

Rubenstein, R. L. and Roth, J. K. *Approaches to Auschwitz*. Atlanta: Knox/London: SCM, 1987.

Ruether, R. R. 'Sexism and the theology of liberation'. *Christian Century* 609 (1973) 1224–9.

— *Faith and Fratricide*. New York: Seabury, 1974.

— *Sexism and God-Talk*. London: SCM, 1983/Boston: Beacon, 1984.

Russell, L. *Human Liberation in Feminist Perspective*. Philadelphia: Westminster, 1974.

Saiving Goldstein, V. 'The human situation: A feminine view'. *Journal of Religion* 40 (1960) 100–12.

Sanders, E. P. *Paul and Palestinian Judaism*. London: SCM/Philadelphia: Fortress, 1977.

— *Jesus and Judaism*. London: SCM/Philadelphia: Fortress, 1985.

Sankey, J. *Christian Self-Interpretation in Relation to Modern Judaism*. Diss. Birmingham, 1993.

Saward, J. *The Foolishness of God*. London/New York: OUP, 1961.

Scanzoni, L. and Hardesty, N. *All We're Meant To Be*. Waco, TX: Word, 1974.

Schiffmann, L. H. 'At the crossroads'. In *Jewish-Christian Self-Definition* (ed. E. P. Sanders and others) 2:115–56. London: SCM, 1981.

Schillebeeckx, E. *The Mission of the Church* (1968). ET New York: Seabury/London: Sheed and Ward, 1973.

Schmemann, A. *The Eucharist* (1984). ET Crestwood, NY: St Vladimir's Seminary Press, 1988.

Schoneveld, J. 'Torah in the flesh'. *Immanuel* 24/25 (1990) 77–94.

Schoonenberg, P. *Man and Sin* (1962). Notre Dame: University of Notre Dame/London: Sheed and Ward, 1965.

Schüssler Fiorenza, E. *In Memory of Her*. New York: Crossroad/London: SCM, 1983.

— *Discipleship of Equals*. New York: Crossroad/London: SCM, 1993.

— [see also under Tracy]

Segal, J. B. *The Hebrew Passover From the Earliest Times To A.D. 70*. London/New York: OUP, 1963.

Simpson, G. M. '*Theologia crucis* and the forensically fraught world: Engaging Helmut Peukert and Jürgen Habermas'. *Journal of the American Academy of Religion* 57 (1989) 509–41.

Sölle, D. *Christ the Representative* (1965). ET Philadelphia: Fortress/London: SCM, 1967.

Song, Choan-Seng. *The Compassionate God*. London: SCM/Maryknoll, NY: Orbis, 1982.

Spencer, A. *Beyond the Curse*. New York: Nelson, 1985.

Stamps, R. J. '*The Sacrament of the Word made Flesh*': The Eucharistic Theology of Thomas F. Torrance. Diss. Nottingham, 1986.

Steinberg, J. *All Or Nothing: The Axis and the Holocaust 1941–43*. London/New York: Routledge, 1990.

Storkey, E. *What's Right With Feminism?* London: SPCK, 1985/Grand Rapids: Eerdmans, 1986.

Stott, J. R. W. *The Cross of Christ*. Leicester/Downers Grove, IL: IVP, 1986.

Stuhlmacher, P. *Gerechtigkeit Gottes bei Paulus*. Gottingen: Vandenhoeck, 1965.

— *Reconciliation, Law and Righteousness* (1981). ET Philadelphia: Fortress, 1986.

Suggate, A. 'The concept of sacrifice in Anglican social ethics'. In Sykes 1991, 235–246.

Surin, K. 'Atonement and Christology'. *Neue Zeitschrift für systematische Theologie und Religionsphilosophie* 24 (1982) 131–49.

Swinburne, R. *Responsibility and Atonement*. Oxford/New York: OUP, 1989.

Sykes, S. W. (ed.). *Sacrifice and Redemption*. Cambridge/New York: CUP, 1991.

Theissen, G. *Sociology of Early Palestinian Christianity*. ET Philadelphia: Fortress, 1978. = *The First Followers of Jesus*. ET London: SCM, 1978.

Thelen, M. F. *Man As Sinner*. New York: Kings Crown Press, 1946.

Thielicke, H. *I Believe* (1965). ET Philadelphia: Fortress, 1968/London: Collins, 1969.

Thiselton, A. C. 'Knowledge, myth and corporate memory'. In *Believing in the Church* (Report of the Doctrine Commission of the Church of England) 45–78. London: SPCK, 1981.

Thistlethwaite, S. B. *Sex, Race, and God*. New York: Crossroad, 1989/ London: Chapman, 1990.

Tillich, P. *Systematic Theology*. Vol. 2. Chicago: University of Chicago/ London: Nisbet, 1957.

Torrance, T. F. 'The paschal mystery of Christ and the Eucharist'. In *Liturgical Review* 6 (1976) 6–12.

— *The Mediation of Christ*. Exeter: Paternoster, 1983.

— *The Trinitarian Faith*. Edinburgh: Clark, 1988.

— *The Ministry of Women*. Edinburgh: Handsel, 1992.

Tracy, D. and Schüssler Fiorenza, E. (eds.). *The Holocaust As Interruption*. Concilium 175 (1984).

Travis, S. H. *Christ and the Judgment of God*. Basingstoke: Marshall, Morgan and Scott, 1986.

— 'Wrath of God (NT)'. In Freedman 1992, 6:996–98.

Trible, P. *Texts of Terror*. Philadelphia: Fortress, 1984/London: SCM, 1992.

Trigg, R. 'Sin and freedom'. *Religious Studies* 20 (1984) 191–202.

Turner, V. *Dramas, Fields and Metaphors*. Ithaca, NY: Cornell UP, 1974.

Vandervelde, G. *Original Sin*. Lanham, MD/London: UP of America, 1981.

de Vaux, R. *Ancient Israel* (1958). ET New York: McGraw-Hill/London: DLT, 1961.

Vermes, G. *Scripture and Tradition in Judaism*. Leiden: Brill, 1973.

Walker, A. (ed.). *Different Gospels*, Revised Edition. London: SPCK, 1993.

Wallace, R. S. *The Atoning Death of Christ*. London: Marshall/Westchester, IL: Crossway, 1981.

Warfield, B. B. *The Person and Work of Christ*. Philadelphia: Presbyterian and Reformed, 1950.

Watson, D. L. 'The church as journalist'. *International Review of Mission* 72 [285] (1983) 57–74.

Weil, S. *Gravity and Grace* (1947). ET New York: Putnam/London: Routledge, 1952.

Wenham, G. J. *The Book of Leviticus*. Grand Rapids: Eerdmans, 1979.

— 'Christ's healing ministry and his attitude to the Law'. In *Christ the Lord* (D. Guthrie Festschrift, ed. H. H. Rowdon) 115–26. Leicester/Downers Grove, IL: IVP, 1982.

— *Genesis 1—15*. Waco, TX: Word, 1987.

Westcott, B. F. *The Epistle to the Hebrews*. London/New York: Macmillan, 1903.

White, V. *Atonement and Incarnation*. Cambridge/New York: CUP, 1991.

Whiteley, D. E. H. *The Theology of St Paul*. Oxford: Blackwell/Philadelphia: Fortress, 1964.

Whitford, M. *Luce Irigaray: Philosophy in the Feminine*. London/New York: Routledge, 1991.

Wilcox, M. ' "Upon the tree" '. *Journal of Biblical Literature* 96 (1977) 85–99.

Wiles, M. F. 'The unassumed is the unhealed'. *Religious Studies* 4 (1969) 47–56.

Williams, J. G. *The Bible, Violence, and the Sacred*. San Francisco: Harper, 1991.

Williams, R. R. 'Sin and evil'. In Hodgson and King 1982, 168–95.

Willmer, H. 'The politics of forgiveness'. *Third Way* III/5 (May 1979) 15–20.

Wistrich, R. *Anti-Semitism: The Longest Hatred*. London: Methuen/New York: Pantheon, 1992.

Wren, B. *Faith Looking Forward*. Oxford/New York: OUP, 1983.

Wright, N. T. *The Great Acquittal*. London: Collins, 1980.

— 'Jesus, Israel, and the cross'. In *SBL Seminar Papers* 1985 (ed. K. H. Richards) 75–95. Atlanta: Scholars, 1985.

— *The Climax of the Covenant*. Edinburgh: Clark, 1991/Minneapolis: Fortress, 1992.

Young, B. 'The cross, Jesus and the Jewish people'. *Immanuel* 24/25 (1990) 23–24.

Young, F. M. *Sacrifice and the Death of Christ*. London: SPCK, 1975.

— *Can These Dry Bones Live?* London: SCM, 1982.

Ziesler, J. *The Meaning of Righteousness in Paul*. Cambridge/New York: CUP, 1972.

— *Paul's Letter to the Romans*. London: SCM/Valley Forge, PA: Trinity, 1989.

Zizioulas, J. D. *Being as Communion*. London: DLT/Crestwood, NY: St Vladimir's Seminary Press, 1985.